MORAL EDUCATION
FOR AMERICANS

Robert D. Heslep

PRAEGER

Westport, Connecticut
London

25.95

Library of Congress Cataloging-in-Publication Data

Heslep, Robert D.
    Moral education for Americans / Robert D. Heslep.
      p. cm.
    Includes bibliographical references and index.
    ISBN 0-275-95073-5 (alk. paper).—ISBN 0-275-95197-9 (pbk. :
alk. paper)
    1. Moral education—United States. 2. United States—Moral
conditions. I. Title.
LC311.H47   1995
370.11′4′0973—dc20   95-3327

British Library Cataloguing in Publication Data is available.

Library of Congress Catalog Card Number: 95-3327
ISBN: 0-275-95073-5
     0-275-95197-9 (pbk.)

First published in 1995

Praeger Publishers, 88 Post Road West, Westport, CT 06881
An imprint of Greenwood Publishing Group, Inc.

Printed in the United States of America

The paper used in this book complies with the
Permanent Paper Standard issued by the National
Information Standards Organization (Z39.48-1984).

10 9 8 7 6 5 4 3 2 1

Contents

WITHDRAWN

Introduction

This book tries to help solve a profound problem that has emerged in the United States since the middle of this century: the widening and deepening decline of the control of our behavior toward one another. The piece of the solution presented here is a conception of moral education. This conception, developed through a method that means to be dialogical in spirit even if not in form, is discussed at the practical as well as the theoretical level.

Since World War II, the regulation of conduct in the United States has become problematic. This condition, which has been recognized for some time by ordinary citizens as well as social commentators, is suggested by familiar facts: soaring crime rates; the enormous growth in illegitimate births; a decline of concern for the public good along with a huge increase in regard for special and individual interests; a growing preference for fame, fortune, and power along with an absence of a sense of shame; gross immoral acts by public figures; and the fascination of people and the media with spectacles of evil. The troubled control of social behavior in the nation is suggested also by the fact that our society has no commonly accepted set of standards by which to comport ourselves. The nation today is a bazaar of competing normative principles, running from those of extreme individualism to those of cultural pluralism, communal unity, and divine will. To be sure, the United States has suffered serious normative lapses during much of its history. Widespread drunkenness, child labor, slavery, the unequal treatment of women, the destruction of native societies, entrepreneurial greed and fraud, lynchings, political corruption, and gangsterism are only some of the most notable episodes. Moreover, some of these episodes occurred in clusters, thereby threatening the normative fabric of the nation. Perhaps America will survive its present values crisis; it certainly got through the ones in the past. We might even survive the current situation just by muddling along and hoping for improvement. It would make more sense, however, if we tried doing something to help strengthen the nation's normative structure.

One thing we will do well to try is to formulate a character education for Americans. Standards that regulate only under the threat of force are not very effective. What are needed are standards that will become internal to Americans, that will become a part of ourselves. People will follow given norms as a matter of course only if they are habituated to follow them and if they appreciate them. Habits of following the standards constitute a basis for regularity, and appreciation for the norms reinforces the regularity and guards it from challenges. While norm-shaped habits and appreciations for standards of conduct are rather different from one another, they are major elements of character and have to be learned.

But what action guides should American character education involve? Interpersonal conduct is subject to various kinds of norms: cultural, social, civic, and moral. While we ultimately would have to identify all four types of principles and rules as the basis of a complete character education for Americans, we will presently assume the more manageable project of locating norms of only one sort. Those we will seek are moral standards, that is, the values, rights, duties, and virtues that pertain to people as moral beings. They are superior to cultural, social, and civic principles in that they may serve as criteria for ultimately overriding the latter, and in that none of the latter may serve as criteria for ultimately overriding the former. By restricting our inquiry to moral standards, we will in effect be looking for a basis of moral character. Hence, the character education we intend to recommend for Americans will be a moral education.

We do not mean to conceive just any set of moral norms; we hope to formulate one that is defensible on rational grounds. In other words, the principles to be sought and the method to be used will be consistent with the canons of reason at the level of practice as well as that of theory.

In the past decade or two there have been attacks on rationalistic morality by Post-Modernists. Such morality, according to these critics, frequently stresses the intellect and ignores feeling and other mental factors. It often allows only one method for moral knowledge and assumes that a totally objective viewpoint is possible. It involves a masculine bias and sometimes presumes that all human behavior is explainable by appeal to natural law. While these allegations apply to certain views of rational morality, they do not apply to the one taken here. Our conception does not imply that feelings have no cognitive significance, for it allows that they may be regarded as possible signs of acts, interests, and norms relevant to moral inquiry. Moreover, our idea is compatible with different methods for obtaining moral knowledge, for instance, moral judgment as well as moral philosophy. While our interpretation of rational morality takes the principles of reason as the markers of objectivity in knowing, it grants that these principles have historical origins and thus are subject to revision and replacement from one era to another. Moreover, while our position recognizes that some theories of rationality have had a distinctive antifeminist bias, it holds that these theories thereby show their own irrationality rather than any gender bias of the canons of reason. Finally, our idea of rational morality does not pretend that all human behavior is explainable by appeal to natural law. As we shall show, the position entails that moral behavior is fully explainable only if there is an appeal to freedom and, thus, to some absence of natural necessity.

Nonrationalistic morality in the United States throughout this century has been of two dominant types. The type known by philosophers as *Emotivism* holds that moral standards are based on feelings in that they ultimately are to be accepted or rejected for no other reason than that one has a favorable or unfavorable feeling toward them. Thus, the fundamental reason that one can offer for altruism, according to Emotivists, is that one has a positive attitude toward it. The kind of nonrationalistic morality known by philosophers as *Fideism* insists that moral directives are founded on religious faith in that they finally are accepted or rejected simply because they are believed, without even the possibility of evidence, to represent divine truth. Consequently, the fundamental reason that one can offer for altruism, according to Fideists, is one's unsubstantiable belief that altruism is commanded by divine will. Nevertheless, both the Emotivist and the Fideist implicitly are committed to reason as the bedrock of moral standards; for each is wedded to the Principles of Identity and Noncontradiction, which generally are recognized as primary principles of reason. The Principle of Identity says that something is what it is and not something else. On pain of nonsense, any Emotivist must concede that any feeling is what it is and not something else. Likewise, the Fideist must admit that one's faith is what it is and not something else. Along with their reliance on the Principle of Identity, these professed nonrationalists have to accept also the Principle of Noncontradiction, which says that a statement and its contradiction cannot both be true. There is no getting around the fact that any self-contradictory statement, whether of feeling, faith, or anything else, is nonsensical and, consequently, cannot count as a good reason for a moral standard or anything else.

In seeking rationally defensible moral standards, we will employ the method of normative conceptual analysis. More specifically, we aim to show, in Chapter 2, that the very concept of a moral standard commits any and all moral agents to certain fundamental principles of moral value, right, duty, and virtue. These principles all relate to the major features of moral agency: freedom, knowledge, purposefulness, evaluativeness, deliberativeness, and judgment. While the standards of moral agency are necessarily quite general, they are feasible, we shall maintain in Chapter 3, as the basis of American morality. They are relevant to American traditions, and they appear to be generally acceptable to Americans today. In the respect that these standards are acceptable and applicable to Americans, they are the tie that binds Americans in moral fellowship; but they allow individual and cultural diversity. After we have argued for the norms of moral agency, we will use them in constructing a theory of education for moral character. That theory will be presented in terms of the purpose (Chapter 4), content (Chapter 5), and pedagogy (Chapter 6) of character education for moral agents.

After setting forth the theory, we will compare and contrast it with several character education policies recently proposed in the United States (Chapter 7). Then we will apply it to two fictional cases relevant to America today. One case is that of a child of the underclass (Chapter 8); the other is that of a clique of white teenage males from the middle class (Chapter 9). As discussion of these cases will reveal, our theory is no panacea or quick fix for the moral education of Americans. The education that it recommends for Americans is differential, complex, and difficult. The education is differential in that it should vary from one kind of situation to another. It is complex in that it should involve parents, neighborhood action, and social agencies as well as schools. It is difficult because many obstacles must be overcome and because unanticipated events might threaten it. While these features of the education might be disappointing to some people, they are not weaknesses of it. They are, rather, functions of social conditions in the United States. Finally, we will analyze the implications of our theory for nonmoral types of character education and for various American institutions (Chapter 10).

1　A Dire Need for Moral Education

This inquiry invites classroom teachers, school administrators, parents, clergy, policy makers, philosophers, and all other interested parties to join me in conceiving a moral education for Americans. The conception is to have a theoretical framework containing a set of moral norms and a view of the end, content, and pedagogy of education resting on that set of norms. The norms, I hope, will be feasible for the United States as well as logically sound. The view of moral education is to be applied to American education in a broad way. For the sake of further practical clarification, the view will be applied also to cases of individual Americans facing moral difficulties.

Certain individuals have already contributed to this project. They are, among others, my colleagues Carl Glickman and Duncan Waite, my one-time graduate research assistants Peggy Geren and Steven Smith, and the students of my Spring 1994 class in Ethics and Education. It is not possible, however, for many people to join me in this project in a strict sense. I am the one actually conducting the project, and few are present to talk with me about the work as it proceeds. Nevertheless, people may cooperate in a looser sense of the term. What I have in mind is a dialogue at a distance. In developing the theory of concern, I will use the published literature relevant to moral education as a basis for anticipating questions and objections that other people presumably would raise if they were present. Moreover, readers can inform me and discuss among themselves whether or not all of their questions and criticisms have been addressed, and whether or not those discussed were resolved satisfactorily. I will attempt to prevent my prejudices from distorting the investigation, while readers can endeavor to keep theirs from unduly interfering with their responses to it.

While the purpose of this investigation probably will be readily acceptable to a few people, it certainly will not be to all. Those cognizant of the unsettled conditions of the world in which we all live will be pleased to see that the inquiry is concerned with the application of moral education theory rather than with such theory as an end in itself. Even so, they might want to know why we should focus on moral education only for Americans rather than include other peoples as well. Others will demand to know why we should concentrate on moral education rather than on another sort of normative education. Indeed, some of them will seek to learn why we mean to propose a normative education of any kind for the United States rather than remedies for the nation's social and economic problems. Still others will insist upon learning why we should build yet another theory of moral education rather than use one of the many already available. Finally, some will want to know the specific sense in which this inquiry is to be one of conception. Let me, then, take up these questions.

WHY MORAL EDUCATION FOR AMERICANS?

There is no doubt that education in values, duties, and other norms is important for any society. When human beings act, they frequently affect one another, not just their respective selves. They are inclined, therefore, to be as interested in guiding the actions of others as they are in directing their own. The principal means that they have devised for controlling one another's actions are norms, or standards to which actions are to conform. While human beings have not shied away from employing coercion in the regulation of conduct, they have not viewed it as the foundation of norms. Rather, they have seen it as a supplement to action guides, e.g., for dealing with violators and for settling urgent conflicts where commonly accepted directives are absent. The members of a society, however, do not automatically act according to its principles and rules of interpersonal conduct. They have to learn to do so over a period of years with the aid of various institutions. Consequently, societies find it necessary to make provisions for the normative education of their members.

Moreover, there is little doubt that normative education is a pressing need in the United States today. Since the middle of this century there has been a sharp increase in violations of widely accepted standards, such as acts of murder, narcotics abuse and trafficking, rape, sexual molestation of children, and fraud.[1] There has been a marked growth in uncertainty over standards that once were generally accepted, notably, norms strictly opposing abortion, homosexuality, venereal disease, bastardy, suicide, and euthanasia.[2] There have been pronounced symptoms of social irresponsibility, as exemplified by the selfishness of the 1980s, the widespread apathy toward those living in the rotted areas of central cities, and the persistence of racial and ethnic tensions.[3] Finally, the violation of social regulations in America has spread from such familiar types as gangsters, juvenile delinquents, local politicians, and Wall Street operators to many once thought to be the personifications of rectitude: clergy, bankers, judges, librarians, directors of charities, school administrators, school teachers, university presidents, university faculty, and occupants of the White House.

For some scholars, the normative situation in the United States has become so bad that the nation has had to lower its standards in order to survive socially.[4] For other commentators, the situation is not that we have lower public standards, but that we have fewer and fewer public standards. Regardless of their differences, both sides probably would agree with the comment that America, once the promised land, seems headed for dystopia.[5] That the United States appears to suffer anomic conditions does not mean that the normative structures of other societies are not in disrepair. The situation here, however, does call for special attention. According to a recent national survey, 76 percent of the respondents "think that the United States is in a moral and spiritual decline."[6]

Despite the gravity of the situation, there are people who respond passively and thoughtlessly. Some simply wait for a Jim Jones, Sun Myung Moon, David Koresh, or another spiritual leader who will reveal a code of conduct. Others do nothing more than try to muddle through with the hope that things will straighten themselves out. Still others minimize their interpersonal lives and content themselves with purely personal pursuits, convinced that life has gotten so complicated that human beings cannot get along with each other. With some reflection, however, we might see, however dimly, that there are ways to deal actively with the normative malaise in America. Character education comes to mind as a necessary means.

A society's norms work most effectively when they are second nature to the society's members. As the history of tyranny shows, standards that regulate only when the police are present are not very effective. People, it is widely agreed, will follow given norms of behavior as a matter of course only if they are habituated to follow them and if they appreciate them. Habits of following the standards constitute a basis for regularity, and appreciation for the norms reinforces the regularity and guards it from challenges. While norm-shaped habit and appreciation for standards of conduct are rather different from each other, they are major elements of character and have to be learned. People without habits reflecting standards of conduct are said to lack character, and the same is said also of those who do not value such standards. By definition, habits are had by people only if they are learned by them. As a matter of fact, appreciations of any sort are held by people only if they are learned by them. So, because a society will have members inclined to act according to its norms of conduct only if they acquire the necessary habits and appreciations, it will do well to provide its members with an appropriate character education. If, therefore, the United States is to rectify the disarray in its interpersonal life, it has to furnish its members with a suitable character education.

There are philosophers and educators who are opposed to any proposal of character education, for they regard it as necessarily involving coercion, imposition, indoctrination, conditioning, or other pedagogical methods that exclude or at least minimize the freedom and autonomy of students. Such a notion of character education might be unfounded, however. It might be possible to develop the character of students in a way that is consistent with freedom and autonomy as central moral principles. In any event, we simply must wait to see whether or not our inquiry can develop a conception of character education that concords with freedom and autonomy.

Character education is not the only area that needs to be examined in a comprehensive effort to correct America's troubled state. The nation's social institutions and economy also are in need of major repairs. Nevertheless, character education is one that has to be addressed. Philosophers as diverse as Plato, Aristotle, St. Augustine, St. Thomas Aquinas, Spinoza, Immanuel Kant, John Stuart Mill, and John Dewey have viewed character education as vital to the life of any worthy society. Moreover, it is common sense that how people behave toward each other is partly, perhaps largely, a function of education. So, until people are trained to follow norms of conduct, they will persist in violating social, political, legal, and moral standards despite efforts to restructure their social and economic institutions. Finally, the reconstruction of America's social and economic institutions must go hand in glove with a conception of character education for the nation's members. It makes no sense to rebuild our social institutions and our economy without considering what impact they might have in shaping the members' character. Also, it makes no sense to try to discover this impact without knowing the kind of character Americans today should have.

But even if it is true that any society requires normative education, and that the United States in particular urgently needs to do something about this education for its members, it does not follow that such education should be moral. First, a society may impart its action guides through something other than moral education, mainly cultural, social, or civic education. Cultural education passes on to the members of a society the standards of their culture. Social education teaches the members their roles and manners in the society. Civic education furnishes instruction in a political society's laws and ideals. Second, it is not immediately evident to everyone that moral education should necessarily be in the public domain. Some people hold that it is under the authority of the family; others do not concede even that much. Third, and last, it might be that a public moral education is practically impossible today; for it might be that no formulation of moral education can gain appreciable acceptance at this time.

Alternatives to Moral Education

On its face, a normative education program resting on some combination of cultural, social, or civic standards might be sufficient for the United States today. Is it not likely that the nation would not be suffering the recent increase in social deviancy if the bulk of its members had embodied its culture, if they had learned to perform their roles and act politely, and if they had learned to respect the nation's laws and ideals? Indeed, a long-standing criticism of normative education following a developmental model is that such education does not pay due attention to the importance of the social control or law-and-order stages of normative development.[7] Nevertheless, there are serious difficulties with a program that rests on nothing more than cultural, social, and civic criteria. One is that cultural education presupposes a uniform culture for a society or, in the case of a society with several cultures, significant overlap among different sets of cultural norms. Such education, therefore, might not be workable in present-day America, whose numerous and diverse cultural groups might not share a core of values. Another difficulty is that it might not be desirable for the normative education of a society to be grounded on nothing more than the society's cultural or social standards. Standards of either sort are not beyond reproach. America's esteem of rugged individualism, for instance, has been a subject of attack during much of this century. The roles and manners expected of women and children in virtually all past societies and many current ones have also been subjects of criticism in recent decades.

But civic education, it might be objected, is different from cultural and social educations in a crucial respect: it rests on a hierarchy of norms that enable it to be self-correcting. The governmental laws of a political society are subordinate to the society's constitution, and the latter is subordinate to the society's political ideals, which supposedly are the ultimate norms of the society. The governmental laws, then, may be evaluated and changed according to the constitution, while the latter may be criticized and amended according to the ideals. In fact, the review of the constitutionality of governmental laws is a very familiar process in the United States; and both the Bill of Rights and the Reconstruction Amendments clearly reflect the ideals of the nation. So, even if cultural or social education contains no mechanism whereby a society's members may learn to be critical of their cultural values or social roles and manners, civic education does comprise a mechanism whereby the society's members may learn to be reflective about their governmental laws and constitution.

This argument is appealing as far as it goes, but it certainly does not go far enough. The problem is that civic education, according to the argument, does not provide a way for people to learn to ponder the political ideals of their society. Such ideals, it should be remembered, are liable to evaluation. Thus, Karl Popper regarded those of the Open Society as good and those of the Closed Society as bad.[8] Many people condemn the ideals of Nazi Germany while praising those of democratic nations. Therefore, because civic education, as traditionally understood, presents a society's political ideals as the ultimate standards of life in that society, it does not prepare the society's members to be critical of those ideals. Even civic education in a nation whose political ideals happen to be truly fundamental and irreproachable will not enable that society's members to judge those ideals. To help them in this respect, it would have to transcend its limits and become some other sort of education.[9]

Moral Education as Not Public

Those who claim that moral education does not necessarily belong in the public domain have a long history and reflect a wide variety of viewpoints.[10] Presently, two groups who frequently appear in public discussions on educational policy are advocates of family morality and individual liberty, respectively. The *Familialists,* who presuppose a moral theory similar to *Communitarianism,* which we will examine below, hold that instruction in moral standards is ultimately under the authority of the family.[11] The *Liberalists,* who presuppose a moral theory similar to *Individualism,* which we also will explain later, maintain that no person has the authority to impose moral norms on another.[12] To be sure, both parties agree that a society may provide supportive conditions for the learning of morality. Hence, Familialists insist that public school policies and practices should conform with the regulations favored by the family, and Liberalists maintain that the public school should provide whatever conditions and curriculum will help students become individually capable of developing their own moral ideals and ways of life. Nevertheless, the Familialists deny that the public school has the authority to teach any norm contrary to those advocated by the family, and Liberalists reject the notion that the public school may impose any way of life upon students. If, then, families regard homosexuality as evil, the public school, according to Familialists, must ignore it or portray it as evil; it cannot present it as just another alternative life-style. For the Liberalists, however, the school may depict homosexuality as an alternative way of life but never as an evil (nor even as a desirable) one.

Plainly, there are difficulties with the Familialist position. The moral principles and rules of families are of numerous sorts, for instance, those of fundamentalist Christians, the Nation of Islam, orthodox Judaism, old-order Amish, and secular humanists. When, therefore, Familialists refer to morality as under control of the family, which morality do they have in mind? If they intend any morality that any family espouses, then they make it practically impossible for public schools to have policies and practices that will be agreeable to all familial moralities, which are quite likely to conflict with one another in extensive and serious respects. The Familialist solution to this problem is that families with sets of moral norms that cannot be accommodated by public schools have the right to instruct their children at home or place them in suitable private schools. But there is an additional difficulty. On first glance, the Familialist seems to regard any moral code of a family neither better nor worse than any other. Yet, one doubts that all moral codes are equal. Some might view medical treatment of disease as evil. Others might deem slavery, child molestation, or the subordination of women as worthy. Still others might obligate their subjects to destroy families following other codes.

If Familialists allow the point that some sorts of moral codes are better or worse than others, they put themselves in the position of assuming moral authority and thus undermining the moral authority of the family. But they do not have to concede the point. What they might do, and often have done, is to seek a resolution based on the distinction between the moral beliefs of a family and the actions that actually follow from those beliefs. By virtue of this distinction, Familialists might insist that a family may teach whatever morality it wants as long as the family does not harm those with other beliefs. The members of the Nation of Islam may regard Jews as evil, and Jews may regard the members of the Nation of Islam as evil. Neither familial group, however, may harm the other. In short, the Familialist's solution is moral tolerance among family groups. This solution too is problematic, however. It leaves open the question of what counts as harm to the members of another group: physical injury, intimidation, threat, insult, innuendo, stereotyping, or something else? It also ignores the issue of what is to be done about a family's treatment of its own members in the name of morality. Is a family to be prevented from practicing incest, withholding medical treatment from its children, flogging members, killing its hopelessly infirm members, or conducting sacrifices of members? If so, are there moral norms by which intervention in a family's affairs may be justified? If there are, are they authorized by the family subject to intervention? If these criteria are not authorized by the family of concern, Familialists must now admit that they were wrong in maintaining that morality is primarily under the authority of the family.

Liberalists avoid these problems because they do not insist that just any way of life may be chosen by an individual or groups of individuals. Because, for the Liberalists, any autonomous and free individual or group is logically committed to autonomy and freedom, none may, on pain of contradiction, choose a way of life that is inconsistent with the autonomy and freedom of any other autonomous and free individual or group. Thus, the Liberalists have fundamental norms regulating the moral characters that people may assume for themselves.

In avoiding the problems of Familialists, however, Liberalists pose a difficulty for themselves. While they have insisted that moral education is not necessarily a public matter, they have argued that education in skills, knowledge, and feelings which enable students to become capable of choosing their own ways of life might be of public concern. But, say Liberalists, even if the public school teaches these matters to students, it does not shape their characters; it leaves students free to choose their characters for themselves.

Yet, are not Liberalists missing a crucial distinction here, namely that between the general character of autonomous and free individuals and the specific character that an autonomous and free individual might assume? If I teach a student the skills of critical thinking, inquiry, evaluation, and deliberation in addition to a fund of concepts and information as well as an appreciation of autonomy, freedom, practical reasoning, and tolerance, have I not, for all practical purposes, instilled in that student the character of an autonomous and free person even though I have not instructed the student in any specific character of such a person? Having overlooked this distinction, Liberalists also fail to recognize their theory's implication that moral education in the general character traits of autonomous and free individuals is necessarily a public right. Because the principles of autonomy and freedom are fundamental not only for autonomous and free individuals, but also for societies of such individuals, is not the enculturation of those principles necessarily of public interest? Thus, does not a society necessarily have the right to develop in its members the general character features of autonomous and free individuals? That society necessarily has authority over the general character education of its members does not entail that it has control over what specific characters its individuals will assume. But it does mean that general character education is moral education necessarily under public authority even if the development of specific characters in autonomous and free individuals is necessarily under their authority.

Disputes Over Moral Education

Few things are more contentious in the United States than morality. As groups and as individuals, we differ in our particular moral standards; but we also tend to disagree over the nature of such standards. Some people maintain that moral principles may be absolutistic, while others insist that they necessarily are relativistic. Many contend that they should be religious, while numerous others claim that they ought to be secular. We also disagree over moral judgments and moral inquiry. While many hold that moral judgments may be objectively true, others maintain that they may be only subjectively true. Philosophers often maintain that moral issues and problems are so complex and subtle that they can be adequately understood only with the aid of experts. Many people allow, however, that one person's ideas about moral standards and judgments are no better or worse than anybody else's. With all this contention about morality, is it not likely to be a waste of time to advance a proposal for moral education? Who will care about it? Will it not be just another piece in the nation's moral education menagerie?

I grant the two points of this concern: Disputes over morality are pervasive and deep in the United States, and they threaten to prevent a general acceptance of any proposal for moral education in the nation. Nevertheless, we do not have to regard the situation as hopeless. Despite the disagreements it is possible that the positions of the various contenders might overlap sufficiently that they provide a significant, albeit restricted, basis for moral education. It is even possible that, upon reflection, the contenders might recognize that they are each committed to a comprehensive conception of morality which they share with one another. If such is the case, this conception can serve as the foundation of a comprehensive program of moral education that people generally find acceptable. As long as either of these possibilities lies before us, there is no good reason to believe that another attempt to set forth a proposal for moral education will meet with nothing more than indifference in the practical world.

WHY ANOTHER THEORY?

Many who want to know why we aim to construct yet another theory of moral education rather than employing one already available probably will allow that the theories of ancient, medieval, and early modern times are not apt to be highly relevant to the contemporary era. Indeed, they are likely to acknowledge that even the theories of early twentieth-century philosophers might have to undergo significant revision before they can be very pertinent. What these inquisitors will definitely insist, however, is that the various theories of moral education put forth in the past several decades bear in all likelihood upon current conditions and thus render redundant an effort to develop now another theory. What significant features can a new theory have that are not possessed by one of the recent ones? There is no doubt that the theories appearing in the past several decades are relevant, but there is a question about the adequacy of these theories. To indicate their weaknesses, we will examine a sampling of the chief types of theories that have been advanced in the United States in the past 30 years or so.

Values Clarification

Values Clarification takes values to be the central fact of moral and civil life.[13] Through and from their experiences, this approach claims, human beings normally acquire guides of behavior. These guides may take the form of purposes, attitudes, feelings, beliefs, or other psychological factors, and they may or may not be consciously held. Accordingly, a value is simply any psychological factor that tends to direct some of the behavior of any person. While the proponents of Values Clarification do not claim that any set of values a person holds must be acceptable according to a given moral standard, they do agree that the set of values held by a person should be internally consistent. Hence, the objective of moral education in a democracy is to help students to develop internally consistent sets of values and to live deliberately by whatever such sets they individually develop. The method for attaining this objective is *Values Clarification,* which enables students to identify their respective values and to spot and eliminate inconsistencies among their respective values.

Major faults of this theory concern its conception of a value and its statement of the purpose and method of moral education.[14] One problem with the theory's view of a value is that it is overly broad. More specifically, it includes as values psychological factors that normally are distinguished from values. It applies, for instance, to whims, which guide actions but are not values. Nobody ever spoke of a worthy whim. Another problem is that the view fails to distinguish between standards of value and valued objects. Hence, it does not clarify if psychological factors that guide actions are valued objects or standards of value. An additional difficulty is that the view fails to recognize that action guides do not have to be psychological factors. The Ten Commandments, for instance, are not psychological factors. Indeed, any statement that serves to guide action may count as a standard of value. In any event, the advocates of Values Clarification do not explain why it fails to acknowledge as values those action guides that are not psychological factors.

The problems with Values Clarification's ideas of the purpose and method of moral education are related to the theory's conception of value. To be sure, people do need to learn to clarify their likes, desires, and other psychological action guides so that they can spot inconsistencies among them and thereby eliminate conflicts within their lives. But there must be more to the aim of moral education than an internally consistent agent. If a student discovers that his or her psychological action guides are all consistent with each other, it does not follow that the student should retain those guides and live deliberately by them. The most that can be said about the student is that he or she is consistent. But Al Capone and Adolph Hitler were consistent, too. Moreover, the pedagogical method provided by Values Clarification is inadequate for enabling students to eliminate the inconsistencies within their psychological action guides. If a student discovers that some of his or her action guides are inconsistent with each other, the student will not know which guides to keep and which to discard. They all are equal as values. How, then, can the student view any of them as worthy of retention or elimination? To determine that one rather than another psychological action guide should be retained or discarded, a person must appeal to more than inconsistency. One also must appeal to some criterion of value beyond those psychological factors. What that criterion might be Values Clarification does not say.

Moral Development

In its most sophisticated version, by Lawrence Kohlberg,[15] Moral Development is strikingly different from Values Clarification. It holds that there are absolute values, that justice is the central moral value, that people at different levels of moral development have special interpretations of justice, and that interpretations at the later stages are superior to those of the earlier stages. The courses of action that persons might entertain in a given situation are contingent upon their psychological equipment and the historical milieu in which they live. The moral precepts and rules they follow in deciding what to do are typically products of the culture in which they live. But the standpoints from which persons view moral precepts or rules—whether standpoints of power, self-interest, social rules, statutory law, a social contract, or moral autonomy—are functions of social-psychological stages in which they are when they consider precepts or rules. The purpose of moral education is to help students attain the highest levels of moral development of which they are individually capable. The method of such education is to enable students to solve, through reasoning from the conceptions of justice appropriate to their present individual moral stages, problems about what is just in given practical situations.

While Moral Development was well received by numerous educators as an alternative to the relativism and presumed moral neutrality of Values Clarification, it has undergone serious criticism during the past decade or so.[16] One charge is that Kohlberg's focus on justice is unwarranted. While justice is an important moral principle, it certainly is not the only major one with which human beings have been concerned. Wisdom, courage, compassion, and moderation are a few of the other candidates; and that they can be reduced to justice is highly doubtful. Another criticism is that Kohlberg's idea of justice (concern for the welfare of others and for the equal treatment of others), which certainly is not the only such idea, has not been adequately defended. While, for instance, some might agree that justice certainly includes the equal treatment of others, they might argue that the extension of justice to a concern for the welfare of others confuses it with compassion. An additional objection is that Kohlberg's notion of practical reasoning is rather narrow, thus limiting the intellectual responses that teachers may permit students to make to posed moral problems. There are other interpretations of practical reasoning, e.g., those of Aristotle and Dewey. Why should not students be allowed to reflect according to these other interpretations? Finally, critics have charged that Kohlberg's work contains an insidious and enervating masculine bias.[17] The emphasis on rights and fairness, despite an acknowledgment of the need for concern for the welfare of others, reflects masculine proclivities. Moreover, the treatment of practical reason as being highly "linear" also betrays a masculine bias.

Individualism

Whereas Moral Developmentalists take autonomy as the distinguishing feature of the highest stage of moral development, but regard justice as the highest moral principle, Individualists regard autonomy as the supreme principle as well as the highest good of morality. For Individualism, autonomy is the capacity of an individual to develop a rational life plan for him- or herself.[18] This capacity is not something natural, independent of human experience. It arises fundamentally because of the conflicts that individuals have with one another in efforts to control their bodies and environments. More specifically, the capacity issues from an individual's rights, or claims that the individual may justify to other individuals through dialogue.[19] Because an individual's autonomy is the highest good, nobody may interfere with it. As Bruce Ackerman has stated the point: "The liberal state does not abolish scarcity or assure happiness; after establishing his rights through Neutral dialogue, a person may use his power to make a mess of his life, and nobody has the right to stop him from going to hell in his own way."[20] In view of the individual's highest good, then, education is not to instill any moral character into students. Its aim, rather, is to help students acquire moral autonomy, that is, to gain the capacity to devise and choose rational life plans for themselves. The pedagogical method for doing this is to provide students with "a sense of the very different lives that could be theirs—so that, as they approach maturity, they have the cultural materials available to build lives equal to their evolving conceptions of the good."[21]

There are several problems with Individualism. One is with its conception of the highest good, which is an individual's capacity to devise and choose rational life plans. It has been long recognized by philosophers that the highest good logically cannot be a capacity or disposition. Thus, Aristotle faulted virtue as the definition of the highest good for the reason that virtues are habits and thus not as valuable as a combination of virtues and the actions to which they lead.[22] Individual autonomy, then, cannot be the highest good for the reason that it, being instrumental to the actions of an individual's life, is not as valuable as a life of action determined autonomously. Another problem is with Individualism's contention that no individual has the right to interfere with any other individual's autonomously chosen way of life, even if that way of life is the pathway to hell. Bluntly, the contention is self-contradictory. On the one hand, nobody does have the right to interfere with another's life that has been autonomously chosen; for that life, being defensible through dialogue on rational grounds, is something to which the individual of concern has a right. On the other hand, any individual who chooses a life leading to hell, at least in the sense of negating his or her autonomy, has no right to that life. It is rationally indefensible to hold that autonomy is the highest good and that, in the name of that good, an individual may choose a life that destroys his or her autonomy.

The other problem with Individualism we suggested in our discussion of the Liberalist's opposition to the idea is that the public has a distinctive authority over moral education. Individualism fails to distinguish between the general features of autonomy and the specific features of the autonomy of a given individual. Because the former are of positive interest to all individuals, they are a public good; and the development of the general traits of autonomy in students is a character education over which the public must have control. Hence, Individualism is wrong in claiming that character education is of private concern only. In any event, the curriculum and instruction proposed by Individualism, which are geared to the development of the general features of autonomy in students, is a kind of character education under public authority.

Communitarianism

According to Communitarians, the proponents of Individualism fail to understand the relationship between people and their social situations.

While all human beings necessarily grow up in social groups, they may grow up in those groups in various specific ways. Nobody, however, ever grows up in social groups in a detached way, not acquiring a character absorbed from their norms, but rather simply nurturing one's powers and options for choosing a rational life plan. The fact of the matter, according to Communitarians, is that the characters of individuals are products largely of their families, neighborhoods, and other primary communities.[23] Characters are shaped also by regional and larger societies. Individuals might eventually reject the norms of their native communities and modify their characters, but they will not grow up with blank slates waiting to be stamped by their choice of character. As products of their social groups, individuals have communal obligations as well as rights.[24] As long as an individual is a member of a community, he or she has the duty to help sustain that community, to repay it for the benefits received from it, and to render aid to its other members. These duties hold no less for individuals whose primary communities have helped them become autonomous. Similar obligations even are binding on individuals who are members of large and impersonal social groups, such as political societies.

For Communitarians, then, the purpose of moral education is to help instill and develop in students the ideals of their respective social groups; to help students understand their social duties; and to foster in students knowledge, cognitive skills, and feelings that will enable them to reflect on their moral values and duties in the face of changing circumstances and to solve moral problems. The method for accomplishing this purpose is to put moral education in a community setting. Even schools should become communities, fostering the norms commonly shared by the families and neighborhoods represented by the students. The content of moral education should include the history, traditions, symbols, rites, and celebrations of involved communities.[25]

Despite the factual basis of its argument, Communitarianism suffers difficulties. First, there is the question of which are the norms of a given community. Were the norms of ante bellum America those of the abolitionist William Lloyd Garrison or those of Roger B. Taney, the U.S. Supreme Court justice who formulated the Dred Scott decision? Were the standards for black society at the beginning of this century those conceived by W.E.B. Du Bois or those conceived by the U.S. Supreme Court at the time? Communitarians usually try to resolve this issue by distinguishing between the true and the conventional norms of a society, with the former knowable by revelation, reflection, or rational dialogue and the latter by appeal to popular belief, custom, or statute. This answer, however, contains its own problems. To distinguish between the true and conventional standards of a society is to imply that within the context of that society the former are better than the latter. But on what

basis can that be said? Certainly the vast majority of Americans probably believed that the Supreme Court's principle of separate but equal
was preferable to the principle of full equality advocated by Du Bois.
Another obstacle is whether or not the true standards of a society can
be identified. Who had the truth about the ideals of American society,
Alexander Hamilton, Thomas Jefferson, Andrew Jackson, or John C.
Calhoun?

Moreover, Communitarians have to face the problem of possible conflict among a society's ideals. Two American ideals are liberty and
equality. Yet, these ideals sometimes are at odds with one another. If I
am free to do what I want to do, I might create inequalities for other
people; but if I have to respect the equality of all other people, I might
not be able to do all that I want to do. Another pair of American ideals
are equal opportunity and equal results. All other things being equal, if
individuals with the same relevant characteristics have equal opportunity, they will enjoy the same results. But equal opportunity is no guarantee of equal results. Thus, some social commentators are strong advocates of equal opportunity regardless of results, while others are strong
advocates of equal results despite equal opportunity. Finally, Communitarians face obstacles in their educational proposals. Individual students
in America, a highly pluralistic society, are likely to come from primary
communities differentiated by conflicting norms—families, neighborhoods, churches, and peer groups, for instance. It might be practically
impossible to find a significant core of values shared by these groups. In
addition, there is some question that schools would have the authority
to teach all students to be critical of their respective social ideals. It is
just not evident that all communities accept critical reflection as an ideal.
A community with ideals based on divine or charismatic authority is not
apt to look favorably on the assessment of its ideals by all of its
members.

Social Liberalism

Social Liberalism attempts to overcome the deficiencies of Individualism
and Communitarianism by blending aspects of the two. While Social
Liberals are insistent upon the rational autonomy of individuals, they
nevertheless recognize that individuals must live in social groups in order to secure the conditions that will enable them to be autonomous.[26]
These groups may be relatively simple primary communities or highly
complex pluralistic societies. Regardless of their differences, all individuals require certain things from a society in order to be autonomous:
life, freedom, prudence, equality, and justice. These qualities, then, become the core values of all reasonable individuals. Those values that
reasonable individuals in a society do not hold in common lie within the

sphere of the private. But the core values that all reasonable individuals share are the public values of a society. So, while public authorities do not have the right to interfere with the private lives of individuals, they do have the right to interfere with the lives of individuals insofar as their lives relate to public values.

Moral education, Social Liberals argue,[27] must seek to enable students to appreciate the core values of reasonable individuals and to help them acquire the knowledge, skills, and attitudes needed for understanding and appreciating those values and for developing into autonomous agents. To achieve this purpose, teachers must de-emphasize competitiveness among students, which tends to encourage students to perceive one another not just as unequal in individual talents but unequal as persons, too. Teachers must also allow students responsible freedom in their studies and see to it that fairness is a part of the classroom. Finally, teachers have to promote in students tolerance of differences in other people's private lives.

While Social Liberalism avoids major problems of both Individualism and Communitarianism, it nevertheless does not elude all difficulties. There are two stubborn ones. First, why does Social Liberalism restrict its bill of public values to less than all values entailed by the autonomy of reasonable individuals? Why not make moderation, caring, nurturing, and courage a part of the public domain? Surely, we are not to assume that prudent people as such do not have to be moderate, friendly, concerned, and courageous. Second, the kind of rationality presumed by Social Liberalism is prudential reasoning, which is concerned mainly with the good of the individual. While prudence is an important and desirable part of human life, it surely is not the only sort of practical reason that there is. Without considering the different sorts, Social Liberalism fails to show that moral reasoning is just a subclass of prudential reasoning. Moreover, by making prudential reasoning central to its approach, Social Liberalism begs the question by guaranteeing that the individual is logically prior to society, and thus that societies and public goods are mainly instruments for the good of individuals. In view of these two criticisms, the moral education advocated by Social Liberals de-emphasizes certain values that it should not and, moreover, consists mainly in instructing students in self-interest, albeit enlightened.

WHAT SORT OF CONCEPTION?

Even if all of you invited to work with me on this project are now convinced that a new theory of moral education for Americans is needed, some of you still might not be prepared to commit yourselves to the project. Some might have questions about the conception of moral education to be achieved.

Do I already have in mind the moral education to be attained? If I do, then will not my conducting the inquiry be just a matter of doing my utmost to rig our inquiry to issue in this preconceived idea of moral education, thus making the project a deceit? If I do not already have in mind the moral education to be formulated, then will not my conducting the investigation be just a matter of intellectual wandering without any sense of where to go, thus making the project a farce?

To be sure, I do have thoughts about moral education, especially for Americans. Some are entertainments, or ideas turned over in the mind but not involving any belief on my part. Many are opinions, or beliefs for which I have insufficient reasons. A few might pass as matters of knowledge, being beliefs for which I presumably have sufficient reasons. Nevertheless, I do not plan to use any of these thoughts, covertly or overtly, as the outcome of our inquiry. Many of you, I suspect, also have thoughts on moral education that we did not discuss above. If you do, then they are alternatives to mine, perhaps better than mine. Unfortunately, I do not know what they are, and there is no convenient way for me to learn what they are. Moreover, even if it were feasible for me to become acquainted with them, you and I probably would disagree over how to assess them in relation to mine. What I propose, therefore, is that we set aside, at least initially, all of our preferred ideas about moral education and see if there is a way to begin this project without prejudicing it toward one or another of our views.

Two neutral starting points seem to be what are usually recognized in philosophy as fundamental principles of reason, viz., the Principle of Identity and the Principle of Noncontradiction. The *Principle of Identity* holds that any object is what it is and not something else, whereas the *Principle of Noncontradiction* holds that a statement cannot be both true and false at the same time. Because these principles are first principles, they are not susceptible to proof, deductive or inductive. That they can be known to be true is problematic, then. Aristotle and David Hume maintained that their truth could be known by intuition; Bertrand Russell and Alfred North Whitehead simply accepted them for the reason that, in the judgment of these philosophers, the principles helped generate the most fruitful system of deductive logic possible. For our purpose we do not have to establish the truth of either principle; we only have to recognize that there is a pragmatic reason why we should use them. We wish to communicate with one another, and we cannot do that unless we employ these principles. If what we say to each other may be something other than what it is or may be both true and false, then we will be talking nonsense. These principles are not without their critics, of course. But every time a person attempts to argue against the principles, he or she relies on them in order to convey his or her points. If somebody ever shows how we can communicate with each other without employing the principles, we might not have to use them.[28] Meanwhile, the Principles of Identity and Noncontradiction exclude from our dialogue only those who believe that they can engage in dialogue without accepting those principles.

Another starting point is what may be called the *Principle of Justifiability,* which holds that any idea advanced for others to accept should be defensible according to the canons of reason, whether those of deduction, induction, scientific inquiry, judicial reasoning, moral reasoning, or some other sort. According to this principle, you should not accept any of my proffered views unless I provide adequate reasons for them, or unless you can think of such reasons on your own. For instance, you should not accept a moral norm submitted by me if I can support it only by appeal to some divine will or to some feeling on my part. I need to explain at least that the standard in question is actually willed by some divinity or that the feeling of concern is a source of moral guidance for people besides myself. The justification for the Principle of Justifiability may be put rather simply: We all presumably understand what it means to give adequate reasons for a statement; we all presumably are capable of giving such reasons; and we all presumably would accept statements put forth by any of us that are defensible on grounds of reason. Some of us might be inclined to accept statements that are not justifiable, but most of us probably are not so inclined. Moreover, that a person might accept an unjustifiable statement does not preclude that person from agreeing to accept whatever statements we advance on grounds of reason. Hence, the Principle of Justifiability necessarily excludes from our dialogue only persons who do not desire to accept any statement supported by reasons.

Because we do not know that any of the starting points of our project is true,[29] we cannot claim that any moral education theory which we develop in relying upon them is true. However, we have tried to justify these starting points; and if we have succeeded in justifying them, we might be able to maintain that any theory we develop in view of them is at least justifiable. John L. Austin, the late English philosopher, reportedly once expressed a doubt about the importance of importance. He said that truth is important, but he was not sure about importance. It might be, therefore, that a true theory of moral education is much more important than a merely justifiable one. Even so, it appears that if this project is to be undertaken conjointly, it must settle for nothing more than a justifiable theory and thus for something that might be less important than a true theory.

But why should the project be social? Why should the present inquiry invite all interested persons to participate? There are three reasons. The first is that this inquiry is philosophical, and philosophical inquiries ultimately are dialogical. Ever since the days of ancient Greek philosophy, when Plato said that a true idea must run the gauntlet of all objections, philosophical inquiry has constantly involved dispute, analysis, criticism, and other modes of intellectual intercourse. Even when Descartes conceived a metaphysical system allegedly through acts of meditation, he had to contend, despite his solitude, with Aristotelian specters lurking in his mind. Moreover, he reported the meditations to the intellectual community, which has subjected them to much discussion ever since. The second reason is that by making this inquiry a cooperative effort, I hope to be in a better position for avoiding mistakes that I otherwise would make. The third reason is practical. The outcome of the inquiry, if it is successful, must be not only applicable but also acceptable to Americans; that is, it must be something with which they can live. By consisting of interactions among all who want to participate in this inquiry, even at a distance, the inquiry will help ensure that whatever justifiable moral education theory might be established will be acceptable.

NOTES

1. Theodore Caplow, Howard M. Bahr, John Modell, and Bruce A. Chadwick, *Recent Social Trends in the United States, 1960–1990* (Montreal, Canada: McGill-Queen's University Press, 1991), pp. 496–504.

2. Ibid., pp. 213–214.

3. Sharon Zukin, "The Hollow Center: U.S. Cities in the Global Era," in *America at Century's End*, edited by Alan Wolfe (Berkeley, CA: University of California Press, 1991), pp. 245–261.

4. Daniel Patrick Moynihan, "Defining Deviancy Down," *The American Scholar* (Winter 1993), pp. 17–30. While Moynihan has held that the American public has lowered its standards on illegitimacy, crime, and mental illness as social deviances, Charles Krauthammer has maintained that the standards of deviancy for some conduct have been raised. Thus, practices that used to be acceptable are now referred to as child abuse, date rape, and politically incorrect speech. Charles Krauthammer, "Defining Deviancy Up," *The New Republic* 209:21 (November 22, 1993), pp. 20–25.

5. Michael Barone, "Slouching Toward Dystopia," *U.S. News & World Report* 115 (December 20, 1993), p. 34.

6. The Newsweek Poll, June 2–3, 1994. As reported in *Newsweek* 123 (June 13, 1994), p. 31.

7. See, for example, R.S. Peters, "A Reply to Kohlberg," *Phi Delta Kappan* 56 (June, 1975), p. 678.

8. Karl R. Popper, *The Open Society and Its Enemies*, 2 vols. (New York: Harper & Row Publishers, 1962).

9. Critical Theorists will argue that their conception of civic education is exempt from the criticism I have just made. The civic education advocated by Critical Theorists is critical civic education; it characteristically includes an ex-

amination of the ideology of a society. The Critical Theorists, I believe, are correct here. It should be noted, however, that they are right not because I am wrong in what I have said about civic education, but because critical civic education transcends the limits of civic education as the latter is usually portrayed.

Critical civic education, however, has a problem of its own. While Critical Theorists hold that people acquire their ideologies from their cultures, they do not fully explain how people learn to criticize their ideologies without cultural influences. Indeed, Critical Theorists do not adequately explain why Critical Theory itself is not simply the ideology of a certain culture, perhaps the culture of radical social theorists.

10. For a convenient survey of the "anti-moral education tradition," see Barry Chazan, *Contemporary Approaches to Moral Education: Analyzing Alternative Theories* (New York: Teachers College Press, 1985), pp. 91–102.

11. This position is described, but not advocated, by Amy Gutmann, *Democratic Education* (Princeton, NJ: Princeton University Press, 1987), pp. 5–6.

12. See, for example, Bruce Ackerman, *Social Justice in the Liberal State* (New Haven, CT: Yale University Press, 1980). Also see Eamonn Callan, *Autonomy and Schooling* (Kingston and Montreal, Canada: McGill-Queen's University Press, 1988).

13. Louis Raths, Merrill Harmin, and Sidney Simon, *Values and Teaching: Working with Values in the Classroom*, 2nd ed. (Columbus, OH: Charles E. Merrill, 1978).

14. For a survey of critical comment on Values Clarification, see Chazan, *Contemporary Approaches to Moral Education*, pp. 45–67.

15. Lawrence Kohlberg, *The Philosophy of Moral Development: Moral Stages and the Idea of Justice*, Vol. 1 of *Essays on Moral Development* (New York: Harper and Row, 1981).

16. For an overview of many critical reactions to Kohlberg's work, see Chazan, *Contemporary Approaches to Moral Education*, pp. 68–90.

17. See Carol Gilligan, *In a Different Voice: Psychological Theory and Women's Development* (Cambridge, MA: Harvard University Press, 1982). Also see Nell Noddings, *Caring: A Feminine Approach to Ethics and Moral Education* (Berkeley, CA: University of California Press, 1984).

18. Ackerman, *Social Justice in the Liberal State*, pp. 367–368.

19. Ibid., pp. 3–19.

20. Ibid., p. 377.

21. Ibid., p. 139.

22. Aristotle, *N. Ethics*, 1095b30–1096a4: ". . . for possession of virtue seems actually compatible with being asleep, or with lifelong inactivity, and, further, with the greatest sufferings and misfortunes; but a man who was living so no one would call happy, unless he were maintaining a thesis at all costs."

23. Betty Sichel, *Moral Education: Character, Community, and Ideals* (Philadelphia, PA: Temple University Press, 1988), pp. 113–134.

24. Amitai Etzioni, *The Spirit of Community: Rights, Responsibilities, and the Communitarian Agenda* (New York: Crown Publishers, 1993).

25. Sichel, *Moral Education: Character, Community, and Ideals*, pp. 135–165.

26. The most influential statement of Social Liberalism in recent years is prob-

ably by John Rawls, *A Theory of Justice* (Cambridge, MA: Harvard University Press, 1971).

27. The Social Liberal view of moral education is extensively discussed by Amy Gutmann in her *Democratic Education*.

28. Thus, Deconstructionists are caught in a bind when decrying either principle. They must utilize both principles in order to convey their position, or they must try to communicate it without using them. As far as I know, nobody has explained how communication can take place without relying on both principles.

29. Two of our starting points are the same as two of Bruce Ackerman's. Our Principle of Noncontradiction is his Principle of Consistency, and our Principle of Justifiability is his Principle of Rationality. He does not explicitly state the Principle of Identity but does presume it. We do not explicitly state an equivalent of his Principle of Neutrality; we regard that principle as entailed by the Principle of Justifiability. See Ackerman, *Social Justice and the Liberal State,* pp. 4–12.

2   The Norms of Moral Agency

Before we can clearly conceive a theory of moral education, we must determine the moral principles ingredient to that theory. Those standards will help shape the purpose, content, and pedagogy of the education covered by that theory.

In trying to delimit a set of moral principles, however, we appear to face an insuperable obstacle. In order to be practically operable in the United States, the principles should be generally agreeable to Americans. Yet, American society is pluralistic, containing many groups with diverse norms. It seems hopeless, then, to search for a set of norms that are commonly acceptable. But maybe the task is not actually hopeless. It might be that, by and large, Americans implicitly subscribe to a certain body of moral standards, but they are just not clear about what these norms are. If there are moral principles to which Americans are committed, more or less vaguely, and if those principles satisfy the Principles of Identity, Noncontradiction, and Justifiability, then they perhaps can serve as the moral foundation for a theory of moral education for Americans.

Before attempting to see whether or not there are moral norms to which Americans commonly subscribe, we should reach an understanding of what we mean by a moral standard. We cannot tell what moral standards Americans do or do not accept if we do not know what a moral standard is. Also, the understanding of a moral standard that we do reach might contain implications for the specific content of moral values, rights, and duties.

Any concept, it is widely held, functions to sort things out, or to identify them by the kinds they are and are not. Paul Hirst and R.S. Peters, for instance, have held that a concept is a linguistic rule by which we classify and distinguish things.[1] But even if this function is the essence of concepts, it is not the only use concepts might have. They might serve also as a source of principles for guiding conduct beyond the pale of classifying and distinguishing. Thus, Aristotle found ethical norms in the notion of the ultimate end of action.[2] Immanuel Kant located precepts of moral duty in the idea of moral duty.[3] Finally, Alan Gewirth has uncovered moral values, rights, and duties in the concept of voluntary action.[4] Not every concept, it should be noted, can function as a depository of ethical norms. The concept of a rectangle, for example, does nothing more than identify planes as rectilinear or not.

Because the conception of a moral norm that we define might have substantive moral implications, it needs to be one that we construct with great care. If it does turn out to involve such implications, it will contribute much to the body of moral standards that we establish for our theory of moral education. We then must be prepared to show that the involved content is acceptable to Americans in general. Consequently, it is appropriate to start our search for moral norms with a close consideration of the concept of a moral standard.

NORMATIVE MORAL CRITERIA

In one sense, a standard is a flag; in other senses, it is a rule of quantitative measure or an upright physical support. When we speak of a moral standard, however, we are talking about something else. We are talking about a criterion, which, as is usually understood, is a test by which the quality, worth, or correctness of something may be judged. The test consists of defined conditions that a given object must meet to satisfy the criterion of concern. Thus, the conditions may be those that an action must satisfy if it is to be judged as being courageous, good, or right. The criteria by which one judges matters as possessing or not possessing moral qualities, such as mercy and friendliness, are purely descriptive. They enable us to determine that the qualities are or are not present, but they do not enable us to judge the goodness or rectitude of anything. While descriptive moral standards are important, normative ones are of greater importance. Ultimately in morality, we want to know not just if a person or action has certain moral characteristics, but if that person is good or that action is right because of those characteristics. It is normative, not descriptive, moral standards on which we are focusing in this inquiry.

Two terms we have used in discussing the ordinary concept of a moral norm need extended clarification. They are *moral* and *judgment*.

Moral Being

There are two major senses of *moral,* descriptive and normative.[5] In the *descriptive* sense we refer to something as having certain features, such as when one says that abortion is a moral, as well as a legal, topic. In the *normative* sense we refer to something as satisfying normative moral standards, such as when one says that reasonable self-sacrifice is moral. An object cannot be moral in the normative sense unless it is moral in the descriptive sense. By contrast, an object can be moral in the descriptive sense without being moral in the normative sense, for it might be immoral. Something without moral features may be described as *nonmoral,* but not as immoral; whereas something morally improper may be described as *immoral,* but not as nonmoral.

What, then, are the commonly acceptable criteria by which actions may be simply described as moral or nonmoral? One of them is *voluntariness,* or being in control of one's actions. Two essentials of voluntariness are freedom and knowledge. We all allow that doers of moral actions are subject to praise and blame only if they act voluntarily, but we also insist that nobody acts willfully unless he or she acts freely and wittingly. An action is free if the agent performing it is not compelled to do so. It is knowing under these conditions: the agent knows who he or she is, is aware of what he or she is doing and why, is conscious of the end toward which the action tends, knows who are the recipients of what he or she is doing, and is aware of the immediate outcomes of his or her action.

Voluntary actions may be matters of decision. To decide on an action is not to select it because there is no alternative, nor is it to pick an action blindly. Rather, to decide on an action is to choose it from alternatives on the basis of a standard of correctness and of what one knows about the chosen action and its alternatives. A decision, however, need not yield a voluntary action; for it might be made from only a Hobson's range of alternatives or with less than all relevant knowledge.

Decisions, however, are certainly not the only generators of voluntary actions. People do many things more or less from habit, without the benefit of decision making. Upon reflection, they might regret some things done from habit and not regret others. Habitual actions, such as some instances of cigarette smoking, which are regretted by their agents are presently not voluntary even if the habits from which the actions sprang were originated by voluntary action on the part of the agents. Habitual actions, such as those of proper sanitation and nutrition, which are not regretted by their agents are voluntary even if the habits from which the actions sprang were initiated by involuntary action on the part of the agents.

But are we prepared to conclude that freedom and knowledge are sufficient for distinguishing moral actions? Suppose that what a woman voluntarily does has one, and only one, of the following for the only recipient of her action: a river, a rock, a tree, a nonhuman animal, herself, another actual voluntary agent, a human infant, a senile man, or a divinity. Probably everyone will agree that if her action affected another occurrent voluntary agent, it would be, in the descriptive sense, a moral action. Also, somebody somewhere will likely hold that the action is moral if it has any of the other recipients; but somebody else might disagree, too. If, for instance, I maintain that willfully polluting a stream, apart from any consequence for other voluntary agents, is morally wrong, I might meet objection from somebody who denies that morality is ever an affair strictly between a voluntary agent and an involuntary object, such as a stream, a rock, a tree, or a horse. Voluntary actions toward the nonhuman environment might be described, apart from any impact on voluntary agents, as natural or unnatural, but not as moral or nonmoral. Moreover, a secular humanist might insist that any voluntary action allegedly toward a divinity, for instance, an act of sacrifice, penance, or gratitude, is religious but nonmoral.

But what about the woman's action toward herself, a human infant, or a senile man? Does anyone have a problem with any of these recipients? There appears to be one with each of them. There is a philosophical tradition, going back at least to Aristotle, which holds that, in the respect that the impact of a voluntary action is upon the person performing it, the action is a matter of prudential, not moral, consideration. According to this tradition, then, the woman's action would be strictly of prudential interest in that it affected only herself. While we all acknowledge that human infants are not occurrent voluntary agents, we commonly recognize that they usually are potential, or prospective, voluntary agents. Hence, we would allow that if the woman's action is toward a human infant, it could be a moral action, although in a derivative sense of the term. Also, while we all acknowledge that senile people are neither occurrent nor prospective voluntary agents, we allow that they most often are retrospective voluntary agents in that they by and large used to be occurrent voluntary agents. Thus, we would tend to grant that if the woman's action is toward a senile man, it could be a moral action, although in a derivative sense.

Let us say, for convenience, that a voluntary action is interpersonal when it has for a recipient some voluntary agent, occurrent, prospective, or retrospective, other than its own agent. Consequently, we are maintaining that to be of moral interest, an act must be interpersonal as well as voluntary. While these traits appear to be sufficient for distinguishing any action as moral or nonmoral, they also are useful for marking more than actions as moral or nonmoral. A moral agent may be understood as the agent of a voluntary and interpersonal action. A moral decision is a decision made by a moral agent; that is, it is a decision that issues in a voluntary and interpersonal action. A moral quality, value, duty, right, or virtue is whatever is a quality, value, duty, right, or virtue for a moral action or agent. Moral rectitude is the conformity of a moral decision or action to a sound moral judgment. Normative moral judgments are determinations of what is good or right, bad or wrong, for agents of voluntary and interpersonal actions. In addition, normative moral standards are criteria by which what is good or right, bad or wrong, may be judged for agents of voluntary and interpersonal actions.

Moral Judgment

The term *judgment* is ambiguous, referring as it does to an activity or its end. The activity is a matter of thinking, while the end is a conclusion reached through the thinking. This ambiguity is reflected in the term's verb form. When we say that a person *judged* an object, we may intend that he or she either engaged in the activity of judging or simply stated a judgment about the object. In clarifying both senses of moral judgment, we will find it easier to begin with such judgment as an end.

The objects on which we pass moral judgments are myriad: actions, persons, character habits, social institutions, economic conditions, art, warfare, police practices, statutes, precepts, rules, and all other things pertaining to interpersonal voluntary agency.[6] The objects may be general and abstract, particular and concrete. Thus, we might judge honesty in general as being morally good, or a particular act of honesty as being morally right.

What we judge about moral objects are their qualities, values, and correctness. Qualities of moral interest are determined ultimately in order to assess the moral goodness of the qualities themselves or of the objects in which they inhere. Take politeness, for instance. In the abstract it might be judged to be morally good, and a concrete action might be judged to be polite and, thus, morally worthy. Which objects may be judged as morally right depends on the meaning of *right* intended. When propriety is meant, then a wide variety of objects may be deemed as morally right or not. Actions, character traits, economic institutions, and many other sorts of objects may be judged to fit or not to fit, according to moral norms, a situation. But when satisfying all relevant moral standards for an action is the intended meaning, only actions, of course, may be judged as right. The latter sense of moral correctness is the one at stake for us.

To judge an action as morally correct is not necessarily to allow that it is morally good. The action might be correct simply because it is the least of evils.[7] But to judge an action as morally good also is not necessarily to allow that it is morally right. When we say that an action is morally right, we mean, as already indicated, that it satisfies all relevant moral standards for acting and, therefore, that it should be performed. But by itself the moral goodness of an action need not be sufficient to make an action one that satisfies all relevant moral norms. An alternative action, for instance, might have greater moral worth and, thus, greater moral force as one that ought to be performed; or another alternative action might be the one that ought to be performed simply because it meets some criterion of moral necessity.

A judgment that an action is morally right is not the same as a decision to perform the action. Judgments of moral correctness guide moral agents to moral decisions; that is, they serve as reasons for selecting actions for performance. But picking out an action for performance is not the same as a reason for selecting it. Hence, moral literature frequently refers to the possibility of not deciding to perform the actions that are judged to be morally right. For example, St. Paul says, "For the good that I would I do not: but the evil which I would not, that I do."[8] The possibility is implied also in the precept, "Do right," which is, according to some commentators on America's moral scene, the chief moral principle of both white Southerners and urban African Americans. For Florence King, the white Southern version is, "You got to do right, you hear?"[9] And, according to Spike Lee, the urban African American version is, "Do the right thing, man."[10] Either way, the precept plainly allows that one may or may not decide to do what one knows to be right. If, of course, Good Ol' Boys and young African American urban males, as well as St. Paul, had an ample supply of moral fortitude, they, like all other ideal moral agents, necessarily would decide to do that which they know to be right. But because they, like the rest of us, suffer some deficiency in moral strength, they have to be reminded to do the things they have judged to be morally right.

The activity of moral judgment involves one's relating the object under consideration to a moral criterion.[11] Like any other kind of criterion, a moral standard applies to a class of objects. A complete statement of such a standard would include a description of that class. Thus, a full statement of the Golden Rule would indicate the class of persons to whom it pertains: Christians only, all people, adults only, rational people only, or some other class. But a moral criterion does not relate to a class of objects in isolation; it applies to those objects within specified circumstances. Accordingly, a comprehensive statement of the criterion must include a description of the circumstances in which the objects are subject to the standard. So, when Kant put forth truthfulness as a normative moral principle, he explained that the principle applied to all rational beings in all circumstances where telling a lie is the only alternative to telling the truth.[12] A part of what one does, then, in relating an object to a moral standard is to compare the object's identity and circumstances with the class characteristics and circumstances included in the standard. If one sees the object's identity and circumstances as matching those of the standard, one must regard the object as subject to the standard.

Another part of what we do in relating objects especially to a moral norm pertains to the normative component of the standard. Besides a description of the objects to which the standard applies, and a statement of the circumstances under which the criterion bears on those objects, a complete statement of the standard also contains a norm, which may be, most notably, a value, duty, or right. Aristotle, for instance, makes happiness the ultimate good of all human action. F.H. Bradley makes the performance of one's social role the moral duty of each and every human being. And virtually all moral philosophers have regarded life as an object of moral claim. A moral standard may be so general that it refers to no object specifically, or it may refer to a specific one. For instance, St. Thomas Aquinas' First Moral Law of Nature is, "Seek the good," which refers to no specific action as leading to any specific end that is good. Also, Kant's Categorical Imperative, "Follow a rule of action only if you logically are willing for all other rational beings in similar circumstances to follow it," refers to no specific rule. Highly general standards may be fundamental ones in that they may be used in judging the worth of standards that do refer to specific norms. The Categorical Imperative, for instance, purports to be a normative standard of rules; that is, it intends that a moral rule can be a good one only if it is one that an agent entertaining it is logically willing for all other agents in similar circumstances to follow.

As indicated, making a normative moral judgment may proceed simply by telling whether or not a single object does or does not satisfy a given standard apart from other objects and standards. Or it might proceed in a more complicated way, examining various people, actions, and circumstances; ranking values and disvalues; and taking into account various rights and duties. The process might be further complicated in that it must determine not if an object is good entirely, but if it is good on balance. People and their actions typically are a mixture of good and bad qualities.

BEING MORAL: THE CRITERION OF MORAL VALUE

We have defined a normative moral norm as a criterion for judging the value or rectitude of matters pertinent to moral agents. A moral agent, we have explained, is one who willfully does something that bears influence on another voluntary agent. So, because the concept of a normative moral standard logically involves that of a moral agent, it also obviously contains those of voluntariness and interpersonalness. There are, however, other elements embedded in the concept. When people do things freely and knowingly, they do them with purpose. That is, they employ the actions for attaining ends in view, which may be separate from the actions themselves or may be nothing more than the performance of the actions. Because moral agents are purposeful, they also are deliberative. They do not select just any actions to attain whatever ends they have in mind; they weigh alternative actions and, in view of all available moral knowledge, decide on those that will rightly fulfill their purposes. Moreover, because moral agents are purposeful, they are evaluative. That a moral agent's purpose is necessarily an object of evaluation is not immediately evident. People acting voluntarily and interpersonally sometimes pursue goals by whim; they fix on them without considering their worth, not even implicitly. Yet, when actual moral agents have their objectives capriciously, they do so only as imperfect voluntary agents. To be completely in control of their actions, people have to pursue ends they value. Unevaluated goals will prove innocuous, harmful, or beneficial. People, it is commonly thought, do not willfully seek goals toward which they are indifferent or which they see as harmful. If unevaluated purposes prove beneficial, they will do so by luck, not by any volition on the part of those with the purposes. In sum, because the concept of a normative moral criterion embodies that of a moral agent, it entails purpose, action, deliberation, and evaluation in addition to freedom, knowledge, and interpersonalness.

There might be other matters contained within the idea of a moral action guide, but those we have just identified appear to be the major ones. So, rather than continuing to look for others, we now shall determine which, if any, of those just identified are moral norms. What we shall soon see is that nearly all of them logically are criterial conditions by which normative moral judgments must be made.[13] In other words, we have constructed a conception of a moral norm that implies certain moral norms. We did not set out to build such a conception; we wanted nothing more than to reach a common understanding of what a moral norm is. Regardless, because we have agreed on a conception that entails normative moral criteria, we eventually will have to determine whether or not those criteria are generally acceptable to Americans.

As moral agents, we have explained, people value their respective purposes and the actions they have severally chosen for attaining them. Consequently, they also prize the particular voluntariness, deliberation, and evaluation involved in their individual agencies. That they necessarily prize the interpersonalness of their given actions is doubtful, for it might involve such rueful relations as those between enemies, between victims and exploiters, and between the grieving and the dying. At any rate, each moral agent also recognizes the worth of the purpose, action, voluntariness, deliberation, and evaluation included in all other instances of his or her moral agency, prospective as well as occurrent.

Each and every moral agent, however, logically has to esteem these conceptual elements of a moral norm as they also are related in general to the agencies of all other moral agents. Even though individual moral agents are different in particulars of purpose, action, freedom, knowledge, deliberativeness, and evaluation, they are the same in certain general respects, for they all have some freedom, some knowledge, some purpose, and so forth. So, because a moral agent esteems these factors as they pertain to his or her agency, he or she must prize them also as they relate to the moral agencies of all others to the extent that their agencies and his or hers are the same. In other words, any moral agent must value these elements of the concept of a moral norm as they pertain to moral agency in general.

In saying that moral agents as such have to appreciate purpose, action, freedom, etc., as features of moral agency, we intend that they have to value as well the psychological and social conditions that help make it possible for moral agents to formulate morally worthy purposes, decide on morally correct actions, enjoy morally estimable freedom, acquire morally worthwhile knowledge, and engage in sound moral deliberations and judgments. Moral agents do not produce purposes, perform actions, have freedom, and so forth in a vacuum. People are able to act as moral agents only because they have talents and dispositions for so doing, and because they live within social circumstances that support them in so doing or at least do not prevent them from acting as moral agents. Hence, moral agents can prize moral purpose, action, voluntariness, etc., only if they value as well the psychological and social conditions that enable them to enjoy these factors.

Because we jointly hold that any moral agent as such is logically committed, by the common idea of a moral norm, to esteeming the major elements of moral agency, we have to concede that each and every moral agent must accept as a moral norm the Criterion of Moral Value (CMVa): *Any person who is a moral agent should value the central elements of moral agency not only as they pertain to his or her own agency, but also as they relate to the moral agency of all other persons.* That this is a basic standard of moral value is derived from two facts. First, the criterion, which involves the major values of moral agency, encompasses values entailed by any and all moral agencies. Second, the norm may serve to determine the moral rectitude of all other criteria of moral values used by people. Thus, if pride, or self-esteem, is a morally correct norm, as Aristotle maintained, then it must be consistent with the CMVa. Or if, by contrast, meekness is a morally right norm, as Jesus maintained, then it must be consistent with the criterion.

Even though the CMVa follows from our analysis of what a moral norm is, it is nontrivial in practical life. It is a standard for moral valuations by actual moral agents, not by ideal ones. Hence, it is a standard that rationally must be followed by people who are moral agents, but it is not one that they necessarily will follow. Some defect in their makeup as moral agents might cause them to violate the standard. With appropriate word changes this point about the practical nontriviality of the CMVa and that about the standard's being basic will apply to the other moral criteria we will formulate.

Lastly, it is important to observe that the CMVa treats the various major elements of moral agency as being of equal worth, which might cause concern for some moral theorists. Treating these elements as having equal value presupposes that they will never be in conflict with each other and thus will never prompt an agent to have to prefer one to another. Yet, this prospect, it might be charged, is unrealistic. Many moral situations in life call for decisions not between the good and the bad, but between greater and lesser goods, greater and lesser bads. Hence, if a standard of moral worth is to be useful, it should include a mechanism for rank ordering moral goods.

The reason why we do not formulate the CMVa in such a way that it rank orders the moral worth of the major elements of moral agency is simply that for moral agency the elements logically are of equal value. Without any one of them, there cannot be complete moral agency; and with them all, interrelated with one another, there is an integral whole, moral agency. Thus, to sacrifice moral freedom for moral knowledge, to emphasize moral action at the expense of moral deliberation, to weigh moral judgment over moral decision, or to do the reverse of any of these is to violate moral agency. On the other hand, the CMVa certainly allows that there might be difficulty in determining which particular freedom, which knowledge, which purpose, which action, and so forth belong to a given instance of moral agency. But trying to determine which freedom, which knowledge, which purpose, which action, and so on fits an instance of moral agency does not depend on a rank ordering of the values of these various elements.

BEING MORAL: OTHER MORAL NORMS

The CMVa is not the only normative moral standard implied by our understanding of the concept of a moral norm. There also are standards of moral rights, moral duty, and moral virtue.

The Criterion of Moral Rights

Because the major elements of moral agency are essential to it, they are part and parcel of any instance of moral agency. Hence, the person who is a moral agent in a given instance may have a moral right to the chief traits of moral agency in that particular instance. As is normally understood, a right is a justified claim to an object;[14] and a claim is a demand that something is due, or owed, to oneself by others. To say that something is due oneself by others with regard to an object is to insist that other people should not interfere with one's access to that object, and to insist that on occasion others should help one gain access to it.

In attempting to justify claims, moral or otherwise, people rely on a variety of reasons, for example, desire, need, merit, kinship, harmlessness, and law. To justify a moral claim, however, we must appeal to need or merit and to harmlessness. That is, a moral claim is established only by appeal to what one needs or deserves as a moral agent and to harmlessness to the moral agency of others. In other words, to justify a moral claim, one has to show that one needs or deserves as a moral agent the object of the claim and, in addition, that one's access to the object will not violate the moral agency of others in an unjustifiable way. If, for instance, Sue Ann neither needs nor deserves a college education for developing as a moral agent, she has no moral right to it even though her having it might violate no other person's moral rights or interfere with any other person's performance of moral duties.[15] If, on the other hand, Charles morally needs and deserves to go to college, but can do so only by leaving his invalid mother without care, he does not have a moral right to go.[16] While voluntary agents occasionally might make claims for reasons of desire, kinship, law, or prudence, they do not thereby justify them morally. Any of those reasons may be overridden by moral need or merit and moral harmlessness.

The sorts of objects which moral agents can show that they need or deserve are the major elements of moral agency. That any moral agent ever earns a given freedom, knowledge, purpose, evaluation, deliberation, et cetera, is contextually dependent. Furthermore, whether or not any moral agent ever needs a given freedom, knowledge, purpose, and so on is contextually dependent, too. But that each and every moral agent needs *some* freedom, knowledge, purpose, and so forth is logically true; for no person conceptually could be or act as a moral agent without some freedom, knowledge, purpose, and so on. Hence, even when a moral agent does not deserve or need certain particular components of moral agency, he or she has a right to other ones as long as his or her enjoying the latter does not harm other moral agents. That a moral agent has a right to the major constituents of moral agency does not imply that he or she must exercise that right. If that fact did imply that obligation, it would mean that a moral right is logically one and the same as a moral duty.[17] But because a moral agent does value the main components of moral agency, he or she is inclined to exercise his or her right to them.

There are, then, two reasons why moral agents logically respect each other's rights to the major features of moral agency. One is that each agent expects all others to respect his or her rights to these objects. The other is that they all accept the same principles of justification for claims to the objects. We derive, as a consequence, the Criterion of Moral Rights (CMR): *Each person who is a moral agent should respect the rights of all other persons to the major elements of moral agency.*

The respect involved in this standard concerns the correlative duties of noninterference and assistance. When a moral agent exercises a moral right, other moral agents are obligated not to interfere with that agent. Moreover, they are bound to assist the agent if need be and if helping the agent does not impose an unreasonable burden upon themselves.[18] When a person does receive aid in the exercise of a right, he or she might incur the reciprocal duty of repaying certain individuals or moral society in general for that help.[19] Thus, sons and daughters are morally bound to repay their parents for sacrifices made by the latter on behalf of the former, providing that the sons and daughters are in a reasonable position to repay and providing that the parents need the repayment. In any event, the sons and daughters are morally bound to be grateful to their parents for any sacrifice made on their behalf.

To be sure, application of the CMR requires close attention to the degree in which persons are moral agents. Prenatal and neonatal human beings surely are not occurrent moral agents; but insofar as their prospects for development as moral agents look promising, they have rights as prospective moral agents to those conditions, such as life, nutrition, health, and education, that will help them develop into full-fledged moral agents.[20] While adolescents are typically closer to being occurrent moral agents than are children, they usually fall short of moral agency in some respects, thus having fewer moral rights, and responsibilities, than occurrent moral agents have. The severely mentally retarded, the hopelessly insane, and the senile have human rights; but it is problematic that they, being neither occurrent nor prospective moral agents, have moral rights. If they do, it is because they used to be moral agents or might have been moral agents. Either way, the rights they have are more limited than those had by prospective or occurrent moral agents.

The Criterion of Moral Duty

A moral duty is an action that a person as a moral agent categorically must perform. Even if that person does not want to perform the action, he must perform it. The necessity expressed here by "must" is not physical or psychological compulsion. It is, rather, the logical necessity that the person is under as a moral agent. In recognition that a person really does not have to follow a moral obligation, people commonly use "should" or "ought" rather than "must" in stating moral duties.

We have already mentioned some moral duties, namely, the correlative and reciprocal obligations associated with moral rights. But any person who is a moral agent has obligations logically independent of any consideration of moral rights. Because a moral agent, by its very concept, values the major elements of moral agency, such an agent seeks to maintain and foster those elements. From this logical fact follows the Criterion of Moral Duty (CMD): *Any person who is a moral agent is bound to secure and nurture the major constituents of moral agency.*

This criterion applies strictly to occurrent moral agents and to prospective ones only to the extent that they are free and knowing. Moreover, it means that a moral agent is obligated, insofar as the agent is free and witting, to maintain and foster the major elements of moral agency for him- or herself as well as for all other persons who are moral agents. The CMD entails also that, in securing and encouraging these elements, people are to be concerned with social and economic institutions, political and legal practices, health care, schools, and other structures and conditions affecting the elements generally and indirectly as well as any matters influencing them specifically and directly. Finally, the CMD in addition implies that a moral agent has responsibilities for maintaining and promoting the major factors of moral agency even if the agent has no duties connected with any moral rights. Ensconced in this implication is the point that the CMD, like the CMR, provides a basis for moral intervention. If a person who is a moral agent fails to perform a moral duty, he or she, failing as a moral agent, is subject to reproof by another moral agent. Thus, the responsible person who does not perform a correlative or reciprocal duty associated with a moral right is subject to chastisement. And the responsible person who, irrespective of any moral right, fails to secure and encourage the major constituents of moral agency, is liable to rebuke also.

The Criterion of Moral Virtue

Moral virtues are the character dispositions that are of moral worth; that is, they are the habits that are elements of the moral agent's character.[21] Because moral virtues are morally worthy, they at least implicitly fall under the Criterion of Moral Value. I think it appropriate, however, to separate our consideration of the norm of moral virtue from that of the norm of moral value in general. Virtue is widely recognized, by philosophers and the moral laity, as quite important in moral life[22]; also, it is commonly regarded as important to moral education, which is the ultimate concern of our inquiry.[23]

Since ancient times, moral virtues have been conceived as involving cognitive as well as affective aspects of oneself. Plato, for instance, spoke of the virtue of wisdom as well as those of courage, temperance, and justice.[24] Aristotle explicitly distinguished between the intellectual virtues and those dealing with the appetites, or what he called the "moral virtues."[25] Contemporary philosophers view the moral virtues as involving intellectual excellences as well as worthy habits related to the feeling side of ourselves.[26] Accordingly, we set forth the Criterion of Moral Virtue (CMVi): *Any person who is a moral agent should have those dispositions of character, in both its cognitive and affective aspects, that are contributive to the major factors of moral agency.*

The intellectual disposition that we take to be of special moral worth is moral reasoning, which consists of the knowledge, skills, appreciations, and psychical energy needed for making decisions consistent with the CMVa, CMR, and CMD. While we take this form of practical reasoning to be special for morality, we do not thereby intend that other intellectual dispositions cannot have moral value. The intellectual habits associated with philosophy and science, natural and social, as well as technological and aesthetic reasoning might contribute to the character of moral agents. These dispositions might contribute to moral reasoning, and they might help produce worthwhile conditions for moral life. None of this is to say, however, that each and every intellectual disposition in and of itself is necessarily a moral virtue. The habits connected with scientific thinking, for instance, are not virtues or vices in the abstract; they become moral virtues or vices only when they become part of some morally good or bad character. The stories of Drs. Frankenstein and Strangelove stand as reminders of this point.

Some affective moral virtues are self-regarding. In order to be capable of moral autonomy, a person needs dispositions contributive to physical and psychical maintenance and growth. For instance, he or she plainly requires dispositions for a healthy diet, sanitation, and exercise. He or she also needs hopefulness and moderation in pleasure. People have to be hopeful if they are to conceive worthy purposes and proper means for attaining them. If people are not to be enslaved by pleasure, they must not set it as a goal. Rather, they must learn to have it simply as a quality that accompanies some right actions for the attainment of worthy purposes.

Other affective moral virtues are other-regarding. Empathy, or interpersonal sensitivity, is putting oneself in the other person's place. Charity is helping others toward whom one has no direct ties and insofar as one reasonably can. Politeness is treating all people in whom one has no particular interest, including complete strangers, as fellow moral beings unless one has good reason to believe that they lack respect for morality. In addition, there are justice and friendship. Compensatory justice is making amends to people whose rights have been violated. Distributive justice is seeing to it that people receive their fair share of the things that they need and deserve. Lastly, retributive justice is calling people to task for violating the CMR and the CMD. Friendship consists largely of the intimate sharing of interests and the equal respect that individuals have with each other. People do not have to have friendships for moral motives; they may have them, rather, simply because they enjoy certain persons as individuals. Even so, there are moral reasons for having friendships when they are consistent with the basic norms of morality.[27] The qualities that individuals share as moral agents provide a basis for morally worthy mutual interests and morally proper equal respect. Friendship makes it possible for moral agents to understand and to be sensitive to one another as moral agents. Finally, it enables moral agents to appreciate and enjoy moral life in one of its richest forms. Like intellectual dispositions, affective dispositions are not moral virtues in the abstract; they have to fit in with the character of moral agency. Aristotle notwithstanding,[28] friendship is not in and of itself a moral virtue. It is a moral virtue only if it is a quality of the moral agent's character. Thus, the possibility of a friendship between Hitler and Himmler is a moral anomaly for only those who treat certain dispositions as morally good in and of themselves, apart from any context of moral character.

There are, of course, other moral virtues. Political leadership and family management are such when they rest on the basic values of morality. Truthfulness is one insofar as it expresses the knowledge and moral equality esteemed by a moral agent. We will not try, however, to give an exhaustive list of the moral virtues. Indeed, such a list may be practically impossible. As Aristotle noted, some virtues emerge from experience; and how many virtues there are and what they are will depend on experience, which is subject to change.

It might be that not all persons who are moral agents, occurrent and prospective, can possess the known moral virtues to the same degree and range. Only a few persons are likely to possess all recognized moral virtues in full perfection. Some persons, for instance, will develop scientific but not moral reasoning easily, and exercise the former but not the latter with proficiency, while others will do the reverse. And some will be much less receptive, for instance, to politeness and friendship than others will be. Thus, moral agents have to know how to deal with deficiencies in the moral character of their fellow beings; and teachers have to take the individual differences of their pupils into account in moral education.

THE MORAL SOCIETY AND THE MORAL COMMUNITY

In arguing that the norms we have proposed for moral agents have their logical origins in our concept of a moral norm, we plainly have not followed the Communitarian's claim that the moral norms and identity of an individual reside in the latter's community. At the same time, we have not followed, either, the Individualist's position that individual moral agents are related to one another mainly in atomistic and instrumental ways. While we started our analysis of the normative dimension of the features of moral agency by considering the individual moral agent's valuation of those features as they pertain to him- or herself only, we did not assume thereby that an individual moral agent is logically independent of others. As a matter of fact, we established that all individual moral agents will see, upon reflection, that they are closely tied to one another through their kinship as moral agents and thus through the norms they share with one another.

There are two major modes of association among moral agents. One is the moral society. This society is informal: Its regulations are not codified, and none of its members is in an official position of authority. To function as members of the society, therefore, people have to rely on their moral autonomy. They have to discover the norms of their moral agency through their powers of reasoning. They have to judge for themselves if they and their fellow members have followed or violated these standards. And they have to praise and reprove one another for their moral accomplishments and shortcomings. The members of the moral society do not have sustained and widespread contact with each other. They interact with each other only intermittently; they often are unacquainted with one another. They are two strangers walking past each other on a dark street; they are sales clerks and customers. They are one family quarreling with another; they are one nation contending with another.

The other mode of association among moral agents is the moral community. A moral community involves enduring and comprehensive contact among its members. Like a moral society, a moral community includes recognition by its members of one another as moral agents and thus of the fundamental norms of moral agency that they share. But the community also includes recognition by its members of whatever moral norms are special to itself. Still further, it comprises customary ways whereby moral problems are examined and settled through rational dialogue. Finally, it contains persistent effort on the part of its adult members to pass on the life of moral agency to its younger members.

It is relatively easy to have moral communities when people live with each other in face-to-face groups. As sociologists and philosophers have long noted, however, people in this century increasingly have associated with each other at a distance and indirectly.[29] We are concerned with injustice, poverty, starvation, disease, pollution, and ignorance in Africa, Asia, eastern Europe, and Latin America as well as in our own neighborhoods and cities. If people who interact with each other by and large, distantly and indirectly, are to constitute a moral community, they at least must be in steady communication with each other so that they can share their interests as moral agents. This in turn means that they have to have a common language and communications technology.

That a great moral community can exist without support from formal institutions is doubtful. The moral community of medieval Europe was sustained by the Roman Catholic Church as well as by various state governments. The moral community of Islam today depends on political as well as ecclesiastical structures and policies. Lastly, the collective wisdom of political philosophers is that human life cannot fully prosper outside political society. It might be, then, that a vast community of moral agents will have to rely on formal structures, practices, and policies. If we are to figure out how to educate the members of the United States in the norms of moral agency and thus to transform them into a large moral community, we might have to consider what formal arrangements will be needed to sustain and promote such a community.

NOTES

1. P.H. Hirst and R.S. Peters, *The Logic of Education* (London: Routledge & Kegan Paul, 1973), p. 4.

2. Aristotle, *N. Ethics,* Book I.

3. Immanuel Kant, *Fundamental Principles of the Metaphysic of Morals,* translated by Thomas K. Abbot (New York: The Liberal Arts Press, 1954), first and second sections.

4. Alan Gewirth, *Reason and Morality* (Chicago, IL: The University of Chicago Press, 1978), Chapter 1.

5. William K. Frankena, *Ethics* (Englewood Cliffs, NJ: Prentice-Hall, 1963), pp. 5–8.

6. For a taxonomy of moral judgments, see Frankena, *Ethics,* pp. 8ff.

7. Nicholas Rescher, *Introduction to Value Theory* (Englewood Cliffs, NJ: Prentice-Hall, 1979), pp. 63–72.

8. *Romans* 7:19.

9. Florence King, *Lump It or Leave It* (New York: St. Martin's Press, 1990), p. 10.

10. At least, this version is suggested by Spike Lee's movie title, *Do the Right Thing.*

11. C.D. Broad, "Ought We to Fight for Our Country?" in *Introductory Readings in Ethics*, edited by William F. Frankena and John T. Granrose (Englewood Cliffs, NJ: Prentice-Hall, 1974), pp. 29–30.

12. Immanuel Kant, "On a Supposed Right to Tell Lies from Benevolent Motives," in *Kant's Critique of Practical Reason and Other Works on the Theory of Ethics*, 6th ed., edited and translated by Thomas Kingsmill Abbott (New York: Longmans, Green and Co., 1954), pp. 361–365.

13. Cf. Gewirth, *Reason and Morality,* pp. 49–54.

14. Cf. Joel Feinberg, *Rights, Justice, and the Bounds of Liberty* (Princeton, NJ: Princeton University Press, 1982), pp. 139–142.

15. But while Sue Ann might not have the education as a matter of moral right, she might have it as a matter of moral privilege or license. Rich relatives might extend her a privilege by enabling her to go, without harming herself or other moral agents, to a college that specializes in students who do not necessarily need a college education and who are not necessarily capable of obtaining

one without extraordinary efforts by, say, a battery of tutors. If Sue Ann does not have parents with sufficient funds, she might be permitted by moral society to attend a public college with an open admissions policy as long as she, while attending there, performs satisfactorily and harms neither herself nor other moral agents. When a moral right conflicts with a moral privilege or license, the former logically prevails. Moral privileges and permissions are bestowed upon moral agents, while moral rights are had by moral agents simply by their being such. Hence, moral privileges and permissions, but not moral rights, carry with them the duty of their bearers to be grateful to the bestowers of concern.

16. But what if there is a conflict between need and merit? Suppose that only two students apply for a scholarship. One student has great financial need for it but has only middling qualifications. The other student does not financially need it but has superb qualifications. The institution awarding the scholarship wants to help needy students but also wants to attract students with superior qualifications so as to enhance itself as an educational milieu, but it has resources for only the one scholarship. Several points have to be considered. What does each student intend to do with his or her education: to benefit him- or herself primarily or to make substantial contributions to moral society? Is the proportion of quality students at the college sufficiently large or woefully small? Can the college change its awards policy so as to rotate the scholarship on a yearly basis between needy and quality students, or so as to award financial aid primarily for need and secondarily for academic qualifications and honorary distinctions primarily for academic excellence? In sum, conflict between a claim based on need and one based on merit often has to be resolved casuistically, as does conflict between competing claims based on need or competing claims based on desert.

17. Ronald Dworkin says, in *Taking Rights Seriously* (Cambridge, MA: Harvard University Press, 1977), p. xi: "Individual rights are political trumps held by individuals." But that rights are trumps does not mean that they have to be exercised indiscriminately. Just as there is a difference between having a trump and playing it, there is a difference between having a right and exercising it. And just as trumps have to be played only under certain conditions, rights should be exercised only with sensitivity to the moral good of others. As Feinberg observes in *Rights, Justice, and the Bounds of Liberty,* p. 142, a person may decline to exercise a right for reason of self-sacrifice.

18. In his *Morality and Reason,* p. 135, Gewirth sets forth the conditions under which one is obligated to render assistance: The bearer of the right of concern cannot successfully exercise the right without the assistance, and providing the assistance will not involve cost for the provider that is comparable to that which the bearer would face if the bearer did not successfully exercise the right of concern.

19. By editorial policy, the journal *The Responsive Community: Rights and Responsibilities* is especially concerned, along with other issues about the community responsibilities of individuals, with whether or not national service is a good way to increase opportunities for repayment to the community for its assistance.

20. We must immediately caution the reader that this explanation does not intend that abortions necessarily are morally wrong. A fetus with poor medical

prospects for developing into a moral agent has a tenuous hold on any rights as a prospective moral agent. Moreover, if a pregnant female is an occurrent moral agent, and there is a profound conflict between her physical or psychical well being as a moral agent and the life of her fetus, she has a stronger case for her right to this well being than the case that might be made for the fetus. A fetus is morally innocent in a sense, but its innocence is not sufficient for making abortion morally wrong in principle. Yet, the innocence factor must weigh in judgments about the moral rectitude of abortion. Even if the taking of a particular human fetus's life is morally right, it is not morally good insofar as the fetus is a prospective moral agent. It is simply the lesser of two evils.

21. The concept of the character of the moral agent is analyzed in Chapter 4.

22. For example, Alasdair MacIntyre, *After Virtue*, 2nd ed. (Notre Dame, IN: Notre Dame University Press, 1984). Howard Fineman, "The Virtuecrats," *Newsweek* 123 (June 13, 1994), pp. 31–36.

23. For instance, William J. Bennett, ed., *The Book of Virtues: A Treasury of Great Moral Stories* (New York: Simon & Schuster, 1993).

24. Plato, *The Republic,* Book IV.

25. Aristotle, *N. Ethics,* Books III–VI.

26. Betty A. Sichel, *Moral Education: Character, Community, and Ideals* (Philadelphia, PA: Temple University Press, 1988), p. 94.

27. To be sure, a friendship need not concord with the CMVa, the CMR, and the CMD. If there was a friendship between Hitler and Himmler, for instance, it almost certainly involved concerns contrary to these standards.

28. Aristotle, *N. Ethics*, Book IV, Chapter 6.

G.E. Moore is both vague and confusing on the status of friendship as a moral virtue. Defining a moral virtue as a habit "to perform actions which generally produce the best possible results," he insists that no moral virtue has intrinsic value. He maintains, however, that human affection does have intrinsic worth. Does he, then, not regard friendship as a moral virtue even though it leads to conduct of a moral sort? Or does he mean that it is a moral virtue under some circumstances but not others, thus leaving open the possibility that friendship can both have intrinsic value and be a moral vice? See G.E. Moore, *Principia Ethica* (Cambridge, England: Cambridge University Press, 1954), pp. 171–173, 188–189, 203–205.

My own view of the matter is that moral virtues, apart from any instrumental value they might have, have constitutive value. That is, they have value as constituent elements of a whole, namely, the moral agent's character. Hence, friendship may but need not be a moral virtue; and when it is a moral virtue, it necessarily has constitutive moral value in addition to any instrumental moral value it might have.

29. A classic on the topic is John Dewey, "Search for the Great Community," in *The Public and Its Problems* (Denver, CO: Alan Swallow, 1954), Chapter 5, pp. 143–184.

3   The Feasibility of the Norms

We began this inquiry by observing that the people of the United States, facing an impending breakdown of their moral life, sorely need moral education. This education is to habituate the nation's members to act according to moral norms and induce them to appreciate such norms. We then undertook to locate defensible moral norms for that education. The norms of moral agency, or the Criterion of Moral Value (CMVa), the Criterion of Moral Rights (CMR), the Criterion of Moral Duty (CMD), and the Criterion of Moral Virtue (CMVi), have been identified as logically defensible.

The argument in the preceding chapter by which we justified these as moral norms was simple in outline: If one accepts the ordinary conception of a moral standard, and if one fully grasps all the implications, direct and indirect, of that conception, then one logically must concede that the CMVa, CMR, CMD, and CMVi are fundamental moral norms. It might be, of course, that the common idea of a moral standard was not accurately stated; and it might be that some of the implications we attributed to the idea that we did state are not actually there. But even if the argument suffers no faults in these or other aspects, it still does not show that the norms of moral agency should be the core of morality and moral education for the United States. That principles are impeccable at the level of theory does not necessarily mean that they are applicable to each and every practical situation, maybe not even any practical situation. Thus, Plato was quite aware that the ideal society he set forth in *The Republic* might not be feasible in this world. A point frequently made about democracy is that it will not work in all societies. A criticism often made of some versions of Christian ethics is that they are unrealistic.

So, before we may conclude that the norms of moral agency should constitute the heart of morality and moral education for America, we have to consider their feasibility as moral standards for the nation. We will proceed by taking up two questions: Are Americans likely to be receptive to the norms of moral agency as moral standards? Do American traditions support the norms of moral agency? Positive answers to these questions might not mean that the standards of concern are feasible, for there might be other questions that need to be addressed. Nevertheless, the two questions before us plainly are major ones; for a negative answer to either will mean that the criteria are impracticable.

WHAT OBJECTIONS ARE AMERICANS LIKELY TO HAVE TO THE NORMS?

It is important that the norms of moral agency be acceptable to the American people if those norms are to be central to the morality and moral education of Americans. If the norms of moral agency are not agreeable to the individuals of this nation, they will be largely learned and followed by them reluctantly, perhaps involuntarily. While some coercion might be desirable as an auxiliary in the moral education of children and in restraining dangerous conduct by adults, it should not be the chief means for implementing the norms of moral agency in the lives of people. Those norms, after all, are criteria for voluntary, not forced, action.

To determine whether or not Americans are likely to be open to the norms of moral agency, we should not rely exclusively on empirical data about the normative views of Americans. This is not because there are no relevant facts available. Indeed, there are surveys which show that many Americans hold values that are compatible with the criteria of concern.[1] On the other hand, the known facts show also that many Americans rate private affairs over public ones.[2] Thus they might not be open to those implications of the advocated criteria that stress a commitment to support public conditions and institutions favorable to moral agency. The difficulty with the gathered data, in short, is that they do not clearly establish that Americans are or are not willing to live by the norms of moral agency. To try to resolve the issue of acceptance, let us begin by examining the objections that the American people are likely to raise against these norms. What we will find is that the objections do not hold up under scrutiny.

Not Open to Considering Moral Criteria

Immediately, some might charge that the mere existence of our inquiry means that numerous Americans are not of a mind to entertain moral standards of any sort, let alone those of moral agency. A salient reason for the inquiry, it will be remembered, is the claim that, during recent decades, Americans increasingly have committed morally dubious acts and assumed principles of selfishness. True or not, this claim does not portray Americans as ready to listen to anyone's moral teachings, albeit sound. To wonder if people in such a frame of mind are likely to consider taking the norms of moral agency as their standards of moral conduct is like wondering if the members of an Omaha steak club are open to following the Prittiken diet. Aristotle made a similar point when he explained that people without good moral habits will not be good students of moral teaching.[3]

This objection, however, rests on a misunderstanding. If we had contended that all, most, or a large minority of the nation's people were vicious or hopelessly selfish, we should not expect them to welcome advocacy of any moral principles. But we did not make that contention. We simply held that there has been a remarkable increase in morally dubious behavior and in selfishness during the past several decades. Also, while we inferred from this increase that there has been a weakening in the normative structure of the nation's social life which warrants remedial efforts, we did not imply that the populace has become predominantly evil or selfish, and thus that those who formulate moral norms for the nation will be like prophets crying in the wilderness.

In fact, if one assumes that the rate of police arrests in the United States indicates anything about the number of the nation's people involved in serious immoral acts, one must conclude that the number is quite small. Between 1960 and 1987, the number of arrests for all manner of offenses, ranging from criminal homicide to runaway and suspicion, increased from 4,000,000 to 10,800,000 of the total population,[4] a jump from 2.2 to 4.3 percent. This does not mean that in 1987 only 10,800,000 people committed arrestable offenses, nor does it mean that in 1987 4.3 percent of the nation's members were arrested. Some culprits in any year do not get caught, and some individuals in any year undergo multiple arrests. But even if we assume, as a caution, that 10 percent of the population today commits arrestable acts, detected or not, and that those acts violate the norms of moral agency, we still have 90 percent of the population that has not committed such acts. Even if we assume that every morally accountable member of the nation commits each year one or more acts that violate those norms, we still need not conclude that the populace as a whole is hardened against entertaining those standards or any others. Many sinners are willing to listen to preachers. So, while the rate of increase in morally suspect conduct and selfishness in the United States is seriously disturbing, it is not yet at a level that makes hopeless the consideration of moral principles by the nation's members.

Moral Agency Is Godless

Even though the American people might be willing to entertain moral principles, a large number of them are likely to object that the norms of moral agency are unacceptable for the reason that they constitute a secular, or Godless, morality. We have defended the norms of moral agency, it will be remembered, on the ground of reason rather than faith; and we have argued that faith alone is not an adequate basis for accepting moral criteria. Nevertheless, there are many people in the United States who hold that true moral principles must represent the Divine Will and rest simply on faith in what that will is. Evangelicals alone make up 20 to 33 percent of the nation's population,[5] but they probably are not the only ones who insist on a Fideist morality. Regardless of their exact magnitude, Fideists surely will reject any morality founded on reason alone.

I am not certain that they will, however. If the point of concern were our justification of the norms of moral agency, it would mean that Evangelicals and other Fideists would reject those criteria along with the justification. The point of concern, however, is something else; it is the norms themselves. The issue is not whether or not Fideists will accept our defense of the norms; it is whether or not they will accept the norms. In order to accept the norms, they need not buy our justification of them; for they might see them, despite our purely rational defense of them, as expressions of God's will.[6] Is there anything about the criteria of moral agency that could be construed by Fideists as opposed to the Divine Will? Yes, there are several things. Anyone who believes in the divine predestination of each and every human act supposedly would spurn these criteria in the respect that they treat freedom as a moral value or an aspect of moral right. Any who believe that human beings should not be seriously concerned with material things supposedly would reject these standards in the respect that they recognize biological, economic, and social conditions and institutions as highly important for moral values, rights, and duties. And any who believe that human beings must show their faith by letting God alone protect them from physical harm supposedly would refuse to accept these norms in the respect that they portray human beings as having the right and duty to guard against all manner of danger to their well being as moral agents.

The number of Fideists in the United States holding any of these beliefs is unknown to me. Many of us probably have held one of them at one time or another, and some of us might express one of them during a time of crisis, for example, a life-threatening illness of a child. But just how many Fideists consistently espouse such beliefs is simply not known. My impression is that the number is small. Reports on strict Christian Scientists and others who deny medical treatment to the gravely ill are rare. Accounts of snake handling as a test of faith treat the matter as an oddity. And Americans are notorious for maintaining that their problems can be solved by individual effort and teamwork. So, while we are prepared to allow that some people will find our proposed moral norms unacceptable on religious grounds, we doubt that their number will be large enough to render these criteria as unacceptable to Americans in general.

The Norms Are Too General

Even if the people of the United States find nothing definitely religiously offensive in the criteria of moral agency, they will not necessarily regard them as positively expressive of the Divine Will. They might see them as too vague or ambiguous to determine that they do or do not express that will. Fideists, however, would not be the only ones who might charge that the criteria of moral agency are too general to accept; many others are likely to agree that these norms are too broad. To accept them as they are, it might be said, would be like buying a pig in a poke: One would not know which specific actions one would be committed to by the norms. Many people today have deep-seated opinions about current moral problems, for example, homosexuality, abortion, euthanasia, suicide, capital punishment, drugs, and poverty; and they might not be prepared to follow any moral precepts unless they perceive that the latter agree with their opinions on these problems.

No doubt, numerous Americans have their minds firmly made up on these and other topical moral problems, and they are likely to use these convictions as standards by which to assess any moral principles proposed to them. This is wrong, of course. One is supposed to use moral norms for establishing solutions to moral problems, not the other way around. This logical backwardness, however, is not at stake here. What is in question is whether or not the norms of moral agency are too general to address specifically the moral problems with which the nation's members are concerned. To be sure, the norms do not provide ready solutions to these or any other problems. If, however, one were to reject them for not containing immediate solutions to his or her problems, one would have to reject all other moral principles, too. As indicated by the Golden Rule, the Categorical Imperative, and Bentham's Utilitarian Principle, it is not the nature of moral norms to entail proximate answers to life's moral problems. It is their nature, rather, to provide answers mediated by the process of judgment: They guide us in making moral judgments on moral cases.[7]

That the norms of moral agency furnish guidance for making judgments about the moral problems with which people are urgently concerned may be seen from the fact that these standards pose questions

which must be answered in efforts to reach judgments on these problems. With reference to homosexuality, as well as heterosexuality, questions about maturity, freedom, knowledge, character, purpose, and the
public good arise. For abortion, the value of life for a merely prospective
moral agent compared with that for an occurrent moral agent is of special concern. Also, whether or not the given pregnancy is a result of a
voluntary act by the pregnant person is a pertinent question. With respect to euthanasia, obvious questions are whether or not the act would
be voluntary for the given person and whether or not the person is presently a moral agent and has prospects for a life of moral agency. The
possible impact of the person's death on others and the likelihood of
abuse of euthanasian procedures have to be considered as well. For suicide, questions of motive, voluntariness, prospects for a life of moral
agency, and impact on others are at issue. Capital punishment involves
such questions as whether or not the intended subject has committed an
act so heinous as to waive his or her right to life, whether or not alternative punishment would be equally fitting, and whether or not execution
of the person is necessary for the protection of the public good. For
drugs, there are questions of the loss of freedom and health, the undermining of virtuous character, and the endangerment of the public
good. Finally, with regard to poverty, one has to ask what are the minimum material conditions needed for a person to grow and function as a
moral agent, how much each person is responsible for providing those
conditions for him- or herself, and how much others can provide without
undermining the material conditions needed for their own lives as
moral agents.

The judgments that one would reach after answering the questions
pertinent to each sort of moral problem would have to be made on a
case-by-case basis, for they will depend on the facts of each situation as
well as the norms of moral agency. It is conceivable that some acts of
homosexuality would be morally right, for example, those between consenting adults, posing no danger to the public good, and in no other way
threatening the central elements of moral agency. It is conceivable also
that some acts of abortion would be morally wrong, for example, those
where persons who willfully become pregnant want abortions for no
other reason than personal convenience. It is conceivable also that some
drug use is morally right while some other is morally wrong. Smoking
pot is radically different from shooting heroin. People who cannot abide
the complexities and uncertainties of case-by-case moral judgment will
reject the approach to current moral problems offered by the norms of
moral agency. But they will have to reject as well the approach posed
by any other set of moral criteria. What such people are against is not
this or that set of moral standards, but the process of moral judgment
itself, for it is in the nature of that process to judge each case on its own

merits. To be sure, rules about types of cases may be formulated and employed, for instance, rules about lying, privacy, and stealing. Nevertheless, one still would have to determine whether or not given cases fall under the given rules.

Our Cultural Diversity Opposes the Norms

Finally, the norms of moral agency are likely to be criticized in connection with the vast cultural diversity of the United States. The American population is racially variegated and becoming more so.[8] Religious groupings, language affinities, and cultural perspectives are equally diverse.[9] A large majority of the Los Angeles population, for instance, consists of Hispanics, African Americans, Asians, Pacific Islanders, and Native Americans.[10] While there is evidence that many recent immigrants from Latin America and Asia have assimilated into the mainstream of American society,[11] there also is evidence that many other people have retained much of their respective original cultural identifications. Even people whose ancestors migrated to this country over 100 years ago frequently have kept alive or revived their old cultural ways, including the values embodied in those ways. The Amish, orthodox Jews, and African Americans are only a few strains of such people. Given this enormous cultural variety, a person has to allow that there are some, perhaps many, opposing sets of cultural values strongly held by Americans.[12] Hence, it is naive to think that the norms of moral agency or any other single body of moral standards will be acceptable to Americans in general.

For the sake of argument, let us concede that the United States is so culturally varied that no single set of moral norms will be as agreeable to the cultural values of most Americans as those values now are. This point does not mean, however, that it is ingenuous to think that most Americans are not ready to look beyond their cultural identities for moral principles. In truth, the point might mean that they are quite prepared to do so. If people in different cultural groups belong to the same society, they have to get along with one another. Even groups that strive to be apart from all others, for example, the Amish, occasionally have to interact with outsiders. The standards by which diverse cultural groups must guide their conduct toward one another must be common to all groups. Behavior led by standards special to one or more groups can lead only to conflict or imposition. If there is, then, extensive and deep cultural diversity in the United States, it indicates that the various cultural groups need and well might want a common set of moral principles by which they may interact with each other. The norms of moral agency, I believe, should be attractive to them as such a set of principles. To accept these norms, the members of a culture only need to hold the ordinary concept of a moral standard and understand its logical implications, or, alternatively, to recognize that freedom, knowledge, purpose, and the other elements of moral agency are values for the members of all or most American cultural groups. Neither alternative seems outlandish.

WHAT POINTS MIGHT BE IN FAVOR OF THE NORMS?

But not only is it the case that the objections Americans are likely to lodge against the norms of moral agency are not insuperable. It also appears that Americans will recognize that their acceptance of these norms has several attractive points.

Minimal Disturbance

The first point is that acceptance of the criteria of moral agency will create minimal disturbance in the lives of the nation's members. According to these criteria, individuals and groups may act toward one another as they freely and knowingly want to as long as what they want to do is consistent with voluntary action for all. Some people will find the constraint of the mutual respect of one another as voluntary agents unacceptable. Those who believe that abortions should be available without good moral reasons, that medical intervention to deal with a life-threatening disease is necessarily wrong, that it is wrong for their children to be reared to choose their own lives freely and knowingly, and that freedom and knowledge are reserved for their own ilk will be profoundly upset in living according to the norms of moral agency. Such people, however, appear to be relatively few and with only isolated pockets of influence. The vast majority of Americans, I believe, would be happy to live by a morality that organizes the interpersonal conduct of the whole nation and at the same time asks of them only that they respect one another as moral agents. Such an arrangement would enable them to do a lot of what they already want to do and at the same time assure them that each would be respected by the others. Historically, once antagonistic religious groups in the United States have managed to reach a similar accommodation with one another. Mormons and their opponents have mutually adjusted their differences. Roman Catholics and Protestants have made large strides in reaching a common understanding. And Christians and Jews have also modified, for mutual benefit, their views of each other. That bitter religious differences in America have been reconciled suggests that many Americans should not find it unbearably painful to adjust their current ways of life to the norms of moral agency.

An Alternative to Extreme Relativism

The second attractive feature is that these criteria will provide Americans with an alternative to the vicious relativism that has haunted morality for several decades. Until recently, there was a growing tendency to hold that moral standards are a matter of individual preference. This position had gained academic respectability in the first half of the century due to its advocacy, under the banner of Emotivism, by Positivists and other philosophers. During the generational revolt of the 1960s, which occurred a decade or so after the demise of Emotivism in philosophy, the position became a part of the nation's youth culture. It was plainly expressed by a slogan of the time, "Do what you like just as long as you do not bother me." Unlike typical symptoms of youthful exuberance, this highly individualistic relativism did not go away. The generational revolt was successful, but the new generation had nothing with which to replace the older generation's morality except the precept of individual preference. By the late 1980s, the widespread acceptance of this principle was an object of attack not only by TV Evangelists, but also by social philosophers.[13]

This simplistic relativism appears to be losing favor, as indicated by the rash of talk about values, duty, and character in recent political campaigns.[14] But recently proposed alternatives to the precept have not been very persuasive. One proposal, known as the "Ozzie and Harriet" alternative, has nothing going for it beyond its power to evoke a nostalgia for the middle-class way of life in the 1950s. Another recommendation, which is to return to the absolutistic moralities formulated by such giants of Western philosophy as Plato and Hegel,[15] asks us to assume that these moralities are relevant today and otherwise defensible. The proposal by Critical Theorists, who maintain that people share a common humanity but at the same time hold moral beliefs opposed to that humanity because of their respective ideologies,[16] fails to explain how we can discover what the values of our humanity are without being unduly influenced by our respective ideologies.

The norms of moral agency reject individualistic relativism. While they insist on individual freedom and the consideration of the facts of each moral situation, they do not allow that whatever one wants to do is right as long as it does not hurt others. They hold that there are definite values—knowledge, freedom, purpose, evaluation, deliberation, etc.—to which we all as moral agents are committed regardless of our wants. They maintain that there are certain duties binding on us irrespective of our likes and desires. They also insist that there are certain character habits which we all should have regardless of our preferred life-styles. Moreover, as we have tried to show, these criteria appear to be theoretically defensible. They are, then, norms that Americans should be disposed to consider seriously as a replacement for the individualistic relativism of which they have lately despaired.

Something Besides Individualism and Communitarianism

The final attractive point to be mentioned is that the criteria of moral agency furnish the nation with an alternative to Individualist and Communitarian moralities. Since the founding of the United States, Americans have placed much emphasis on the moral importance of individuals.[17] They have held that the happiness of individuals is a primary value. They have established legal arrangements to protect the rights of individuals, not only from one another, but from government and other institutions as well. They have praised the rugged individualism of frontiersmen, business tycoons, inventors, and scientists. They have spoken also of self-reliance[18] and self-actualization[19] as moral goals. On the other hand, Americans have favored social membership.[20] They have treasured patriotism, spoken highly of teamwork, cautioned one another about "rocking the boat," and at times have been disposed to conformity and blind obedience.[21] Accordingly, many Americans have been confused and frustrated by the inevitable conflicts arising from their tendencies toward being both individualistic and social.

While moral thinkers have spoken about this conflict, they have not always helped. Some, in the tradition of John Locke, Adam Smith, Thomas Jefferson, and Henry David Thoreau, have come down hard on the side of the individual. They have maintained that individuals have certain rights, and that the proper function of societies is to enable individuals to exercise those rights. In recent years they have spoken in the terms of entitlements,[22] free markets,[23] self-fulfillment,[24] and the minimal state.[25] If Individualists could agree on a motto, they just might settle for, "Everyone for himself and no one for anybody else." Other moral thinkers, however, in the tradition of Georg W.F. Hegel, Frances Herbert Bradley, and Josiah Royce, have come down hard on the side of society. They have contended that our individual identities and worth come from the groups in which we live, and that our proper functions in life are to perform social roles. Lately, they have been speaking in the language of community,[26] social responsibility,[27] and institutions.[28] If Communitarians thought a motto socially necessary, they easily might agree on, "All for one and one for all." The difficulty with the Individualist and Communitarian positions, of course, is that they simply replicate at the intellectual level the conflicts between individualism and sociality that bedevil most Americans at the practical level. Thus, they leave most Americans confused and frustrated at the level of moral theory.

The theory of moral agency offers a position that mediates between those of Individualism and Communitarianism. To be sure, the theory begins with the individual voluntary agent and interprets interpersonal action from the individual's standpoint; and it definitely allows for prudential considerations. But the theory does not formulate moral principles in terms of the individual voluntary agent's interest, for example, enlightened self-interest, as Individualism does. Rather, the theory constructs such principles in the terms of moral agency itself, thereby eventually establishing the commonality and community of individuals who are moral agents. So, rather than locating morality in either the individual or in the community, the theory locates morality in the interaction among individuals who make up a moral group. Accordingly, the norms of moral agency contain a criterion of moral rights and a criterion of moral duty that provide guidance for the reconciliation of seeming conflicts between individual interests and social goods. Any moral agent may exercise a moral right as long as in so doing the agent does not infringe on the rights of other agents, including the weakening of the social conditions of moral agency. At the same time, any moral agent is bound to maintain and foster the social conditions of moral agency. Therefore, rather than leaving decisions about seeming conflicts between individual interest and the social good pending, the two criteria specify the limits within which individuals may exercise their rights and at the same time make clear that individuals are obligated to look after the social good.

DO TRADITIONAL AMERICAN VALUES CONCORD WITH MORAL AGENCY?

Even though the receptivity of the individual members of the United States to the norms of moral agency is vital for that morality's workability here, it is no more crucial than is the support that the morality might receive from the nation's traditional values. The traditional values of a society help shape the mindset of its individual members toward a given body of moral standards. Moreover, the support given by such values to a given body of moral standards seriously influences the chances of those standards taking hold in a given society. If a set of norms is opposed to those values, it must overcome the resistance of a vast accumulation of practices, customs, and blind habits before it can take hold. Even if the standards face only indifference from the values, they then must establish roots without the sustenance of practices, customs, and habits already present. Whatever the causes of the collapse of the Soviet Union, the fact remains that the values of Marxist–Leninist Communism, which were largely opposed to the traditional values of Czarist Russia and its imperial lands, developed only shallow roots after cultivation for three-quarters of a century.

In examining the connection between the norms of moral agency and

American traditional values, we shall focus on several salient points about moral agency that relate to three well-known American values. Two of the latter are robust, but the third is in decline. What we will discover is that the norms of moral agency are continuous with the vigorous values and important for the conditions surrounding the enervation of the third.

Freedom

Freedom is perhaps the most famous traditional value of the United States.[29] Liberty was the watchword of the nation's revolution and the driving force of its civil war. It has been the magnet that has attracted refugees from oppression in foreign lands and one of the ideals for which we have fought world wars and conducted foreign policy. It is the central principle of the Constitution's first ten amendments. And it is the principle underlying the hope of individual Americans to be what they want to be. Not just any freedom, however, is traditional in America. As Hobbes remarked, freedom can belong to a society without belonging to its members.[30] Ancient Sparta, for instance, was free of foreign domination for centuries, but its members enjoyed little liberty. The liberty embedded in American practices, customs, and habits is that of the individual as well as that of society. While the United States has sought to maintain the independence of some countries with authoritarian regimes, it has done so not for the oppression of the subjects of such but for its own self-interest. Also, it has chastised some authoritarian regimes, such as the present-day one in the People's Republic of China, for severely restricting its members' freedom. But the liberty of the individual that is traditional in the United States is not that of doing whatever one wants to do. Locke, unlike Hobbes, distinguished liberty from license. License is doing whatever one wants to do, whereas liberty is doing whatever one wants to do that is consistent with the moral law of nature, which is known by reason.[31] Traditional American freedom is similar to what Locke had in mind by liberty. It is reasonable, which means at least that it may not unjustifiably diminish the freedom of others or that of oneself. Moreover, it is consistent with and at times entails social responsibility. Hence, Americans have placed restrictions on alcohol, drugs, automobiles, and waste disposal without losing any of their freedom. In their long-standing fascination with outlaws of the Old West and gangsters of the 1920s and 1930s, Americans have tended to see them as embodiments of evil or as victims of society, not as exemplars of liberty.

The freedom integral to moral agency is consistent with that traditionally prized in the United States. It pertains to the individual, and it is reasonable. So, insofar as the norms of moral agency mesh with the tradition of freedom in the nation, they should flourish here.

Knowledge

The knowledge that was traditionally esteemed in the United States until recently was empirical and practical.[32] Americans usually looked askance at knowledge derived purely from reason. They relied on personal experience and, except on basic questions involving religion, natural science. Despite their admiration of science, they were impatient with scientific research for its own sake; they expected it to have a payoff. This tradition had its origins in pre-revolutionary America with the advent here of the Enlightenment, as personified by Benjamin Franklin. It was nourished later by John Adams, Thomas Jefferson, Benjamin Rush, and other early leaders of the nation.[33] It came to full force during the century and a half of the nation's industrialization. It inspired Pragmatism, which is the indigenous American philosophy,[34] and later it nourished Logical Empiricism, a variety of Positivism imported into the United States.[35] It thrives today under the banner of high technology.

Opposition to this view of knowledge is long-standing and accumulative. The Enlightenment was opposed in America by the Great Awakening, which was followed by waves of other religious revivals putting emphasis on Divine Wisdom. Romantics, such as Emerson and Thoreau, not only criticized industrialization but held that science pales in comparison with the wisdom to be gained through communion with nature. Progressive Reformers, such as Henry George, Richard T. Ely, and Jane Addams, decried the inhumane conditions of industrial society. Albert Einstein, Robert J. Oppenheimer, Hans Bethe, and others connected with the development of the atomic bomb warned that science had potential for the destruction of humankind.[36] Critics of Cold War policies saw science as having become the handmaiden of the military–industrial complex.[37] Post-Modernists have persistently charged, with wide-ranging impact, that the American tradition of knowledge emphasizes objectivity, quantity, and specialization while ignoring individual, cultural, and gender perspectives; discounting the qualitative aspects of life; and fostering fragmented thoughts, institutions, and experiences.[38] Because of the enduring and accumulating nature of this criticism, it is doubtful that knowledge as typified by natural science prevails today as *the* American view of knowledge. What appears to be the case is that epistemology in the nation is unsettled. There is a plurality of approaches to knowledge, and there are as yet no commonly accepted principles for settling disparities among them all.

It might be contended that the knowledge integral to moral agency belongs to the late epistemological tradition of the United States. After all, the inquiry by which we constructed the theory of moral agency maintained that each and every moral principle must rest on reason, and that the values, rights, duties, and virtues of moral agency were determined objectively. The inquiry was not scientific, to be sure; but its insistence upon reason and objectivity betrayed a strong influence by the scientific tradition.

Such a contention, however, would be misguided. For one thing, reason and objectivity are not peculiar to modern science; they are elements also in other epistemological traditions, for example, Rationalism, which dates back to ancient Greece. For another thing, as we have suggested already, any cognitive claim that rests entirely on something other than reason is unsatisfactory. Still further, the objectivity entailed by our theory of moral agency is not that of Scientific Realism, which holds that there is a physical world independent of observers but observable as it is through the use of the experimental method. The objectivity of our theory, rather, consists of adhering to the canons of reason, such as the principles of identity and noncontradiction and the principles of induction. While this objectivity is presupposed by science as well as all other intellectual endeavors, the theory of moral agency, even if it is incompatible with an ontology that excludes any measure of free will, is open to many varieties of ontology and epistemological methodology, including those of Aristotle, St. Thomas Aquinas, Kant, John Dewey, and Martin Heidegger.

Still more, the knowledge constitutive of moral agency allows for the importance of individual, cultural, and gender perspectives. My perceptions of your purposes are likely to differ from yours. People imbued with Western culture do have different values and give different weights to rights and duties than do those imbued with Eastern culture. Men and women historically have seen moral situations in different ways. But the knowledge associated with moral agency is not just some sort of perspective. Moral agency distinguishes between mere personal beliefs and rationally defensible beliefs held by individuals, mere cultural beliefs and rationally defensible cultural beliefs, and beliefs historically held by males or females and rationally defensible beliefs held by males or females. Finally, the knowledge belonging to moral agency is not the disembodied and unfeeling intelligence sometimes attributed to science; for it is enmeshed in interplays among the cognitive, affective, and physical aspects of the moral agent. Desires, evaluations, purposes, and deliberations are the occasions for seeking practical knowledge. A person's search for practical knowledge is shaped by his or her love for practical inquiry as well as by his or her intellectual skills and physical abilities in such an inquiry. And the practical inquiry in which one engages, and the knowledge obtained through it, reinforce some feelings, habits, and attitudes and modify others.

We conclude, then, that the knowledge integral to moral agency fits in with the epistemological situation of the United States today. While it is not a child of the tradition inspired by modern science, it insists upon reason and methodological objectivity, which are features of that tradition. While it respects individual, cultural, and gender perspectives, it provides a way by which perspectival positions might be assessed. And while it holds that the moral life must be a rational life, it recognizes that the moral life also contains affective strands interwoven with practical reason. In sum, even though the knowledge involved in moral agency might not be totally supported by any one epistemological approach presently found in the nation, it can be more or less partially backed by a wide variety of such approaches.

Equality

Having become a force in America through the Declaration of Independence, equality has contributed to the practices, customs, and habits of Americans almost as long as freedom and knowledge have.[39] The idea, of course, did not pervade the nation's social conditions quickly and on an unbroken front. Starting with its inception, equality has been resisted by libertarians and cultural elitists, who regard it as promoting conformity and mediocrity at the expense of individuality and excellence. And of course it has been rejected by racists. Despite these and other obstacles, however, equality has gained popular and legal acceptance in the United States. The rootedness of the value does not mean, to be sure, that inequalities have vanished from our society. They are plentiful in many sectors of our lives. But while the general esteem of the principle does not mean that real equality is pervasive in the nation, this valuation does indicate that any moral standards which are to work as the core of this society's morality must be consistent with the principle.

The equality usually associated with American life is a complex idea, a constellation of tenets. One belief, reflected by Jefferson's renown statement that "all men are created equal," is that all human beings share the same traits as human beings. Thus, no individual or group is more or less human than another. Another tenet, which presupposes the previous one, is that all human beings are of the same worth as human beings. Hence, there are no superior or inferior human beings as such. The third belief, which is complementary to the first one, is that individual or even groups of human beings might differ in degree from one another in their human traits. For instance, some may be stronger or faster than others; some may be brighter than others. The fourth, and last, tenet, which presupposes the first three, is that all human beings should have equal opportunity in pursuing social positions.

Only hard-nosed racists in America take exception to the first two tenets. While the third belief is commonly accepted, it has raised disputes, yet to be settled, over what is the explanation of individual and group differences, and over whether or not an individual's or group's deficiencies in some human trait may be remedied.[40] The last tenet has been the focal point of dissent in the past several decades from the traditional American conception of equality. That dissent, shared perhaps by only a minority of the nation's members, has called for a new conception of American equality by replacing the tenet of equal opportunity with one of equal results.[41] The usual reply to this dissent is that there is no sufficient ground for replacing equal opportunity with equal results as a principle for guiding the distribution of social positions in the nation. Equal or unequal results may, but need not, be indicators of equal or unequal opportunity. But concentration on equal results without attention to equal opportunity ultimately leads to questions about the lesser qualified gaining preference over the greater qualified, and to questions about whether or not social positions in the nation will be occupied by the best talent available. Even many ardent supporters of affirmative action programs, which concentrate more on results than on opportunity, allow that such programs are not rejections of equal opportunity but rather are expedients for creating breakthroughs in a historical impasse.[42]

The standard conception of equality in America coheres completely with the equality implicit in the norms of moral agency. According to the theory underlying those criteria, all moral agents are specifically identical and of the same worth insofar as they are voluntary and interpersonal agents. Moreover, people may differ in degree from one another in their moral agency. Some may be closer than others to being fully developed moral agents. Some may be more perceptive than others. Some may be better able than others in forecasting consequences of action. Some may be keener than others in applying principles and rules. Finally, as far as equal opportunity goes, any moral agent has the right to develop fully his or her cognitive, affective, and physical features as a moral agent with a view to occupying social positions within his or her society. Moreover, such an agent has the right to compete under fair conditions for positions of his or her choice, which is to be consistent with the agent's duties controlled by the Criterion of Moral Duty. The theory involved here is silent on whether or not individual or group differences in moral traits are matters of genes, environment, or some combination of the two. It purports to be compatible with whatever rationally defensible position is offered, if ever. Also, the theory is not oblivious to results in talk about equal opportunity. It sides with those who hold that results are a source of data to be employed in estimating whether or not equal opportunity obtains in given cases.

CONCLUSION

Our argument for the feasibility of using the criteria of moral agency as the heart of American morality certainly does not *prove* that these norms are workable in this respect. In truth, the argument is not especially powerful. It considers only four objections that Americans might raise against the norms. It provides only three points about the criteria that Americans might favor. And it discusses only three traditional American values that might link positively with the norms. Surely, Americans might have other objections to pose; and neither three favorable points nor three values are very many. Nevertheless, the other objections that might be put forth also might be refutable. The favorable points and the supporting values examined in the argument are important ones. There might be other points about the norms that Americans might favor. For example, in our discussion of the criteria, we indicated that the material aspects of life are important but also that they are subject to definite moral limits. This point should appeal to Americans, who reputedly like material well being but at the same time do not identify it with an unbridled accumulation of material goods and services. There might be other traditional American values supportive of these standards. Democratic government, for instance, resonates with them.[43]

NOTES

1. Theodore Caplow, Howard M. Bahr, John Modell, and Bruce A. Chadwick, *Recent Social Trends in the United States, 1960–1990* (Buffalo, NY: McGill-Queen's University Press, 1992), pp. 555–557.

2. Ibid., p. 561.

3. Aristotle, *N. Ethics,* 1095b 1–8.

4. Caplow et al., *Recent Social Trends in the United States,* p. 504.

5. Ibid., p. 373.

6. B. Mitchell, *Morality: Religious and Secular* (Oxford, England: Clarendon Press, 1980).

7. See Chapter 2, pp. 30–32.

8. Harold L. Hodgkinson, *A Demographic Look at Tomorrow* (Washington, DC: Institute for Educational Leadership, 1992).

9. Sandra Lee McKay and Sau-Ling Cynthia Wong, eds., *Language Diversity, Problem or Resource?: A Social and Educational Perspective on Language Minorities in the United States* (New York: Newbury House, 1988).

10. United States Department of Commerce, *Statistical Abstracts of the United States,* 111th ed. (Washington, DC: United States Government Printing Office, 1991), p. 35.

11. Ibid., p. 491.

12. As a matter of fact, some opposing values have helped promote conflict between groups. For an account of the hostile relations between the Hasidic Lubavitcher community and African Americans living in the Crown Heights

neighborhood of Brooklyn, New York, see David Remnick, "Waiting for the Apocalypse," *The New Yorker* (December 21, 1992), pp. 52–57

13. Allan Bloom, *The Closing of the American Mind* (New York: Simon and Schuster, 1987), pp. 25–43.

14. Nevertheless, moral subjectivity still has staunch defenders among some notable social theorists. See Charles Taylor, *Sources of the Self* (Cambridge, MA: Harvard University Press, 1989).

15. E.g., Bloom, *The Closing of the American Mind*, pp. 194–216.

16. H.A. Giroux, *Ideology, Culture, and the Process of Schooling* (Philadelphia, PA: Temple University Press, 1981).

17. Alexis de Tocqueville, *Democracy in America*, edited by Phillip Bradley (New York: Vintage Books, 1954), Volume II, pp. 104–113.

18. Ralph Waldo Emerson, "Self Reliance," in *The Complete Essays and Other Writings of Ralph Waldo Emerson*, edited by Brooks Atkinson (New York: The Modern Library, 1940), pp. 145–169.

19. Abraham Maslow, *Dominance, Self-Esteem, Self-Actualization: Germinal Papers of A.H. Maslow* (Monterey, CA: Brooks/Cole Publishing Company, 1973).

20. De Tocqueville, *Democracy in America*, Volume II, pp. 114–128.

21. David Riesman, *The Lonely Crowd* (Garden City, NY: Doubleday-Anchor, 1954).

22. Ronald Dworkin, *Taking Rights Seriously* (Cambridge, MA: Harvard University Press, 1977).

23. Milton Friedman and Rose Friedman, *Capitalism and Freedom*, 2nd ed. (Chicago, IL: The University of Chicago Press, 1982).

24. Carl Rogers, *Freedom to Learn: A View of What Education Might Become* (Columbus, OH: C.E. Merrill Publishing Company, 1969).

25. Robert Nozick, *Anarchy, State, and Utopia* (New York: Basic Books, 1974).

26. Michael J. Sandel, *Liberalism and the Limits of Justice* (Cambridge, England: Cambridge University Press, 1982). See also Amitai Etzioni, *The Spirit of Community: Rights, Responsibilities, and the Communitarian Agenda* (New York: Crown Publishers, 1993).

27. Mary Ann Glendon, *Rights Talk: The Impoverishment of Political Discourse* (New York: The Free Press, 1991).

28. Robert N. Bellah, Richard Madsen, William M. Sullivan, Ann Swidler, and Steven M. Tipton, *The Good Society* (New York: Alfred A. Knopf, 1991).

29. This is not to say necessarily that freedom is the value most highly favored by Americans. De Tocqueville maintained that in any democracy equality is more prized than freedom. De Tocqueville, *Democracy in America*, Volume II, pp. 102–103. Bellah and his associates, it must be noted, hold that de Tocqueville is wrong here; they insist that freedom, not equality, has "marched inexorably throughout history." Robert N. Bellah, Richard Madsen, William M. Sullivan, Ann Swidler, and Steven M. Tipton, *Habits of the Heart: Individualism and Commitment in American Life* (Berkeley, CA: University of California Press, 1985), p. viii.

30. Thomas Hobbes, *Leviathan* (New York: E.P. Dutton, 1950), pp. 181–182.

31. John Locke, *Two Treatises of Civil Government; Book II: An Essay Con-

cerning the True Original, Extent and End of Civil Government (London: J.M. Dent & Sons, 1949), pp. 118–120.

32. De Tocqueville, *Democracy in America*, Volume II, pp. 3–8, 19–20.

33. Robert D. Heslep, *Thomas Jefferson and Education* (New York: Random House, 1969), pp. 26, 34–35, 97–98, 103–104, 118–119.

34. John Dewey, *The Quest for Certainty* (New York: Minton, Balch & Co., 1929), pp. 98–104, 125–139.

35. James L. Jarrett and Sterling M. McMurrin,"Logical Empiricism: Introduction," in *Contemporary Philosophy: A Book of Readings,* edited by James L. Jarrett and Sterling M. McMurrin (New York: Henry Holt and Company, 1954), pp. 361–365.

36. E.g., Albert Einstein, "A Message to Intellectuals," in *Out of My Later Years* (New York: Philosophical Library, 1950), pp. 152–155.

37. C. Wright Mills, *The Power Elite* (New York: Oxford University Press, 1956), pp. 216–219.

38. Bruce W. Wilshire, *The Moral Collapse of the University: Professionalism, Purity, and Alienation* (Albany, NY: State University of New York Press, 1990).

39. De Tocqueville, *Democracy in America*, Volume II, pp. 99–103.

40. Arthur R. Jensen, "How Much Can We Boost IQ and Scholastic Achievement?", *Harvard Educational Review* 39 (Winter 1969), pp. 1–123. N.R. Block and Gerald Dworkin, "IQ, Heritability and Inequality, Part I," *Philosophy & Public Affairs* 3 (Summer 1974), pp. 331–409; and "IQ, Heritability and Inequality, Part II," *Philosophy & Public Affairs* 4 (Fall 1974), pp. 40–99.

41. James S. Coleman, "The Concept of Equality of Educational Opportunity," *Harvard Educational Review* 38 (Winter 1968), pp. 7–22.

42. Ruth Bader Ginsberg, "Realizing the Equality Principle," in *Social Justice and Preferential Treatment: Women and Racial Minorities in Education and Business*, edited by William T. Blackstone and Robert D. Heslep (Athens, GA: The University of Georgia Press, 1977), esp. pp. 137–138.

43. Robert D. Heslep, *Education in Democracy: Education's Moral Role in the Democratic State* (Ames, IA: Iowa State University Press, 1989), esp. pp. 77–78.

4 The Goal of Moral Education

After contending that Americans need a character education that rests on defensible moral principles, we argued that the norms of moral agency are defensible on the grounds of feasibility as well as those of logic. Also, in saying that the character education Americans ought to have should rest on the norms of moral agency, we mean that the nation's members should have the character of moral agents. But we have not explained what character is, let alone what the character of a moral agent is. Let us, then, try to make clear the type of educational product we have in mind.

CHARACTER

Of the various dictionary meanings of the word *character,* the one most germane to our concern is, "the aggregate of distinctive qualities belonging to a person or race." In other words, the character of a person is the mass of qualities that distinguishes him or her. This definition clearly derives from the etymology of the word: One's character is what characterizes, or marks, oneself. Even though the definition is common and somewhat useful, it has two serious faults. One is that it leaves up in the air what a quality of a person is. The other is that it fails to indicate how an aggregate of qualities might mark a person. Happily, these gaps can be filled in rather easily.

When we talk about a personal quality, we normally refer to it as some aspect of the individual's being. Thus, we often speak of the quality as what the person *is* in some respect: "She is assertive," "He is rude," "Franco was dictatorial," and "Silas Marner was miserly." It also is the case that the words and phrases we use in referring to qualities have counterparts for describing actions: "She acted assertively" or "She asserted herself," "He acted rudely," "Meryl acted rationally," and "The host acted in a mean spirit." Nevertheless, it should not be thought that personal qualities are just occurrent manners of action. That a person acts courageously does not mean that courage is a quality of that person. Even a weakling, a Casper Milquetoast, might perform courageously at least once in his life. On the other hand, the ways in which we act might signify what our qualities are. A person whose actions are always erratic, irregular, or without pattern lacks personal qualities regardless of the ways in which he or she acts; for that person does things that do not reflect any definite aspect of his or her being. When, however, an individual acts in some way, for instance, sensibly or charitably, not in a few or scattered instances but regularly, that individual *is* a person with a quality (e.g., sensibility or charity) associated with those actions. We take occurrent ways of action as possibly significant of qualities not because we regard the latter as mysterious causes of actions, but because we see them as tendencies to act in specified ways. A sensitive person is disposed to act in a sensitive manner; a friendly person acts friendly as a matter of course.

Individuals typically have many dispositions, including those implicated in their tastes, personal relationships, hobbies, and jobs. But even if the tendencies of an individual are the qualities of that agent, they do not characterize the latter simply by being an aggregate. The tendencies of an individual, no matter how unique, might be in opposition to each other; but a person who tends to act in opposing ways is ordinarily said to lack character. Moreover, even if the inclinations of a person do not oppose each other, they might be unconnected with each other, thereby making him or her fragmented. But character is usually understood to include an integration of its parts. A cluster of inclinations, then, gives an individual a character only if it has structure, that is, only if the dispositions are integrally related to one another.[1] This structure, which may involve feelings, knowledge, understanding, skills, and interests, is definable by the emphasis given to some tendencies rather than others, the relative strengths that the tendencies have, and which tendencies enter into which combinations. Accordingly, there are no disordered characters even though there are disordered personalities.

That structure of dispositions is the key to character explains why people with the same qualities might be distinguishable from one another. Three students, for instance, might all share the same tendencies, for example, those of cleanliness, moderation, industriousness, politeness, civic mindedness, and analytical thinking. But because their respective inclinations might be coordinated with one another in different ways, thereby expressing different understandings and interests, one of the students might have the character of an entrepreneur; another, that of an academic; and the other, that of a politician. The centrality of structure also explains why people with different qualities might have similar characters. The dispositions of those who perform the role of merchant are likely to differ remarkably, albeit not entirely, from one place and time of the world to another, for example, from Phoenicia to Venice, to Singapore, to New York. Yet, the dispositions in one area and era might involve a structure that is quite similar to that in other regions and periods, thus possibly giving people who play the role of merchant in diverse places and times the character of a merchant. Something like this point lies behind the attempts by poets, dramatists, and novelists to universalize the characters in their works.

The association of structured inclinations with character was keenly conceived by John Dewey, who described character alternately as the "interpenetration" and the "integration" of habits.[2] It involves the "mutual modification of habits by one another."[3] Character, however, is not a binary matter. The structure of dispositions is complete in only a minority of cases, which we sometimes call "strong characters." For most of us, character, being arrested in or still under development, is a matter of degree. Incompletely formed characters, to be sure, leave room for some conflict in our tendencies and actions; but they also order our tendencies and actions in general or at least for the most part. Thus, they make us somewhat identifiable even while giving us enigmatic aspects. Dewey took a person's character as being what his or her self is.[4] But even if this notion of the self is challengeable, it compels us to recognize just how profound character is for a person's being. A disposition, we mentioned above, is understandable as an element of one's being. And because character is the structure obtaining among one's inclinations, it pervades, unifies, and forms one's being. Without character, then, we are not much of anything—at most, clusters of tendencies.

What has been said about the character of a single person applies *mutatis mutandis* to groups of people, for instance, the Chinese, the Mandans, and baseball fans. In saying, however, that character is the essence of a person or group, I do not mean that character is an entity, that is, a thing existing in the person or group. I intend nothing more than that character is a concept by which we interpret, or understand, individuals and groups. As far as I can tell, this is what character is normally taken to be. There are instances, to be sure, where orators, historians, and philosophers reify the concept, speaking of the Athenian spirit, the German *Geist,* or the Russian soul as though it were something in addition to the way of life involving the values, customs, beliefs, and practices representative of ancient Athens, of Germany, or of Russia. But we forthwith recognize the oddity of this view of the matter when we wonder what that additional thing might be.

THE CHARACTER OF THE MORAL AGENT

The inclinations that enter into the makeup of a person are varied as well as numerous. There are, for instance, habits of sleep, eating, drinking, sex, hygiene, reading, music listening, TV watching, work, religion, socializing, and exercise. The dispositions of persons may vary from individual to individual, from culture to culture, from era to era. What, however, shall be said about those pertaining to a person insofar as he or she has the character of a moral agent? One might infer from our discussion of the Criterion of Moral Virtue that certain dispositions of moral agents, which we called "moral virtues," are the stock inclinations of a moral agent. Those were such tendencies as moral reason, moderation, interpersonal sensitivity, politeness, and friendship. But one also might infer from our discussion of the concept of character that there are no stock qualities constitutive of the character of a moral agent; for that discussion allowed that people with quite different qualities might have the same sort of character. Are there or are there not, then, qualities that all moral agents must share? The answer, unfortunately, is complicated.

Any occurrent action is particular. It has a particular agent, and it occurs at a particular place and time. Nevertheless, it also has features that are more or less general, more or less specific. While, for example, the deeds of Audie Murphy in World War II were particular acts, they also shared traits of courage with the actions of the Spartans in the battle of Thermopylae. If an action is of a kind that its agent has performed with regularity, it reflects through its features, as we already have mentioned, one or more of its agent's proclivities. Whether singly or in combination, the inclinations that lead to actions, including the ways in which the actions are performed, are what we mean by *habits*. Habits, to be sure, are more or less specific. They are acquired by a particular agent's engagement with specific environmental conditions. Moreover, if they were not specific, they could not account for regularly occurring actions in situations with a close resemblance but not occurring in situations with only a highly general resemblance. But that habits are learned under limited conditions does not mean that they are necessarily fixed and narrow. We commonly speak of habits as being flexible as well as rigid, intelligent as well as thoughtless, controllable as well as compulsive. So, one person's habit of toothbrushing might be adaptable to different circumstances, while another's might lead to the same manner and time of brushing regardless of circumstances.

Despite the rich vocabulary in which we ordinarily talk about habits, some philosophers, perhaps influenced by the special language of psychology, have viewed them essentially as fixed and narrow dispositions. Thus, even though Gilbert Ryle implicitly distinguished between blind and informed habits, between pure habit and attentive habit, he insisted on distinguishing explicitly between habits and intelligent capacities. A habit is learned through drill, he claimed, whereas an intelligent capacity is learned through training, in other words, stimulation by criticism and example of one's own judgment.[5] Also, in contrast with "know-how" skills, habits are single-track and not innovative.[6] These explicit claims by Ryle are confusing, confused, and false. They are confusing for the reason that they run counter to Ryle's implicit claims, which concord, as far as one can tell, with normal discourse. And they are confused because they conflate all habits, contrary to Ryle's own implicit distinctions, to being blind, rigid, and narrow. For instance, they mean that the habits of inquiry, such as those espoused by Dewey, are thoughtless, inflexible, and narrow. Surely, habits may be intelligent in that qualities of intelligence, which are dispositional matters, attach to habits as features of them. An intelligent habit, in other words, involves dispositions to observe, forecast consequences, draw inferences, and make adjustments in performance based on changes in contextual conditions and on past mistakes. Finally, the explicit claims are false in that Ryle's account of how habits are learned is false. It quite likely is true that fixed and narrow habits are acquired through drill. But it is the case too that adjustable and widely applicable habits may be learned through training.

Another part of our answer to the question of whether or not there are dispositions that all moral agents logically must share relates to the attachment of qualities to habits. Qualities that we associate especially with moral agents, for instance, rationality, courage, and friendship, are not habits generic to each and every particular moral agent; they are, rather, features of habits had by moral agents as such. There is, for instance, no habit of moral reasoning that is completely indifferent to all diversities in subject matter, principles, facts, and methods. The moral reasoning had by various agents differs according to variations in the subject matters, facts, principles, and methods that helped shape the agent's habits of reasoning about practical affairs and according to differences in such matters when they are encountered by the agents. While Socrates, St. Thomas Aquinas, Henry David Thoreau, Albert Schweitzer, and Mother Theresa all had or have habits of moral reasoning, they each had or have specifically different habits of moral reasoning. Nevertheless, those diverse habits share several features. When we talked earlier about the virtue of moral reasoning, we were referring to the features shared by habits of moral reasoning. A similar point may be made about each of the other named moral virtues. Insofar as moral virtues are general and stock tendencies of moral agency, they consist of traits shared by habits of all moral agents. A habit special to a particular time and place and no others may be spoken of as a moral virtue; but if it is, it must be regarded as a moral virtue for that time and place, not for any moral agent in any time and place. Thus, moral reasoning modeled after the scientific method of the modern era is a moral virtue within the context of modern times, not that of the medieval or classical period. In sum, the moral virtues discussed above are dispositional features that all moral agents have as features of habits. While these features are similar to one another from agent to agent, other aspects of the agents's habits may vary from agent to agent.

The structure of the habits belonging to a moral agent depends essentially on the sorts of value attaching to the agent's dispositions. That an inclination pertains to a moral agent does not mean that it is an element, general or special, of moral agency; it might simply support such agency. While a tendency to eat three times a day, for instance, is not a part of moral agency, it might help to sustain such agency. Tendencies that simply support moral agency plainly have instrumental moral value. Besides eating tendencies, they might include dispositions to bath daily, exercise frequently, recycle aluminum cans, and to see a psychologist weekly. Proclivities that are elements of moral agency, for example, those involving freedom, knowledge, evaluation, judgment, deliberation, and decision making, have constitutive value. This means that they have value as parts of a worthy whole, but they are not as valuable as the whole itself. The whole of which they are a part, of course, is moral agency, which is intrinsically worthy and, because of the superiority of moral principles to any other normative sort, must always be honored above all other goods. The constituents of moral agency have intrinsic moral value, too, but in a derivative way. The tendency to know may or may not be morally estimable in itself; it might belong to an arch criminal or otherwise be in the service of evil. A proclivity gains intrinsic moral worth only when it becomes a part of moral agency, reflecting the intrinsic value of the latter. But that the dispositions ingredient to moral agency have intrinsic worth does not prevent them from bearing instrumental value also. For instance, evaluation and deliberation, which are for the sake of making judgments and decisions, obviously have instrumental worth. Some inclinations that are merely supportive of moral agency might be appreciated for their own sakes in addition to their utility because of their close association with such agency. Healthiness, for instance, might be accorded intrinsic as well as instrumental moral worth because of its close and common connections with moral agency. Nevertheless, any supportive tendency viewed as having intrinsic moral value ranks lower in moral worth than any tendency with constitutive moral value.

It is quite possible, accordingly, for people to have the general dispositions of moral agency but lack the character of moral agents. They might treat supportive tendencies as though they were constituents of moral agency. They might treat inclinations with constitutive moral worth as having ultimate value. Or they might suffer an obstructive weakness in one of their dispositions. Thus, some people, like many reared during the Great Depression, might treat thrift as though it were an element of moral agency. Others, like gentlemen of yore, might place personal honor at the highest level. Still others, like Hamlet, might be indecisive when facing hard cases.

But that some qualities are only supportive of moral agency and others are constitutive of it does not imply that habits must contain supportive or constitutive tendencies exclusively. As a matter of both fact and logic, supportive habits are blind, narrow, and fixed when they do not involve certain constitutive moral qualities, namely, those of reason. Thus, the habit of eating three square meals a day may be stupid or informed. It is blind or informed when one is or is not disposed to consider, for instance, whether or not such a diet is selfish or healthy. Habits of skill might be narrow when they are first learned, but they remain needlessly narrow only because they do not include tendencies to relate given skills to areas other than those where the habits are presently operative. Habits of smoking and imbibing are fixed in many instances only because they do not contain a disposition to check closely and honestly their consequences for the health of oneself and others.

In saying this about habits, we are talking about habits as they pertain to voluntary agents. Habits might be fixed regardless of reason, for they might be matters of physical addiction or psychological compulsion. Thus, one occasionally hears of physicians who are addicted to narcotics and of psychologists who throw temper tantrums. But neither addictions nor compulsions are part of the character of voluntary and *a fortiori* moral agents as such, whose habits must be within their control. Another aspect of the freedom endemic to the character of moral agents is their moral autonomy. Such agents are inclined to do or not to do things only when they judge for themselves, explicitly or implicitly, that those actions are right or wrong. In judging actions autonomously, moral agents not only rely on the norms of moral agency but also have determined that those criteria apply to themselves.

THE PRIOR CONDITIONS OF MORAL CHARACTER

In the respect that moral character consists of an arrangement of personal qualities, or dispositions, concordant with the norms of moral agency, it is a concrescence of those norms; it is their embodiment. The appearance of moral character, however, is not indifferent to circumstances, social or individual. Some conditions will highly support a person's embodiment of the norms of moral agency; others will tend to prevent it.

The individual circumstances that will strongly favor the development of moral character are obvious. First, the prospective moral agent must be healthy, physically and psychologically. This means that in their prenatal states children must have had adequate sustenance and not have suffered adversely from alcohol, narcotics, nicotine, and other toxic substances in their mothers' bodies. It means also that children must be free from beatings, sexual abuse, neglect, and other causes of trauma.[7] Second, children must come from nurturing and caring homes. To become trusting of others and to gain self-confidence, they must be loved and looked after by their parents, whether biological or just social, and other home members. And to acquire experience with intimate, complex, and developing interpersonal relationships, they must have stability in their home life.[8] Third, children must have parents and regular direct associations with other adults who themselves have morally sound characters. Life with such persons not only will provide moral models for children but will also furnish continuity with the content of moral education that students will encounter at school and other unfamiliar places. Finally, children must be free of severe economic deprivation, which not only would give them a feeling of insecurity but would distract them from being concerned with freedom, knowledge, values, rights, duties, and other central aspects of moral agency.

The circumstances required for individuals plainly indicate some of the social institutions especially supportive of the development of moral character. There have to be health institutions that will provide for the biological and psychological well being of infants and children. There have to be familial institutions that will ensure a safe, caring, and nurturing home for all students. There have to be institutions that promote friendly and enduring face-to-face associations beyond the family. And there have to be institutions that foster economic security for families. Less obvious institutions concern the media and political society. There have to be institutions that inform people of the morally relevant problems of society and entertain them in ways that in both substance and form are consistent with the norms of moral agency. There also has to be a political society whose principles are consistent with these norms and whose conception of the public good is definable by them. Some key practices concordant with all these institutions are needed, too: free inquiry into moral problems, both private and public; coordination of individual judgment and decision making with public judgment and decision making; equal respect for one another's qualities as moral agents; relating to each other, near and distant, through empathy and sympathy; and honoring the values, rights, and duties of moral agency.[9]

The individual and social conditions that we have just outlined are, it should be emphasized, optimal. That is, prospective moral agents under such conditions should have a very strong chance of acquiring moral character. As we have already stressed, individual and social conditions in present-day America are not optimal for moral education; indeed, many of them are a hindrance to it. The grimness of reality, however, should not keep us from understanding the types of conditions that will greatly facilitate the learning of the content of moral education. These conditions can serve as guidelines for determining changes that need to be made in the United States if its members are to be able to attempt to develop the character of moral agents without great obstacles.

THE PUBLIC'S INTEREST IN MORAL CHARACTER

In the early stage of this inquiry, we had occasion to discuss various current theories of moral education. Several of them speak to the extent to which moral character education is of public interest. Individualism holds that while certain intellectual and affective developments of autonomy within youth should receive support from the public, the specific character that an individual assumes is that person's business and no one else's concern, including his or her family's, friends', or government's interest. Communitarianism holds that because any individual's moral character derives from the community in which the individual grows up, the development of such character is of complete interest to the community. Social Liberalism maintains that while much of a person's moral character may be of private interest only, education in the core values of civil society is definitely of public interest. Our own position has similarities and differences with these theories.

In contrast with Individualism, our view holds that an individual's moral autonomy is understandable only within the normative constraints of moral agency. Because, then, an individual's moral character is of interest to all other moral agents, its development is of public interest, both that of the moral society and that of the moral community of which the individual is a member. The learning of the general features of moral character is of concern to all members of any moral society, and the learning of specific features of such character is of interest to the particular moral society and community to which the individual belongs. Some moral virtues, for example, the academic disciplines and politeness, have special significance for moral societies. Others, such as friendliness and friendship, have special importance for moral communities. Moral reasoning, moderation, honesty, and interpersonal sensitivity have equal importance, perhaps, for both sorts of moral associations. To be sure, whatever character a particular moral agent assumes must be within his or her control; but that character has to be consistent with the norms of moral agency. How the public's interest in moral character education can be satisfied without violating the moral autonomy of students will be discussed in the next two chapters.

Even though our position agrees with Communitarianism that the public has an extensive concern with moral character education, it does not agree that the community is the source of moral character. That source is moral agency, which defines the general moral content of moral character. To be sure, the specific moral content of a person's moral character might originate with the moral community of which that person is a member. Even so, the suitability of that specific content for moral character ultimately depends on the norms of moral agency. In short, moral agency is logically prior to moral community. Because the norms of an actual community might conflict with those of moral agency, they might render the community immoral to some extent. Hence, our theory of moral education recognizes that there might be a tension between the character which an actual community might want acquired by its young members and the character which is morally correct for them according to the norms of moral agency. What might be done about that tension will be addressed in subsequent chapters.

Our position agrees with Social Liberalism's claim that education in civic virtues is a legitimate public interest, but it disagrees that the public's concern with moral character education should be restricted to the civic virtues. In truth, we contend that the public has a positive interest in the full range of the development of moral character. The reason for this disagreement has to do with the nature of social arrangements. Social Liberalism, it might be recalled, looks upon a morally proper society as an instrument for promoting the enlightened self-interest of its members; whereas our view is that such a society, while it has instrumental value, derives its worth ultimately not from its members' self-interest but from the norms of moral agency. A moral society or community, therefore, is concerned with its members not just as individuals who through civic virtue can help it better serve their enlightened self-interest, but also as individuals who are bound to have the character of moral agents. Accordingly, that society or community has authority to oversee the development of all aspects of the moral character of its members. As hinted in our discussion of Individualism, the authority of a moral association to oversee the full range of the moral education of its members does not entail authority to violate their moral autonomy. Moreover, which institutions should be involved in moral education, as we will mention again in later chapters, is contingent upon political, cultural, economic, and other circumstances.

NOTES

1. The conception of character just established is generic; it applies to both moral and immoral characters. It also seems applicable to Sichel's idea of moral

character. See Betty Sichel, *Moral Education: Character, Community, and Ideals* (Philadelphia, PA: Temple University Press, 1988), pp. 82–83.

2. John Dewey, *Human Nature and Conduct* (New York: Random House, 1950), p. 38. Also see John Dewey, *Ethics* (Edwardsville, IL: Southern Illinois University Press, 1981), pp. 170–172.

3. Dewey, *Human Nature and Conduct*, p. 39.

4. Dewey, *Ethics*, p. 171.

5. Gilbert Ryle, *The Concept of Mind* (New York: Barnes & Noble, 1949), pp. 42–43.

6. Ibid., pp. 46–47.

7. The literature of psychoanalysis has long maintained that childhood trauma need not stem from malicious behavior. See Bruno Bettelheim, *Love Is Not Enough* (New York: The Free Press, 1950), pp. 277–303.

8. Needless to say, much depends on how the child interprets the well-intended behavior of a home's members toward him or her. See Bettelheim, *Love Is Not Enough*, pp. 13–29.

9. I have suggested elsewhere that these conditions are satisfied in a democratic state when it is understood to be a political society organized according to the norms of moral agency. See Robert D. Heslep, *Education in Democracy: Education's Moral Role in the Democratic State* (Ames, IA: Iowa State University Press, 1989), pp. 69–77.

5 The Content of Moral Education

The goal of the moral education being proposed here is people with the character of moral agents. It is one thing, however, to know what type of person one wants to produce; it is quite another to know how that kind of person is to be produced. One dimension of any educational process is content. Students study something in order to learn something; teachers teach something so that students will learn something. In each of these instances the term *something* refers to content—what is studied, what is taught, and what is learned. If, therefore, we are to explain fully the character education of moral agents, we have to address the issue of the content people should experience if they are to acquire the character of moral education.

The first part of our discussion of content is concerned with the everyday world, especially as it forms the moral character of children. The second part deals with the relevance of academic subjects to moral education. The last part concentrates on the importance of the content of career preparation for moral education.

THE PRACTICAL

Practical content consists of things that people encounter in their everyday lives, that is, things that are particular, concrete, and variable.[1] In the practical world we deal with this or that person or rule, not with persons or rules in general. We experience quantities, qualities, and relations as they exist in and among physical objects, not as they are in the abstract. Contexts, while not necessarily chaotic, are liable to change from place to place, from time to time.

Social theorists have long held that the practical world is crucial in the formation of character. Some have held that the social world serves to provide stimuli which enable one's genetic code to set one's character. Others have maintained that a person's social environment is exclusively responsible for his or her character. Still others have argued that character is a joint product of genes and surroundings. While these positions, which are thoroughly deterministic, are primarily irrelevant to explaining the origin of character in a moral agent, who is a voluntary agent, they do not undercut the point that the practical world is highly important in the formation of moral character. There, students have bodies and individual differences in intelligence, skills, attitudes, appreciations, and interests; they live in particular locations and at particular times; and they have specific cultural, social, and economic backgrounds. There, they have or lack role models, suffer deprivation or advantage, follow or disobey particular rules, face the consequences of their actions, and experience success and failure. There, they encounter many other conditions that also evoke responses on their part. Their responses eventually mold and structure their dispositions. Even the academic content of moral education, which we shall soon discuss, influences moral character only as that content is experienced in a particular, concrete, and alterable situation.

Freedom and the Practical

To see more clearly the crucial place of the practical in moral education, let us consider the significance of practical matters in the development of two features of moral character, freedom and knowledge. When we speak of freedom as a personal quality, we normally do not refer to a specific habit of freedom, that is, a habit of freedom in addition to other habits. The idea of a specific habit of freedom is not only vacuous but also unnecessary for talking about freedom as a personal quality. We get along quite well in conceiving such freedom as just a feature of the habits that a person has, including their structural relations. More specifically, a person has freedom as a personal quality in that the dispositions of that person are freely acquired, freely exercised, and freely retained. When people are made to learn or exercise habits or are prevented from getting rid of them, they are not in control of their habits and thus are not free. We would not describe as free, for instance, the woman who was made to become a concert pianist, who is compelled to perform in concerts even though she does not want to, or who cannot shake her inclination to be a concert pianist even though she would rather pursue another career.

People freely acquire tendencies and the interrelations among them when they freely do the things that establish the tendencies and their structure. Such actions may be freely performed voluntarily, impulsively, or somewhere in between. As explained earlier, people act voluntarily when they act unforcedly and with knowledge of what they are doing. They act impulsively when they act unforcedly but with no or only scant knowledge of what they are doing. In between they act unforcedly but with incomplete knowledge of what they are doing, as in the case of a child who freely uses a hammer without being much aware of the dangers in its use. Tendencies acquired voluntarily are usually found in youth and adulthood, and those learned impulsively are associated with childhood and adolescence. Dispositions gained with incomplete knowledge of what one is about are associated with all phases of life. Even though impulsive actions are spontaneous, they sometimes lead to tendencies; and because impulsive actions are uninformed, the habits to which they lead often are undesired. Hence, parents and school teachers, trusting to their own knowledge of a child's welfare rather than to any luck or natural goodness on the part of his or her impulses, often impose dispositions upon children. But that a person was made to acquire certain tendencies early in life does not necessarily mean that he or she can never be free with respect to the acquisition of those tendencies. A person who was forced to gain certain habits in childhood can in subsequent years become the functional equivalent of one who freely assumed those tendencies. If eventually the former person freely and knowingly approves of having gained those habits, he or she no longer has regrets about having assumed them and insofar is very much like one who had freely learned them. Thus, we can become voluntary agents despite impositions during childhood.

It is one thing, however, to gain a disposition freely and quite another to exercise it freely. While many adolescents and adults take up smoking, drinking, or drugs primarily because of peer pressure and the attractions of commercial advertisements in the mass media,[2] others acquire these habits freely. Yet, even those who started addictive habits freely and continue to control their exercise might find eventually that those habits have become coercive. We all know people who took up smoking, drinking, or drugs freely but now, despite the onset of bad health and the warnings of medical research, cannot get rid of their tendencies.[3] Such people no longer have smoking, drinking, or drug habits; the habits have them. These, to be sure, are not the only dispositions that might bedevil us. Food weaknesses, tempers, twitches, speech mannerisms, and aggressiveness are only a few of the sorts of inclinations that might extend beyond the pale of free exercise.

It is easier to tell when a rational agent is exercising a disposition forcedly than it is to determine when such an agent is exercising one freely. According to the normal concept of the matter, no rational agent freely does what the agent regards as wrong. Hence, no rational person who regards as wrong his or her exercising a given inclination freely acts from that inclination. This explains why anyone whom we know to be rational and to do something habitually that he or she acknowledges to be wrong is always judged by us to be acting under compulsion, either external or internal. On the other hand, the concept of a rational agent does not necessarily imply that an action by a rational agent is performed freely just because the agent regards it as right; for the concept logically allows that a rational agent might do under compulsion what he or she judges to be right. The compulsion might be a matter of physical force or of deep-seated habit. Thus, we occasionally hear of convicts who truly approve of their imposed regimen but who cannot freely live a lawful life. Also, we often hear of clerics, soldiers, spinsters, and other upright and informed people with habits so ingrained that they could never change those habits even if reason dictated that they should.

In trying to tell if a rational agent is freely acting from a disposition, we in effect are attempting to determine if that agent would be acting differently if he or she had sufficiently good reasons for doing so. In answering that question, we consider what would count as such reasons and take into account a variety of factors related to the agent, for example, biological, environmental, and psychological factors. If we cannot establish that any of these or some other factor would keep the agent from acting otherwise if he or she had sufficiently good reasons for so doing, we normally conclude that he or she is freely following the tendency of concern. The conclusion is not apodictic, but practical knowledge never is.

Similar points apply to determining whether or not one freely retains a habit. If Betty June has sufficiently good reasons for getting rid of a behavior pattern but persists in keeping it, she does not freely retain it. If Elizabeth has sufficiently good reasons for holding on to a disposition and persists in exercising it, she might be keeping it under compulsion rather than by free choice. If, however, she is prepared to abolish the habit upon learning of sufficiently good reasons for so doing, she is retaining it freely. Getting rid of a tendency, of course, is usually more difficult than simply not exercising it. With some effort, if not struggle, people can occasionally control their proclivities for consuming fatty foods; but they do not purge themselves of those inclinations just by not exercising them for a short span of time. We have abandoned dispositions completely only when we have no urge the rest of our lives to exercise them. Few, if any, of us can be thoroughly free of our past ways. Sometimes, as with reformed alcoholics, we have to be constantly on guard against the resurgence of an old habit. At best, as with former smokers, we have to contend with nothing more than an occasional mild itch to return to a rejected way. Even St. Paul, who presumably turned from his old life instantaneously, had to contend with the ways of the flesh. Practically speaking, those who suffer only occasional mild urges have eliminated their former tendencies, whereas those who never again act on former tendencies only by dent of struggle simply have those inclinations under control, which may be more or less tenuous, more or less firm. Before judging whether or not a person has abandoned a habit, we usually want to observe over an extended period of time the relevant behavior of the person to detect any evidence of struggle or relapse.

Because freedom is a major trait of moral character, it must always be a principle in selecting and organizing the content of moral education. Except where there are overriding reasons, the integrally related dispositions making up a moral agent's character must be freely learned, exercised, and retained. Overriding reasons might be considerations of physical safety and health, interpersonal behavior, and intellectual immaturity. Regardless of their impulses, children must cross streets safely, eat nutritious foods, and brush their teeth; and they might have to be made to learn to do these things. They may have to be restrained from injuring one another, and they may have to be compelled to be civil and truthful with others. Where they are too immature to grasp the reasons for acquiring basic intellectual competences and have no present interest in learning these abilities, they will have to be required to learn them. In sum, there are overriding reasons when the dispositions of concern are crucial, positively or negatively, for the development of given people as moral agents, and when those people will not freely learn or abandon the inclinations or cannot freely learn or eliminate them when they need to for their moral growth. In any case, imposition is to be employed only when freedom is practically impossible; and any force employed in shaping the dispositions of a moral agent must be justifiable to the agent when he or she is able to see the point of the force.

Ever since Plato, who maintained that subjects for the intellectual development of children should be freely studied by them,[4] many educators have recognized that much of what young children need to learn can be learned freely. To be sure, some traditionalists have contended that the freedom of students is irrelevant to the selection and organization of content; and some progressives have insisted that the freedom of students is the only principle relevant to that end. Between these extremes there have been many educators, for example, from Pestalozzi, Froebel, and Herbart, to Dewey, Montessori, and Flexner, to Jerome Bruner, Jane Roland Martin, Howard Gardner, and Maxine Greene, who have viewed the freedom of students as a major, but not the only, principle for determining what they should study. They have set forth a variety of recommendations for helping to ensure that students will freely learn the content selected and organized for them. Underlying these recommendations is the principle that students will not freely engage any content that is not of positive interest to them.[5]

To be interested in something is at least to pay attention to it. The attention may be superficial and fleeting or close and prolonged. To be positively interested in an object is to like, desire, or value it. To be negatively interested in something is to dislike, take an aversion to, or disvalue it. A like involves a pleasant feeling about something. While likes favorably dispose us toward objects, they do not necessarily lead us to seek the objects. They might be so weak that they leave us passive. Thus, we may like people without loving them or wanting to be friends with them. Indeed, Judy might like Tom upon meeting him at a party but never make an effort to see him again. When we desire, or want, an object, we are inclined to obtain it. To want something, however, is not necessarily to like it. That we desire dental surgery does not mean that we like it. But even if we want something that we do not like, we presume that obtaining it will help us gain something that we do like, such as health. Desire, then, might not anticipate pleasure in possession of its object. As explained in Chapter 2, a desire need not be evaluative, for it might be capricious. To desire something on the basis of a norm is to value that object. However, one may value something without desiring it, for instance, when one judges an object to be good but does not want it, at least at that moment.

As the critics of progressive educators have long pointed out, something need not be morally good or even in one's interest just because one is positively interested in it. Hitler's desire to eliminate Jews and Gypsies was evil. Many things, such as pizza, gin, and orgies, that we like or want might be bad for us. But as the advocates of progressive education have insisted, one's being positively interested in something is a necessary condition for one's engaging the object freely. If I am indifferent toward a subject or negatively interested in it, then I will learn it only if some factor beyond my control makes me do so.[6] Thus, if the content of moral education is not of positive interest to students, it cannot be learned freely by them.

To be sure, one's positive interest in something might be externally induced. Curiosity, likes, wants, and fears frequently are outside of one's control. Nevertheless, this point, which has been ignored by some proponents of progressive education, does not necessarily preclude a person's interest in an object from enabling that person's freely relating to the object. For one thing, our interest in an object may be under our control from the very beginning: We may freely hold standards by virtue of which we like or desire objects. Gourmets, art connoisseurs, mathematicians, and baseball scouts are only some of the types of people who become interested in things because those things satisfy their freely held standards. Moreover, even if we do get hooked or simply aroused by objects, we may freely check our responses to them and then freely decide whether or not to retain our interests in them. Finally, if we, like the hopeless romantic who has forsworn all love only to find himself in love, cannot but be concerned with something even after concluding that we should not be interested in it, we still may freely decide how to act with respect to the object.

As already indicated, the use of student interest as a principle for selecting and organizing the content of moral education does not intend that students are to learn just anything in which they are interested. Whatever they are to learn must not interfere with their acquiring the character of a moral agent, and it must help develop such character. Thus, the activities in which given students participate and the materials that they employ as a part of their moral education need to be not only matters in which they are interested but also matters that maintain and foster moral character in them. To help ensure that this condition will be satisfied in the selection of content for given students, one has to know which habits and interrelations among them constitute the character of a moral agent for the students, which materials, activities, and milieux are available and suitable for learning this character, and in which of these materials, activities, and milieux the students are interested. There is no question that if students experience only those activities, materials, and contexts selected for them at a specific time of their moral education, they will become arrested in the development of their character. They might even remain morally childish. So, if the content of moral education is to enable students to acquire the character of a moral agent as fully as they are likely to, it must be organized with respect to several features of student interests.

Students with an interest in something may lose their interest in it or they may keep it. If they keep it, they may simply pursue it or they may develop it.[7] In pursuing an interest, we rely only on concepts and facts about the object that we already possess, we exercise only skills already in our repertoire, we experience feelings quite similar to ones we have previously had when engaging the matter, and we have no goal other than to enjoy what it is we are doing. By this measure, most of us simply pursue our interests in music, swimming, or gardening. Indeed, many of us eventually diminish our pursuits of these and other activities by increasingly experiencing them casually or indirectly, for instance, listening to music as background, watching televised swim meets instead of going to the Y, thumbing through seed catalogues as a substitute for gardening, and reading book reviews rather than books. When developing an interest in something, we acquire new information about the matter, broaden and deepen our understanding of it, refine old skills and gain new ones, and expand and intensify our feelings about the object. Thus, a person who seriously develops an interest in classical music does not stop with tune recognition and composer identification, but ultimately learns the history, culture, politics, economics, compositional theory, and instrumentation of such music. The one who takes gardening seriously sooner or later learns elements of agronomy, botany, and ecology.

Therefore, in organizing the content of moral education we need to take into account the potential development of the student's interest in that content. More specifically, we should begin by selecting those parts or aspects of the content in which the student is presently interested. Then, in view of his or her present and future character deficiencies, and building on the knowledge, skills, and feelings about the content that the student now has and will have, we should proceed to encourage the student to develop his or her character as well as it might be. In the student's childhood, this organization might be guided largely by his or her natural imaginativeness, curiosity, and social connections. In later years, for those students with a distinct interest in academic matters, it may be guided chiefly by the structure of the intellectual disciplines. For those students with special interests in practical affairs, it also may be guided mainly by the structure of practical problems. There are other modes, too, for organizing content with respect to student interests.[8] The overriding consideration is that whatever design is used, it must enable the student to gain the character of a moral agent according to his or her development of interests in the appropriate content.

As already noted, the cultural, social, and economic conditions of students tend to influence the latter's interests. They frequently limit the sorts of objects in which people might be interested, encourage the pursuit of some interests, the avoidance of others, and help determine who will develop which interests. For this reason Marxists and Critical Theorists might insist that our principle of student interest is anathema to freedom in education of any sort: To the extent that the subjective interests of students are determined by cultural, social, and economic conditions, the former are beyond the control of the students; hence, they lead to a curriculum where student freedom is necessarily inoperative in both the selection and the organization of the content of that curriculum. Content ultimately will be selected and organized according to social-economic class lines or according to cultural groupings.

This criticism does not hold up, however. Through reflection people can raise and expand their consciousness and thereby transcend their economic or cultural interests and gain others. Workers, for instance, can learn to be interested in something other than better wages, fringe benefits, and working hours; they can become interested in what is good for themselves and others as human beings. Similarly, the members of a cultural group can cease to be interested in just what their culture deems worthy and become interested in what is good from the standpoint of all human beings. Thus, even if the interests of students initially are caused by their economic or cultural backgrounds, they do not have to remain merely the products of class or cultural membership. Upon understanding what moral agency is, students may assess their class or cultural interests from the standpoint of the norms of moral agency and then judge whether or not the pursuit or development of those interests is morally right and, therefore, whether or not other interests should be pursued or developed.

Knowledge and the Practical

Besides having an impact on the acquisition of freedom as a feature of moral character, the practical world affects the development of the intellectual facets of moral character.[9] The first opportunities that children have to form cognitive dispositions are strongly influenced by their immediate environments. The facts that they establish early on pertain to their proximate surroundings; and the connections that they soon make are between events at hand, such as the baby's cry and the subsequent presence of the mother. To be sure, imagination rather than cool inquiry drives much of the child's perception of the world; but even though imagination typically leads to an erroneous perception, it can serve children as a vehicle for relating facts and feelings to one another and thus for making sense of things and forces beyond their sight and control. Thus, the philosopher Alfred North Whitehead regarded the cognitive life of childhood as one dominated by imagination.[10] With experience and parental guidance children can begin to gain more facts and understanding of their environments, thereby helping to build tendencies to know. As long as the knowledge that children acquire and the activities in which they engage to learn it are interesting to them, the knowledge and the activities will be prized by them. Thus, the children will have begun a basis for valuing a major feature of moral agency.

Much of what children learn concerns themselves, and something about themselves that they need to know is that their actions have consequences and that these consequences involve other people as well as those performing the actions. This understanding can be facilitated initially through small group interaction, as in families and during play. Another matter that younger children can and should learn is the notion of a rule. This they can start to grasp in play activities and in the routines of their households. In formal games and the household, children are apt to learn that many rules are beyond their, but not all human, control; but in informal games, they can learn that at least some rules are subject to their control. Either way, it is highly important for children to learn that rules are necessary for and integral to the operation of games, households, and other activities.[11]

The child's growing disposition to seek knowledge for him- or herself can serve as a root stock for developing an inclination to help others gain knowledge. Such an inclination can be encouraged through conjoint cognitive activities and by teaching children to be truthful. If children are interested in seeking and sharing knowledge with each other and their older associates, they will strengthen their foundation for appreciating knowledge, including the activities for obtaining it, as a main trait of moral agency. It is important, therefore, that truthfulness be taught to children in such a way that they do not come to see the sharing of knowledge as a threat to themselves. While competition and secrecy might have a vital place in athletics, business, and warfare, they are not essential to moral agency.

Toward the end of childhood and during youth, people have increasing opportunities to develop new types of cognition: details, extensive arrays of facts, classifications, technical information, natural and social laws, and the manipulability of the environment, including people as well as mere things. These avenues can open up because of the addition of new materials to one's world. But they can open up also because of the expansion and refinement of the cognitive resources of the older child and the adolescent, mainly, establishment of a fund of experience, development of abstract reasoning and psychomotor skills, expansion of interests, cultivation of friendships, and engagement in activities without close adult supervision. A well-organized school provides an enriched environment that enables students to use and increase these resources in regular, systematic, and efficient ways; but the school is not the only social institution relevant here. Hobbies, recreation, clubs, the public media, churches, traveling, libraries, museums, and part-time jobs can also help.

The formation of cognitive dispositions does not end with youth. Adults typically continue to add to their stores of information, and they usually tend to note ruptures from the past that are indicated by new facts. Nevertheless, adults can and should be inclined to rely increasingly upon principles—natural, social, and ethical—for their understanding of the world. These will enable them to forecast events and to grasp their causes. They also will help them to judge rules, institutions, practices, and natural and artistic objects as well as people and their actions. With a large store of information and an inclination to rely on principled reasoning, adults can and should develop dispositions to forecast distant as well as proximate consequences and to look for connections between the natural and the human, the private and the public, and the domestic and the foreign. In addition, they can and should acquire tendencies to apply principles to the facts of each case as they are, not as they are prejudged to be, and to recognize that some standards of judgment must be abandoned or amended from time to time because of changes in historical conditions. In brief, adults should become inclined to see the complexities of moral relations in the practical world and to recognize that knowledge of them can be complicated and hard to gain.

Newspapers, movies, radio, and television have been prime vehicles for adult education in this century. Literature, music, drama, and the plastic arts also have been major vehicles. Recent advances in video electronics have opened up other means. Technologies alone, however, will not engender tendencies on the part of adults to acquire and appreciate moral wisdom. Despite the intellectual stimulation of print journalism and TV public affairs programs, despite publications by experts, despite the emotional power of the arts, and despite the possibilities of interactive electronics, these educational instruments by themselves do not help individual moral agents to cultivate habits of moral knowledge. To maintain and nourish these dispositions, people must experience the accumulation and acquisition of moral knowledge as something commonly involved in their particular lives and as something in which they usually and actively engage. Adults can learn moral knowledge in these ways through direct and regular associations with one another where moral knowledge is mutually respected, exchanged, sought, treasured, and acted upon. Associations of this sort can and should raise moral issues, examine facts relevant to them, and identify moral problems; they also can and ought to discuss what values, rights, and duties of moral agency are related to the issues, facts, and problems under consideration. They can take the forms of daily table talk between spouses, chats with neighbors, block meetings, coffee-break talk at the work place, conversations with friends, discussion groups at church, professional conferences, meetings of business executives, and public forums.

Such associations can assume, too, the form of meetings between political leaders and their technical advisers. If they did, they would tend to prevent the blunders of technocracy, which result from policy dominated by narrow expertise. They also would ward off policy dictated by uninformed political ambition.[12]

THE ACADEMIC

Before the middle of this century, moral education in the academic area typically was not a separate subject. It usually was, instead, a dimension of other subjects, most notably, literature and history. Fables, plays, poems, and novels often were selected for the moral lessons, the moral virtues, the moral characters, and the moral inspiration that they presented.[13] Historical figures and events frequently were remarked for the lessons, virtues, characters, and inspiration that they too reflected. It was in college that morality was studied as a separate subject, and there it often was offered as a culminating experience in the development of the student's character. While grades in literature, history, and other subjects with dimensions of moral education usually represented academic attainments only, grades relevant to achievement in moral character did appear under the rubrics of conduct, deportment, attitude, and mental hygiene.

Because of the integrated approach to moral education in academic areas, philosophers, religious leaders, educators, politicians, and others were especially concerned about the moral facets of traditional studies. Thus, not only Plato and the Pope, but also parental groups and school board members, advocated censorship to ensure that the curriculum included content promoting virtue and excluded content cultivating vice. Some critics of schools charged that a curriculum of purely academic subjects implicitly fostered in students a character of secular morality. Populists maintained that a strong emphasis on the moral in academic subjects was necessary to keep people from using their academic talents for selfish ends.

It was possible to teach moral character as a thread interwoven throughout other subjects only as long as there was agreement on what constituted such character. By the 1960s, however, the spread of cultural relativism and the increasing diversification of American culture had begun to undermine the nation's consensus on moral character. The result was that schools and colleges soon abandoned such character as an educational goal. Academic subjects more and more became "value-free."

There is no question that ethics as a separate subject has a place in moral education.[14] If nothing else, it enables teachers and students to concentrate on technical problems in morality, for instance, the logical structure of moral judgment. It also is doubtless, however, that an integrated orientation to moral education generally has decisive advantages over the separate subjects approach when the principles of moral character are agreed upon. This viewpoint anchors morality, as it is in the practical world, in a specific context, even if only that of a simple story or an ancient event. Hence, it does not transform morality into a purely theoretical pursuit. Moreover, the integrated approach emphasizes that morality permeates life in the practical world, whereas the separate subjects perspective suggests that morality is just a pigeonhole in real life, vying with law, business, politics, culture, religion, and personal preference. Finally, the integrated orientation enables students to witness the making of moral decisions, real as well as fictional, and to see the aftermath of those decisions. So, on the ground that we have established the formation of the character of the moral agent as the aim of moral education, we propose to show how this character might be learned, in part, as a facet of the study of academic subjects, mainly literature, history, science, and mathematics.

Literature is rife with material about freedom and knowledge.[15] Jack London's *Call of the Wild* and Frank Norris's *MacTeague* treat the tension between raw nature and individual freedom. Mark Twain's *Hucklebury Finn* and Toni Morrison's *Beloved* ponder the dominance that social institutions can have over individual freedom. George Orwell's *1984,* Solshenitzyn's *The First Circle,* and B.F. Skinner's *Walden Two* portray society absent of freedom, institutional as well as individual. The capacity of the individual to make or not to make choices and accept responsibility for their outcomes is dominant in Ernest Hemingway's *The Old Man and the Sea* as well as Shakespeare's *Hamlet.* Sophocles' *Ajax* and *Oedipus the King* and Shakespeare's *Romeo and Juliet* emphasize just how terrible the consequences of uninformed actions can be. The myth of Prometheus, the story of Adam and Eve, and the aphorisms of *Ecclesiastes* see the possession of knowledge as something that brings suffering and grief along with power and dignity. The second part of Goethe's *Faust* dramatizes the good that enlightened technology can bring to human life, whereas Mary Shelley's *Frankenstein* warns of the evil that can come when science severs its humanistic roots. Plays by Eugene O'Neill and Tennessee Williams deal with self-deception while Dostoyevsky's *Crime and Punishment* concerns itself with conscience and truthfulness as well as moral equality, moral respect, and self-sacrifice.[16]

Being the pageant of human life, history enables students to witness the morally good and bad and the morally ambiguous in a rich variety. It presents them with Pericles, Charlemagne, Elizabeth I, Washington, Gandhi, Martin Luther King, Jr., and other leaders who, despite their faults and difficult circumstances, possessed personal traits that enabled them to enhance the social good. At the same time it puts before students Nero, King John, Richard III, Hitler, Stalin, and other heads of government who, because of evil traits, acted for evil ends and violated their subjects' moral rights. Wars, ancient and modern, offer many examples of courage, cowardice, and foolishness. But so do events in the lives of intellectuals, for example, Socrates, Abelard, Galileo, Milton, Fuller, and Beauvoir; and in the lives of ordinary people, for example, those who held to their religious beliefs despite persecutions, those who coped with natural disaster and economic depression, and those who were victims of conquest. In addition, history presents the dismal picture of man's inhumanity to man: the enslavement of people, their slaughter in the name of God, the exploitation and oppression of women and children, the neglect of the physically and mentally ill and the old, the theft of natural resources, and the conduct of international commerce in slaves, liquor, and narcotics. But history also shows the student that human beings have struggled for and attained ends of notable moral worth, for example, the Protestant Reformation's stress on individual autonomy, the Enlightenment era's call for the application of rationality to human affairs, the abolition of slavery during the nineteenth century, Romanticism's emphasis on the worth and dignity of ordinary people, the rise of democratic government, child labor reform, the feminist movement, and the United Nation's adoption of its Universal Declaration of Human Rights.

There have been many instances where science has gone awry because it has had to conform to religious or political doctrines. For medieval European science, findings had to conform to the teachings of the Christian church. Earlier in this century German and Soviet scientists had to accept certain biological theories that supported the respective political views of Hitler and Stalin even though those theories were manifestly false. Because of these and other distortions of science by religious, political, and other normative principles, the majority of scientists, often marching under the banner of Positivism, have adopted the view that science must be value-free. Its theories must be purely nonnormative; its findings must be so, too; and its methods must be empirical. Accordingly, some people might contend that science should never be a subject with a moral strain and thus should never be a part of moral education. This position, however, is open to challenge.[17] Scientists are moral agents, not automata. They have to face the question of the moral worth of science, they have to concern themselves with the impact of their findings on other human beings, and they have to have moral guidelines for their investigations.

This objection does not mean that scientists do or should force their theories and findings to fit some normative preconception of the universe, but it does mean that science has facets relevant to moral education. Its theories, laws, and facts provide the student with a storehouse of descriptions of the world; they also furnish the student with explanations and predictions of events in the world. These descriptions, explanations, and predictions in turn can help the student establish facts needed in making moral judgments. The methods of science, qualitative as well as quantitative, serve the student as exemplars of how to go about describing and understanding factual features of moral contexts; but they also indicate the limits they have for practical knowledge. A study of the accomplishments of science can show its outstanding contributions to the infrastructure of moral life, for instance, in the control of communicable disease, in nutrition, in medicine, in agriculture, in industrial production, in transportation, and in computer technology. At the same time, a study of the accomplishments of science can reveal that some of them have been morally problematic, for example, the ecological destruction indirectly resulting from the synthesis of nitrates and of phosphates and the dangers posed by the discoveries about nuclear energy. In learning about the morally problematic attainments of science, students should not conclude that science is necessarily or likely to be a force for evil; rather, they ought to conclude that its findings must be applied to human life only with moral care, that is, only in accordance with the norms of moral agency.

If the study of science is on its face remote from moral education, the study of mathematics is even more so. In ancient times Pythagoras and his followers found much in the subject that was normatively significant for human life, but in modern times mathematicians do not see their discipline essentially as descriptive or explanatory of the world, let alone as evaluative or prescriptive of matters within it. There are, however, aspects of mathematics that have relevance for morality. One of them is mathematical analysis. Strictly speaking, moral agents are not numbers, moral values are not quantities, and moral thinking is not a matter of calculation. Nevertheless, morality is sometimes amenable to mathematical analysis. Rankings of values, distributions of goods, and estimates of utility are only a few of the operations in moral judgment that profit from the use of mathematics. Moreover, mathematics is a subject from which students can learn in plain form about some of the basic elements of rationality and hence of morality, notably, the Principle of Identity and deductive inference. Finally, because mathematics can help students to think in abstractions, it can help them to think about moral problems removed from the immediacy of practical situations and thus to think about them reflectively. This does not mean that students should learn to regard the feelings, climates, urgencies, confusions, dilemmas, and uncertainties of real life as irrelevant to moral problems. But it does intend that they must learn to reflect upon moral problems in order to detect and assemble relevant facts, select and apply normative standards, forecast consequences, weigh alternative courses of action, and do whatever else is involved in making moral judgments and decisions. The quasi-detachment obtained through moral reflection saves moral agents from becoming victims of situations, for it enables them to make sense of and thus to gain control of the feelings, climates, urgencies, confusions, dilemmas, and uncertainties of the practical world.[18]

In saying that literature, history, science, and mathematics are relevant to moral education, we want to stress that a purely academic approach to them, by which they are to be learned for their own sakes, is not likely to have an optimal impact on the formation of the student's moral character. Perhaps some students can make learning transfers from pure mathematics to moral reasoning, but that the moral character of all or even most students will necessarily benefit from the study of pure mathematics is questionable. Because mathematics by itself makes no reference to the real world, it makes learning transfers from itself to anything practical especially difficult. Thus, students learn practical applications of arithmetic only because they first encounter it in practical ways; and they typically do not see what is the practical importance of algebra, which they usually encounter apart from practical contexts. Moreover, the strictly academic study of even literature, history, or moral philosophy, where materials of moral significance abound, is no guarantee that students will gain in moral stature. If it did, then teachers of these subjects should have characters of solid moral gold, which they do not.

On the other hand, we do not recommend that traditional academic subjects be given just a practical approach. Students with a strong academic bent who can make learning transfers from the strictly academic to the moral should have the opportunity to pursue and expand their academic interests. Moreover, moral agents, in order to have access to the knowledge provided by the academic disciplines, must rely on specialists in those fields, which people can become only if they study, for a period of time, such subjects in a purely academic way. There are various ways by which the moral and the academic may be balanced with one another. One configuration is to give academic subjects a definite moral orientation until the moral character of students is well established and then to shift to a purely academic approach. Another mode is to stress the moral in some subjects, such as literature and history, and stress the academic in other subjects, such as science and mathematics. A strong academic approach to the former would be provided for specialization in advanced studies. One more way is to pose moral problems in some subjects, for instance, literature and history, and to use knowledge and skills from subjects with an academic emphasis, for instance, science and mathematics, in an analysis of those problems. Which configuration is appropriate depends on several factors, notably, the interests of students, the moral problems facing the moral agents of a given time and place, the special moral virtues needed by those agents, and the nature and status of the academic disciplines available to those agents.

SERVICES, PRODUCTS, AND PROCESSES

Much of adult life is concerned with services, products, and the activities that bring the latter into being. As bank tellers, counselors, physicians, waitresses, truck drivers, accountants, garbage collectors, lawyers, and teachers, many of us perform services. As borrowers, the mentally distressed, the physically ill, restaurant patrons, purchasers of toothpaste and clothing, keepers of business records, producers of waste, parents, and parties to contracts, we all need services. Moreover, we all are users and consumers of houses, food, clothes, medicine, automobiles, cosmetics, and other utilitarian goods; and we all also are readers of literature, viewers of paintings and sculptures, listeners to music, and experiencers of other goods made for their own sakes. Many of us are engaged in manufacturing as workers, supervisors, managers, and owners; and some of us are engaged in the making of aesthetic objects, such as poets, dramatists, actors, novelists, painters, sculptors, composers, and performers.

By the usual understanding of service and production, both involve values and rules. Services rendered are of value to the recipient, and compensation for those services is of value to the provider. Products are supposed to have worth, utilitarian or aesthetic; and the work contributed to the making of an object has worth also. The server and the served conduct their transactions according to rules, for instance, those of fees and procedures; and the physical labor, the skills, and the technologies contained in production also relate to rules, for example, those of execution, operation, and wages. In some instances, the values and rules associated with service and production are economic or technical; in other instances they are cultural, legal, or aesthetic. But service and production may have moral norms as well. Because a service, by its nature, is both interpersonal and voluntary, it is subject to the Criteria of Moral Value, Moral Rights, and Moral Duty. It may be judged as good or bad for the involved parties as moral agents and as to whether or not it accords to the moral rights and duties of those parties. Despite the loneliness of some inventors and artists, production is necessarily interpersonal: The making of a utilitarian or aesthetic object necessarily entails a user, consumer, observer, reader, listener, and so on. While production actually has included many cases of slave labor and mad inventors and artists, it surely is subject to the CMVa, CMR, and CMD. After all, slaves are prospective moral agents, and mad inventors and artists, retrospective ones.

One would have to be a stranger to this planet not to recognize that service and production have a large tie to moral character as well as to moral values, rights, and duties. In Biblical times, money changers were to be fair, not avaricious. In medieval Europe, money lenders were allowed to be prudent but not usurious; later they were permitted by Protestant theology to charge whatever interest the market would bear. Also according to the norms of Protestantism, workers should be industrious, punctual, fair, honest, reliable, and respectful of authority and property; whereas employers should have not only good work habits but dispositions for the socially conscious stewardship of their wealth. In the first half of the twentieth century, the virtue governing the relationship between employers and employees was a truncated version of the Protestant work ethic: a fair day's wage for an honest day's work. But the historical concern with the connection of services and production to moral virtue has born partly on the nature of services provided and goods produced. The concern has focused in addition on the relations between provider and recipient, producer and consumer, and employer and employee. Prostitution, abortion, pornography, alcohol, narcotics, slavery, obscene artwork, weapons, gambling, and other services and products have been variously challenged by moralists, from Plato to John Milton, to Carey Nation, to the Ayatolla Khomeini, and to Mrs. James Brady, on the ground that they undermine virtues and promote vicious habits. Some moralists have contended that such services and products must be eliminated or minimized by governmental intervention; others have held that they should be kept from the young by governmental intervention but left for adults to the forces of the market place. Accordingly, a moral education that did not aim to inculcate moral character related to service and production would be seriously incomplete.

A kind of content that people need to learn in order to develop such character is general to service and production. They have to understand that those engaged in these activities are interpersonal voluntary agents and thus are subject to the norms of moral agency. They must see what services and products may be good or bad for people as moral agents. They need to understand what moral rights of employees must be respected by employers and what obligations are owed by employees to employers. They have to see how service and production contribute to the public moral good. Lastly, they have to learn to recognize compatibilities and resolve conflicts between the moral norms governing service and production and the customs, statutes, and occupational codes governing them. This study of service and production in general can occur in different places. In literature, students can benefit from such works as Chaucer's *The Canterbury Tales,* Shakespeare's *The Merchant of Venice,* Goldsmith's *The Vicar of Wakefield,* Joyce's *The Portrait of the Artist as a Young Man,* Shaw's *Mrs. Warren's Profession,* Woolf's *A Room of One's Own,* Sinclair's *The Jungle,* Steinbeck's *The Grapes of Wrath,* Ellison's *Invisible Man,* Sloan Wilson's *The Man in the Gray Flannel Suit,* John Grisham's *A Time to Kill,* and Michael Dorris' short story collection, *Working Men.*

In history, students can learn about the actual moral conditions of laborers, artisans, artists, writers, musicians, bankers, industrialists, lawyers, physicians, reverends, scientists, engineers, teachers, politicians, and social workers, as well as about the moral quality of services actually rendered and goods actually produced. Exploited apprentices, sumptuary laws, evictions from land, hazardous mines, Renaissance art, Classical music, impressed seamen, white slavery, grimy factories, subsistence wages, long working hours, colonial plantations, electrification, the Suez canal, oil fields, sewers and water mains, unemployment, enormous accumulations of wealth, charitable hospitals, bureaucracy, immigrant and migrant workers, insane asylums, strikes, urban planning and squalor, sexual and racial discrimination, riots, and bank fraud—these and many more conditions and events are present for examination and judgment. In courses organized around current social problems, students can examine the moral aspects of such topics as technology and unemployment, censorship and art, global economics, free markets, cultural perspectives on work, aesthetics and morality, individualism and teamwork, business and the public good, equal opportunity in the workplace, and decision making in the workplace.

The special study of the moral dimensions of service and production has to do with career preparation. Students bent on service occupations must become sensitive to the special moral needs and rights of prospective clients. They have to become cognizant not only of the laws and professional codes bearing on their chosen occupations, but also of the moral correctness of those laws and codes. They need to reflect on the moral quality of their respective motives for wanting to enter their different fields. They should learn how to serve their clients efficiently without violating the norms of moral agency. They must become disposed to inform their clients fully about procedures and share decision making with them where options are available.

Students inclined to engage in manufacturing, as employees or as employers, have to become alert to the moral impact of products and by-products of processes. They must be mindful to design products and processes that will be within the parameters of morality. Prospective employees and employers should learn to see one another as moral beings, not as antagonists. They need to recognize that efficiency and quality must exist in manufacturing, but not at the expense of moral agency. They have to learn to engage in joint decision making, thereby learning to respect multiple viewpoints and to share responsibilities and benefits.

There is a thin line between sermonizing and morally correct art, between moral restraint in art and oppression of the aesthetic. Artists are first and foremost makers of aesthetic works; they require freedom of aesthetic expression as well as skills, concepts, and sensibilities for creating artistic works. Nevertheless, it is quite possible to have aesthetic products that both agree with artistic canons and do not violate the norms of moral agency. Titian, Duerer, Bosch, Goya, Catlin, Remington, Monet, Cassat, Picasso, O'Keefe, and Rothko support the point in painting. Dante, Milton, Goethe, Burns, Whitman, Dickinson, Eliot, and Langston Hughes uphold it in poetry. Vivaldi, Bach, Mozart, Beethoven, Verdi, Stravinski, and Barber support it in music. The person who contends that the artist may let the moral chips fall where they may as long as good art is produced implies that the artist is not a morally responsible agent, and the one who maintains that the artist is bound above all else by the canons of art forgets that moral principles are superior to all others. Accordingly, students who want to become poets, dramatists, painters, musicians, or other sorts of artistic workers must learn to express themselves aesthetically without violating the norms of moral agency. They well might learn to express the dimensions of moral agency without violating aesthetic principles.

NOTES

1. These traits of the practical come from Aristotle. See, for example, his *N. Ethics*, Book VI, Chapters 3–8.

2. About $3.9 billion per year is spent in America on cigarette advertising. From 1977 until 1991 there was no yearly increase in the percentage of American adults who smoked. In 1992, however, there was an increase in the percentage of women who smoked. It was attributed by the Centers for Disease Control and Prevention to advertising. *Athens (Georgia) Daily News*, April 2, 1993, p. 1A.

3. According to one account, 75 million Americans admitted to the "recreational" use of drugs at some time in their lives; 8 percent of these people reported problems stemming from such use. "Morning Edition: Special Report on the Use and Abuse of Alcohol and Drugs," National Public Radio, March 31, 1993.

4. Plato, *The Republic*, 536E.

5. See Eamonn Callan, *Autonomy and Schooling* (Kingston and Montreal, Canada: McGill-Queen's University Press, 1988), esp. pp. 56–87.

6. Paul Goodman, "No Processing Whatever," in *Radical School Reform*, edited by Ronald and Beatrice Gross (New York: Simon & Schuster, 1969), pp. 98–106. That a student does well in a subject does not necessarily mean that he or she is positively interested in it. The student might dislike the subject but be interested in avoiding the disapproval of teachers or parents.

7. See Callan, *Autonomy and Schooling,* pp. 61–63.

8. Allan C. Ornstein and Francis P. Hunkins, *Curriculum: Foundations, Principles, and Issues*, 2nd ed. (Boston: Allyn and Bacon, 1992), pp. 249–254.

9. See Jean Piaget, *The Origins of Intelligence in Children* (New York: W.W. Norton and Company, 1952).

10. Alfred North Whitehead, *The Aims of Education and Other Essays* (New York: Mentor Books, 1955).

11. For a variety of views on the appearance of morality in children, see J. Kagan and S. Lamb, eds., *The Emergence of Morality in Young Children* (Chicago, IL: The University of Chicago Press, 1987).

12. For a recent study related to technocracy and tyranny in the Soviet Union, see Loren R. Graham, *The Ghost of the Executed Engineer: Technology and the Fall of the Soviet Union* (Cambridge, MA: Harvard University Press, 1993). Political leaders, as suggested by Plato's writings, have ignored or rejected expert advice since ancient times. While technocracy is implicit in Francis Bacon's *The Great Instauration* and treatises by Enlightenment philosophers of eighteenth-century France, it did not become a formal movement in the United States until between the world wars.

13. For a recent advocacy of this approach to moral education, see Christina Hoff Sommers, *The Public Interest* 111 (Spring 1993), pp. 3–13.

14. A case for formal moral education in the schools is made by Thomas Lickona, *Educating for Character* (New York: Bantam Books, 1992).

15. For arguments on the significance of literature for moral education, see Martha C. Nussbaum, *Love's Knowledge: Essays on Philosophy and Literature* (New York: Oxford University Press, 1990). Also see Judith Shklar, *Ordinary Vices* (Cambridge, MA: Harvard University Press, 1984).

16. For an anthology of readings on paradigmatic examples of moral and civic virtues, see William J. Bennett, ed., *The Book of Virtues: A Treasury of Great Moral Stories* (New York: Simon & Schuster, 1993).

17. For a discussion of just one issue related to science and morality, see Robert D. Heslep, "Moral Duty and the Academic Scientist," in *Education and Ethics*, edited by W.T. Blackstone and G.L. Newsome, Jr. (Athens, GA: The University of Georgia Press, 1969), pp. 104–120.

18. For a discussion of the moral import of algebra, see Philip W. Jackson, Robert E. Boostrom, and David T. Hansen, *The Moral Life of Schools* (San Francisco: Jossey-Bass, 1993), pp. 75–84.

6 The Pedagogy of Moral Education

In education it is not enough to know about goal and content; it is necessary to know about pedagogical practices, too. Curricular reforms frequently fail to bear fruit when no changes in existing teaching methods accompany those reforms. Schools sometimes utilize conditioning and propagandizing as major ways of fostering democratic values. Teachers at times employ set and mechanical procedures in trying to get students to think critically.

Even if it were not important in all areas of education to be very concerned with pedagogy, it still would be crucial to pay close attention to it in moral education. To be sure, teaching historically has been of moral interest regardless of its purpose, content, and methods. Thus, teachers in any subject area have been required to behave toward their students in morally proper ways; and teachers of mathematics as well as those of social studies have been expected to have sound moral character. Nevertheless, in moral education teaching is especially important. Because moral norms are foremost in the purpose, content, and methods of the teaching involved in moral education but not in other areas, they highlight the positive and negative moral aspects of that teaching. Indeed, they require that teachers in moral education be exemplars of moral character and conduct. A weakness in a science instructor's character or a lapse in his or her conduct need not undermine his or her teaching, but a weakness or lapse by teachers of morality necessarily threatens their work. People demand moral goodness and correctness on the part of the teachers of morality just as they expect religious goodness and correctness on the part of clergy, and they are bothered by moral hypocrisy and other moral shortcomings by teachers of morality just as they are troubled by religious hypocrisy and other religious short-comings on the part of clergy.

Teaching, of course, involves two parties, a student as well as a teacher. So, in discussing the pedagogy of moral education, we shall concern ourselves with the relevance of the norms of moral agency to both the student and the teacher.

THE TEACHING OF MORALITY AS A MORAL ACTIVITY

Before examining the pedagogical relevance of these norms, however, we have to determine that the teaching of morality is itself a moral activity. Until we establish this point, we have no reason to believe that the norms are relevant to the activity.

Each and every teacher, regardless of subject matter, is an interpersonal agent. It simply would not make sense to regard someone as a teacher unless that person was also viewed as doing something, occurrently, prospectively, or retrospectively. Nor would it make sense to think of what a teacher does without thinking of it as having another agent as a recipient. The doing of which a teacher is the agent is, of course, an act of teaching; and the agent who is the recipient of the teaching is, of course, a student.

Teachers, however, are not just any sort of interpersonal agent.[1] They are purposeful, for they pose ends for their actions, namely, their students learning whatever is being taught. They are evaluative, for they take those ends to be worthy, specifically, beneficial to their students. And they are deliberative, for they decide upon their pedagogical acts as likely means for attaining their ends. Being purposeful, evaluative, and deliberative, teachers necessarily are witting interpersonal agents; but they need not be free. A teacher's esteemed purpose and decision might be nothing more than effects of a compulsive disposition; or they might be nothing more than the best of a severely narrow range of options presented to the teacher by a superior. Nevertheless, people commonly allow that teachers might and usually do act freely. As the accountability movement of recent decades strongly suggested,[2] people typically view teachers as responsible for their acts; but agents are not responsible for actions unless they perform them freely. When teachers are free as well as knowing in their actions, they are voluntary interpersonal agents.

Students too may be voluntary interpersonal agents. In kindergarten, their voluntariness is much more prospective than occurrent; in graduate school, it is likely to be occurrent. Some students, for example, moderately retarded ones, have only slim, if any, prospects of acting voluntarily; but they are exceptions. By and large, then, teachers and students both are moral agents. Even those students with few or no prospects of voluntariness are moral agents in a sense, for they would be free and witting if they did not suffer certain handicaps. Accordingly, the interactions between them and teachers who are moral agents are moral actions also.

There are pedagogical reasons as to why teachers of moral education should be moral agents. First, if teachers are moral agents, they will present themselves to students as instances of moral agents, thereby showing students what the features of moral agency look like in the concrete and thus helping the students to acquire such features for themselves. Second, if teachers are moral agents, they will be in a position to comprehend fully what students must experience in order to acquire the traits of moral agency and thus will be in a position, through empathy as well as sympathy, to help students overcome difficulties in developing as moral agents. Third, and last, by being moral agents, teachers will enable their students to have moral experiences in a controlled and nurturing environment, not only with one another but also with their teachers, thereby increasing the students' opportunities for learning morality.

That teachers of moral education should be moral agents for pedagogical reasons means that they must regard moral agency as having instrumental value for their teaching. But this entailment does not mean that they look upon moral agency as being without intrinsic worth or that they degrade it. By conceptual necessity, we have explained, any voluntary agent deems voluntary agency as good not only from his or her own standpoint but also from the viewpoint of any other voluntary agent. Moreover, any interpersonal voluntary agent has to see moral agency as the general and supreme good of all moral agents. It is general because it pertains to each and every moral agent, and it is supreme because there is no other moral value as great. As moral agents, therefore, teachers of moral education are committed to regarding moral agency as the general and supreme value of morality and, thus, as something as good in its own right. In using their moral agency as an instrument of teaching, teachers of morality are far from degrading moral agency. The aim of their teaching is to promote moral agency. And in employing moral agency to promote itself, they explicitly recognize it as having more than instrumental value.

Because of our historical circumstances, we sometimes forget that school teachers are not the only teachers. Parents and clerics also are teachers, at least at times. Athletic instructors are, too. TV personnel and authors of books might be. Comedians, actors, and writers are not teachers if all that they do is try to entertain. Nor are liars and propagandists teachers, who are only trying to use us for their ends. But anyone trying to shape another's behavior or beliefs for the latter's benefit and by respecting the latter's rationality, potential or actual, may be said to be teaching.[3] Thus, the moral agents teaching moral character need not be just school teachers. In truth, it seems desirable for moral instruction to be performed by agents in a wide variety of social roles. Otherwise, students might get the impression that morality does not apply to all sectors of their lives. So, when we subsequently talk in an unqualified way about teachers of moral character, we will be referring principally to parents, clergy, school teachers, pundits, and all other moral agents, regardless of social position, engaged in the teaching of moral character.

In being moral agents, the teachers and students of moral education are subject, occurrently and prospectively, to the norms of moral agency: the Criterion of Moral Values (CMVa), the Criterion of Moral Rights (CMR), the Criterion of Moral Duty (CMD), and the Criterion of Moral Virtue (CMVi). They must value knowledge, freedom, evaluativeness, and the other central elements of moral agency as they relate to the moral agency of all persons. They must respect the rights of all to the major features of moral agency. They are bound to secure and foster the chief constituents of moral agency. They must have those dispositions of character that are compatible with and contributive to the central factors of moral agency.

MORAL VALUES IN THE PEDAGOGY
OF MORAL CHARACTER

Teachers

In compliance with the CMVa, teachers of moral education logically esteem the key features of moral agency as they pertain to moral agents in general. They also must prize them as they relate specifically to all teachers and students engaged in education of any sort. But in addition they necessarily look favorably upon these features as they pertain especially to teachers and students participating in moral education.

1. The teachers of moral education logically cherish the purposefulness involved in their teaching. They prize their purpose, which is to bring about the development of moral character in their students. They esteem the content of that purpose, which is the character of moral agency. They value the process whereby they engage in formulating that purpose for their individual situations. They regard approvingly the competencies they have and need for formulating their purposes. They esteem whatever success they have in attaining their purposes. They treasure the improvement of their goal attainment, both by rectifying past failures and by raising the level of their future aims. And they view as desirable the background conditions required for sustaining and increasing the development of moral character.

That moral educators have a decisive responsibility for formulating their specific aims does not mean that they have to impose those ends upon students and prohibit or ignore advice from parents and other interested members of the society of concern. As stated earlier, the content of moral education must be linked to the likes, desires, and interests of students in such manner that, in pursuing and developing these affective matters, students freely and knowingly acquire the character of moral agents. Teachers of morality, then, must consult with their students about purposes so that the teachers can help assure that the purposes involve the students' likes, desires, and interests. Moreover, because teachers of morality must seek whatever information and understanding are pertinent to conceiving purposes for their specific situations, they should consult with members of society outside the instructional setting so as to obtain such information and understanding. Whom they should consult will vary from context to context. Local business leaders and clergy might be helpful in some situations but not others. Parents might be helpful in most cases but not all. Police and social workers might be useful in special contexts.

2. Moral agents, we said in Chapter 2, do not choose their goals whimsically; they choose them, rather, for the reason that they see them as worthy goals. Moral agents, however, evaluate more than their ends and the conditions that support these ends; they also appraise matters related to actions they ponder as means for attaining their ends. Moral agents, then, prize evaluativeness as it appears across the entire range of the judgment of moral values. While teachers of morality certainly employ and esteem the norms of moral agency as a part of their evaluations, they also prize the other standards they must use in establishing their ends and means. Such standards might be psychological, sociological, political, or some other sort. In selecting these other standards, teachers of morality have to ascertain that they are compatible with the norms of moral agency. This does not mean that the teachers must reject deterministic theories, such as those of John Calvin, Karl Marx, and B.F. Skinner, in a wholesale way. Instead, it allows that the teachers may comb theories of the sort in search of norms that do not oppose those of moral agency.

Besides norms, moral agents value factual knowledge in their judgments of value. They well might contemn some events that are matters of fact, but they always regard facts as a desirable basis of moral evaluations. Thus, teachers of morality regard positively the gathering of relevant facts for judging the moral worth of their purposes and activities. These would include facts about their students' particular capabilities, interests, and backgrounds; general information about human learning, society, and culture; and data on specific economic support and curricular materials available for the teaching of the given students.

As moral agents, teachers of morality necessarily cherish the process of moral evaluation both in general and in their own situations. They regard it as better than any other way for establishing moral values, for example, by revelation or feeling. They also deem as good their participation in the process, including discussions with one another and other interested parties of the soundness of given evaluations.

Because such teachers value their engagement in the process of moral evaluation, they also prize the understanding, skills, sensitivities, and other competencies that they have as judges of moral worth. Thus, prospective school teachers of morality must acquire proficiencies for assessing the moral worth of matters specific to the activities in which they are likely to participate. What they learn in their preservice training about moral judgment probably will not prepare them to comprehend all the particularities and complexities of the actual situations in which they eventually will teach. This prospect is not a condemnation of preservice training in moral judgment, however. It simply recognizes that the likelihood of gaps between preparation and practice, whether in law, medicine, police work, parenting, or any other activity, is a perduring lesson of human experience.[4] Whatever deficiencies in moral judgment the new teacher of morality has may be remedied through a program of on-the-job adjustment, such as mentoring.[5] As particular situations of moral education undergo change, teachers might find that special judgmental competencies which once served in those situations no longer do and thus are no longer desirable. When teachers do reach this conclusion, they also must determine which adjustments in and replacements of these erstwhile competencies are needed. So, because a moral educator, whether new or experienced, can correct deficiencies in his or her competence as a judge of moral worth only through the use of self-evaluation, such an educator must treasure self-evaluation itself as a competence that enables him or her to engage in moral evaluation. To help ensure that self-evaluation does not lag or become biased, one may complement it with peer review, whereby teachers assess one another's talents as evaluators in moral education. Also, one may complement self-evaluation with critiques by older students, who might indicate problematic areas in judgments by teachers.

3. The teaching of morality may be special and separate, or it may be interwoven with the teaching of other contents, such as academic, political, or vocational. Either way, the content of this teaching will be deemed as praiseworthy by teachers who are moral agents only if it satisfies certain criteria. If the teaching is special and separate, its factual content must be empirically correct. Hence, it will exclude claims that smoking marijuana is highly likely to cause lung cancer and that masturbation tends to cause madness. Moral principles and judgments in the content have to be rationally sound. This does not mean that the teacher usually has to present principles and judgments as conclusions of a chain of inferences whose first link is the concept of a moral standard, but it does mean that the teacher should be prepared to help students grasp the reasons for principles and judgments when they need to do so. The content must appeal to the students at hand. It has to be relevant to the development of moral character in these students in particular. Any interpretation of the content, whether by teachers or students, must respect the canons of reason.

If the teaching of morality is interwoven with other areas of education, the integrity of the nonmoral as well as that of the moral areas has to be intact. Moral lessons are not to be had at the expense of history, literature, or science. Nor is morality to be tailored to support any special interests of politics, technology, or business. Like morality, the academic disciplines are supposed to rest on the canons of reason. Hence, any proper theories and conclusions of those disciplines must be respected by moral educators. Moreover, because politics, technology, and business, being practical affairs, are also presumed to be rational, their special interests will be valued by moral educators and other moral agents when they are rationally defensible.

The methods for teaching moral character, that is, the activities employed by moral agents for such teaching, have to meet several criteria. For one thing, they have to be compatible with the learning styles of the students. Different students might be successful in some ways of learning but not in others. Because the point of teaching moral character to students is to help them acquire such character, it entails that pedagogical actions have to allow students to learn in modes in which they are likely to be successful as long as the modes are not morally offensive.[6] Accordingly, teachers must have a rich repertoire of teaching methods. On the other hand, that a student at a given point has acquired only one or two styles of learning marks an educational need to which the teacher must attend when the student is developmentally ready to gain additional styles. An increase in the student's command of manners of learning will enhance his or her opportunities not only to develop moral character, but also to learn in other areas of education.

Also, the methods have to be appropriate to the content being taught. If the content is primarily moral, it allows whatever actions are proper in a given situation for developing moral character, for example, the telling of stories, student discussions of their own moral problems, student interviews with other people to learn how the latter make moral decisions, the assignment of tasks in the moral virtues, lectures on moral theory and practice, and research projects on the moral problems of society. If, however, the content is a combination of the moral with the academic or some other area, it calls for methods that are suitable for teaching the nonmoral as well as the moral. Thus, while it might involve cooperative learning and discussion of the moral implications of the nonmoral, it also might include recitation, memorization, laboratory work, field experience, and frequent written homework assignments.

In addition, the methods must be consistent with the moral integrity of the student. Because the methods address students who are moral agents, albeit largely prospective ones, the methods have to support whatever moral qualities the students presently have and contribute to, and never obstruct, the moral development of the students. Thus, threats, torture, and physical coercion are unacceptable, as are false indoctrination, errant persuasion, and brainwashing. Behavioral conditioning, indoctrination in true beliefs, and persuasion to worthy ends are acceptable only in situations where methods immediately fostering the intellect and freedom of students are not appropriate to the developmental readiness of the involved students, and where what students learn by the former methods will be understandable to students when they are ready for rational and free methods.

Finally, the methods used in moral education must be effective and efficient. They must be effective in that, even upon meeting the three criteria of learning style compatibility, appropriateness to content, and support of student moral integrity, they have to show promise of attaining the given goals of teaching. The methods are to be efficient in a similar sense: Even upon satisfying these four criteria, they must be economical not only in material resources but also in time, effort, and personnel. Teaching methods need to be effective because it is irrational to employ something as a means that is not likely to attain a given end, and they need to be efficient for the simple reason that there is no reason to do and use things that are not necessary. It must be stressed, however, that the moral correctness of effectiveness and efficiency of teaching methods in moral education is contingent. This correctness presupposes the satisfaction of the other criteria of the moral worth of such methods, a point that has not always been addressed by the advocates of effective teaching and educational efficiency.[7]

But if teachers of morality prize their methods according to the standards we have been discussing, they also logically value the process of deliberation by which they decide upon those methods and the competences they possess for participating in that process. That process involves the use of the criteria just mentioned, and it includes also an awareness of relevant facts and a weighing of alternative courses of action. Being deliberative, this process is flexible, or adaptable to the particularities and changes of concrete situations; it is not a routine procedure dictated by detailed and rigid bureaucratic rules. So, the competences of deliberation needed by teachers of morality are not the abilities to follow instructional manuals and central office directives.

They include, rather, an ability to identify important facts, to see which standards of good teaching methods apply to which facts, to conceive various ways of teaching whatever content is of concern, to forecast the respective outcomes of various methods, and to determine which method is most likely to attain a given goal and satisfy all other moral and pedagogical demands. Because the teachers of morality esteem the deliberativeness entailed by their work, they also value organizational structures, professional practices, and all other conditions that maintain and encourage this quality of their moral agency.

4. Teachers occasionally work with their students as isolated individuals. A tutor, for instance, might be inclined to instruct a charge not as a member of a group but as a solitary individual with certain academic needs. Even a classroom teacher might view students not as they relate to one another and his- or herself, but as so many individuals who simply happen to be in the same vicinity while being taught.[8] But because a teacher of morality who is a moral agent sees him- or herself and his or her students as related to one another according to the values, rights, and duties of moral agency, the teacher also regards them along with him- or herself as constituting a moral group, if not community, with its own moral good, which consists of those conditions necessary for the group's members to conduct themselves toward each other in morally proper ways and for them to perform their respective tasks of teaching and learning. These conditions, of course, are estimable to the teacher; but the moral group at hand, which is supported by the conditions, is even more so. In truth, few things could be more valuable to a moral agent teaching morality than a pedagogical group whose members are interacting according to the norms of moral agency and are teaching and learning matters that eventually will enable its immature members to become morally mature members of society.

Students

In their early years, students frequently lack adequate knowledge and a strong sense of standards, and they typically are under impulse or external control. In their later years, they often act voluntarily and according to the norms of moral agency, but they are likely to see themselves as moral agents only in a vague way. It is not readily evident, then, how the CMVa might relate to students of moral education. We should not expect children to appreciate knowledge, freedom, purposefulness, evaluativeness, and so on, as characteristics of moral agency. Nor should we suppose that students who are only vaguely aware of themselves as moral agents will have much appreciation of these matters as features of themselves. Nevertheless, the CMVa does have a definite significance for the students who are to acquire the character of moral agents; for it serves as the criterion by which to cultivate and shape the given interests of students.

In sum, this criterion specifies the kinds of objects such students should like, desire, and be interested in. Long before students are prepared to be interested as moral agents in knowledge, freedom, and the other traits of moral agency, they may like or desire them; they might even prize them prudentially or in some other nonmoral way. Any likes, desires, or appreciations that they have for such objects are to be reinforced and developed. Any that they have in opposing objects are to be discouraged and, where possible, transformed into acceptable attitudes. While this cultivation and shaping of attitudes will have to be externally directed at times, they must not be directed in such a way as to prevent the students ultimately from understanding the moral worth of the characteristics of moral agency. The ultimate way to ensure that the cultivation and shaping lead to such understanding is to encourage and transform the likes, desires, and values of students in such a way that they lead students ultimately to see themselves as moral agents logically committed to valuing these characteristics.

To be realistic, we suppose that some students will have likes, desires, and values which, despite the best of pedagogical efforts, cannot be encouraged and transformed in this way. Even for students of this sort, however, the CMVa may have significance. If any students really cannot learn to see that they as moral agents are logically committed to prizing the traits of moral agency, they might be able to learn at least to see those traits as in their own individual interests. Teaching a student to value these characteristics strictly from a prudential standpoint is not as desirable as teaching him or her to prize them from a moral standpoint. Nevertheless, it does have the virtue of allowing the student to learn to appreciate those features voluntarily. If particular students really cannot learn to esteem the elements of moral agency even for prudential reasons, they might be amenable to being conditioned to like, desire, and esteem those elements. Because conditioning of this sort will not help students become voluntary agents, it should be reserved for students with little or no prospect of development as such agents. It is unfortunate that a person might do no better than learn involuntarily to conform to the CMVa, but it is better that that person learns involuntarily to do this than to learn involuntarily to violate the criterion.

MORAL RIGHTS IN TEACHING MORAL CHARACTER

A moral right, we argued in Chapter 2, is a moral agent's claim to a feature of moral agency that rests on the agent's needing or deserving that feature. As a moral agent, the teacher of morality has moral rights, some of which are specific to the teaching of moral character. Students of morality also have moral rights special to their role of acquiring moral character. We will not provide an exhaustive list of the rights of either the teacher or the student, but we will attempt to itemize the major ones of each party.

Rights of the Teacher of Moral Character

The objects to which a teacher of morality has justified claims involve matters that the teacher prizes, but they certainly do not include all of the latter. Not all prized objects fall within the pale of rights. While a teacher certainly has the right to try to establish a well-functioning moral group consisting of the teacher and his or her students, the teacher does not have a right to be successful in establishing the group. A right, we have explained, entails nothing more than noninterference and reasonable assistance from others in one's efforts to attain an object; it does not ensure success in one's efforts to attain the object, which might fail because of bad luck or incompetence. Accordingly, no needs-based right a teacher of morality might have to a well-functioning moral group, which will relate only to noninterference or assistance in his or her attempts to establish such a group, guarantees that those attempts will be successful. Moreover, no merit-based right, which would be a claim by the teacher to noninterference or assistance in his or her efforts to create such a group for the reason that he or she has certain qualifications for the undertaking, ensures success either.[9] At any rate, teachers of moral character have two major rights.

1. The first right, which correlates with the fact that teachers of moral character value the purposefulness and evaluativeness that are characteristic of their work, is that such teachers have the right to determine, through evaluation, the specific moral character to be learned by their given students. Being voluntary agents, teachers of moral character are prepared for their jobs. Where they are deficient in needed knowledge, they have the competence for obtaining it; and they possess standards required for necessary judgments. Hence, they are capable of formulating worthy ends for their teaching. Moreover, teachers of moral character have a need as moral agents to establish their respective goals. If they are to have objectives as moral agents do, they must have them voluntarily. This means that teachers must construct their objectives or make objectives proposed by others their own through moral evaluation.

Consonant with the right to determine their own purposes, teachers of moral character are to have freedom of inquiry in learning about the moral background of their students. School teachers must have access to required knowledge about the home life of their students and receive reasonable assistance from parents and other interested parties in obtaining that knowledge.[10] On the other hand, parents and other non-school teachers of morality have the right to learn from schools about what of moral relevance happens to their charges. Moreover, teachers of morality are to be permitted to participate in the process of assessing the moral character deficiencies that their individual students have and judging what traits of moral character would be good for them to learn. Also, because of the need for teachers of morality to participate in evaluations involved in deliberations about what actions to perform for attaining their chosen purposes, such teachers are to be free to engage in and receive reasonable assistance for such evaluations.

This right, however, does not entitle school teachers of moral education to ignore other interested parties. Moral guidelines provided by the general public and its representatives should be positively considered by the teachers as long as the guidelines are consistent with the norms of moral agency. Advice as well as information from parents, social workers, clergy, and other local parties must be taken seriously by the teachers. Student expressions of interests, nagging concerns, and viewpoints also have to be respected by the teachers. For the teachers to ignore or discount any of these matters is for them to discount the moral agency of other interested parties.

The right to set purposes and values further indicates that there must be cooperation and coordination among all varieties of teachers of moral character. As we have mentioned, teachers of morality need not be just school teachers. They may be parents, camp counselors, social workers, police officers, or anyone else trying to instill the character of moral agency in people. Because the right to formulate specific goals and values for moral education may be scattered among different people in myriad social positions, it can lead to disagreement and conflict. School teachers might hold that first graders should be told about sexual conduct in explicit terms, whereas parents might maintain that they should not be told until pubescence and church officials might insist that they should not be told in school at any grade anything explicit about sexual conduct. Police and social workers might be working to control adolescent gangs prone to violence while teachers might not recognize that violence is a character deficiency in any of their students with which they must deal. How cooperation and coordination among teachers of moral character may be secured is problematic. A community council on moral education might be effective. So might open discussions at regular school board sessions and special meetings of interested parties called to address pressing moral issues. But what works for one locale might not be suitable for another, and what gets results in a local area might not be effective in a regional or still larger area. Different clusters of teachers have to develop, through practical experimentation and with public assistance, their own institutions for securing cooperation and co-ordination among themselves.

2. The second right of teachers of moral character follows from the esteem they have for content and method: Such teachers have a justified claim to choose the content and methods to be used in their teaching moral character.[11] Because teachers of moral character who are moral agents are qualified and need to select, on the basis of appropriate information and standards, the content and methods needed to attain their respective pedagogical purposes, they should have the freedom to choose the content and methods and receive whatever reasonable assistance they need to obtain this content and implement these methods. Consequently, nobody should impose content and methods upon teachers of moral character or withhold reasonable help from them for acquiring the content and putting into operation the methods that they choose.

As agents committed to being knowledgeable in their work, teachers of moral character are open to and seek information and advice from relevant parties, whether students, academic experts, community leaders, publishers, media specialists, or governmental officials. They also welcome thoughtful criticism. In short, they want open and thorough deliberations about content and methods. But they can have such deliberations only in a social context with organizational structures and institutional practices that encourage them.

Rights of the Student of Moral Education

While the teachers of moral character have moral rights related to their teaching, moral agents who are supposed to learn moral character have moral rights that pertain to their learning it. Because these students frequently do not know what their rights in moral education are, they often must depend on mature moral agents to be their advocates. Those who might function as their advocates might be parents, school teachers, social workers, ministers, clinical counselors, legislators, police, and judges.

The following claims are the major rights of students in learning moral character.

1. Each student has the right to an opportunity to acquire the character of a moral agent. By the CMR, a moral agent has the right to act according to the norms of moral agency, but a moral agent can act regularly according to the norms of a moral agency only if that agent has the character, or organization of habits, that disposes him or her to act according to the norms. By need, then, any moral agent has the right to a chance to assume a moral character. This right implies that a moral agent has a justified claim to the features of moral character he or she already might have and, what is more important here, that a moral agent lacking in such features is entitled to the opportunity to acquire those missing to the degree that the agent is capable of acquiring them.

There might be virtues that a moral agent can, practically as well as theoretically, learn without benefit of teaching; and there might be some that such an agent, for reasons of theory or practical circumstances, must learn with the aid of teaching. If, however, a student of moral education can, theoretically or practically, learn any features of moral character only with pedagogical assistance, that student has the right to be taught those features.

Individual students might differ from one another in the capacities and abilities that they need to learn moral character. Some simply might lack or possess capacities or abilities that others do or do not have, or they might possess those capacities or abilities in a lesser or greater degree than others. While no student can, as a matter of tautology, learn moral character beyond the limits of his or her capacities and abilities to do so, each needs, also as a matter of tautology, to learn it to the full extent of those capacities and abilities in order to act according to the norms of moral agency as much as he or she can. Consequently, each student logically has the right to be taught and try to learn the features of moral character to the utmost of his or her capacities and abilities. It follows that using irrelevant traits or circumstances of a student, such as gender, race, or wealth, as factors determining the extent of the development of his or her moral education is wrong.

A virtue ingredient to the character of a moral agent, we explained in Chapter 4, may be general or special. It is general if it is needed by moral agents in virtually all times and places, and it is special if it is needed in only certain historical contexts. In order to function optimally as moral agents, people have to have the general virtues; but they also have to have the ones special to their respective contexts. Students, therefore, have the right to the opportunity to learn and be taught the moral virtues special to their several historical contexts as well as the general ones.

2. In learning moral character, each student has the right to study whatever relevant subject matter appeals to him or her. This claim is far from frivolous, and it does not rest upon anything more than a penchant for making education "fun." As a matter of logical fact, the claim is justified by a rudimentary student need in moral education. To learn the character of a moral agent, we pointed out in Chapter 5, students have to learn it freely; and to do that, they have to study what they like, desire, or have an interest in. Thus, because their need to study what is attractive to themselves is vital to their moral education, it justifies their claim to study such subject matters.

That students of moral education have this right does not mean that they have to be allowed to study whatever appeals to them. What they study obviously must be relevant to the development of their moral character. So, even if students in a moral education class are most interested in comics, they do not have a justified claim to study comics unless the latter are in some aspect germane to the virtues of moral agency. If certain comics are appropriate to moral education, students who are engaged in such education and most interested in comics have a right to pursue their interests in them in the respect that the comics are relevant; but such students also have a right to develop whatever pertinent interests they might have in the comics. This means, for instance, that they eventually have to see that moral virtues and vices, practical situations, evaluations, deliberations, temptations, rewards, and punishments are not just the two-dimensional, simplistic, stark, and epic matters that they are portrayed to be in comics but can be, and often are, quite complex, ambiguous, subtle, and commonplace.

There probably will be times when content in a student's moral education will be completely unattractive to him or her. This would be unfortunate, for it would mean that if the student did learn the content, he or she would do so involuntarily. Nevertheless, this situation would not necessarily entail that the student's right to study what is interesting would have been violated. The right would have been violated only if the student were prevented from studying what is interesting or if his or her teacher neglected, albeit innocently, to select interesting content or contrived to select uninteresting content. If the teacher chose content that he or she took to be interesting to the student, but which failed to be, then the teacher, as well as the student, was simply unlucky in the choice. And if the student merely happened upon some content relevant to moral character but uninteresting to him- or herself, then he or she just had an unfortunate experience in moral education. In sum, the right of students to interesting content is violated under either of two conditions: when classroom instructors, parents, counselors, or others teaching moral character to students do not conscientiously try to provide the latter with an opportunity to pursue their present interests in moral character, and when they do not furnish those students with a serious opportunity to develop their interests in moral character.

3. Students in moral education have the right to be taught in ways that match their respective learning styles. A student's given learning style, we explained in Chapter 5, might not be compatible with a teacher's given manner of teaching. And if the two are incongruous with one another, then the intended learning will probably not take place. If, therefore, the teaching of moral character to students is to be successful, the modes in which such character is taught need to agree with the various learning styles of different students. That a method of teaching matches a learning style does not ensure successful teaching; factors extraneous to ways of teaching and learning, such as environmental distractions, lack of motivation, and personality conflicts, might prevent intended learning from taking place. Hence, unsuccessful teaching in moral education does not by itself imply that a student's right to be taught in a way compatible with his or her learning style has been breached. Moreover, that a manner of teaching and a way of learning mesh with one another does not entail that the involved teacher respects the concerned student's right to be taught in a compatible way. Teaching and learning might mesh simply by accident. Moreover, a teacher's lack of respect for the student's right does not by itself violate the right. But if that lack of respect is accompanied by a pedagogical manner that conflicts with the student's learning style, then the student's right is infringed.

Because students can acquire only those features of moral character that their ways of learning enable them to gain, they each need to develop a repertoire of learning styles that enables the optimal development of their respective moral characters. For instance, they have to learn to accept prescriptions and admonitions so that they will learn what to do where appropriate habits are lacking and where their powers of practical reason have not yet developed. They have to be able to learn through reflective imitation so that they will pick morally worthy role models. They have to be able to learn through intellectual discourse in order to acquire dispositions for grasping moral principles, determining facts, formulating and judging purposes, conceiving and deliberating about alternative courses of action, forecasting consequences of action, and performing the other tasks of practical reason. They have to be able to learn through vicarious experience of moral situations, imagined and concrete, so that they, under tutelage, can experience, analyze, and reconstruct their emotional and intellectual reactions to such situations. Finally, they need to be able to learn through direct participation in a variety of concrete moral situations in order to learn to experience what interacting with other real moral agents is like and, as a result, to make suitable adjustments in their intellectual and affective dispositions.

4. The students of moral education have a right to the conditions that support and nurture the optimal development of their respective moral characters. Qualified teachers at home and in the community as well as in school, appropriate curricular materials, both an immediate environment and a public media expressive of the norms of moral agency, adequate nutrition and health care, physical safety—all of these are obvious conditions required for maintaining and encouraging moral education.[12] When a society of moral agents and its morally responsible members collectively and individually fail to provide such conditions when they can provide them, they violate the right of the prospective moral agents to these conditions. These students, accordingly, face the practically hopeless situation of having no one to serve as the advocate of their moral education except those who have violated their right to its conditions. Unfortunately, this situation is not just a theoretical possibility. The victims of preventable infantile death, crack babies, malnourished infants, sufferers of physical and sexual abuse, children who are permitted and often encouraged to learn from the public media that material goods, sexual activity, and physical violence are central goods and desirable responses in life—these agents are supposed to be protected by parents, social agencies, the police, the courts, and the law. While some of them are, many others are guarded by nothing more than ineffectual groups concerned with children's rights. Indeed, the existence and ineffectiveness of these groups are themselves testimony that adult members, including officials, of American society have been immoral in their neglect of the right of numerous children to the conditions that would support and foster their moral education.

DUTIES IN MORAL EDUCATION

Duties of the Teacher

Any moral right, we explained in Chapter 2, involves correlative duties, that is, obligations had by any and all moral agents against whom the concerned claim is made. In general, those duties are, first, not to interfere with the efforts of a moral agent to obtain the object of any justified claim by the agent; and, second, to render assistance to an agent when it is necessary for attainment of the objects of his or her rights and when it does not impose unreasonable burdens upon those who would provide it. Accordingly, the moral rights born by students of moral education set duties for the teachers of those students. The right of students to learn moral character binds teachers not to obstruct the students' efforts to gain such character and to assist students in gaining it. The right of students of moral education to study relevant content that is appealing to themselves obligates their teachers to provide it. The right of students to be taught in ways that are compatible with their individual learning styles places upon their teachers the duty to teach accordingly. And the right of students to conditions that maintain and encourage their moral education binds teachers as well as society at large to establish those conditions.

Moral rights, we further explained in Chapter 2, also might involve reciprocal duties. If an agent receives aid in the exercise of a right, that agent might owe compensation to the provider of the help, whether the provider is an individual or society at large. The payment might be in kind, monetary, by service, or by a show of gratitude. In moral education teachers have two types of reciprocal duties. A teacher of moral education supposedly has a moral character; and back when exercising his or her right as a student to acquire that character, he or she received assistance from individual teachers and from society at large. Accordingly, the person who becomes a teacher of moral education especially has an obligation to compensate those teachers and society. The other reciprocal duty of a teacher of moral education concerns the exercise of his or her rights in teaching moral character to students. In exercising their rights to set purposes and select content and pedagogical style, teachers of moral education are likely to have help from other individuals and from society in general. For the help such teachers receive, they have an obligation to repay its providers.

While there might be other ways for a teacher of moral education to help meet these two reciprocal duties, it is arguable that a suitable mode of repayment for both obligations is the teacher's helping his or her students to acquire moral character. This will repay the teacher's debt for past assistance in the development of his or her own moral character for the reason that the providers of that assistance, individual teachers and society at large, necessarily would have to esteem equally their efforts in developing the moral character of that individual moral agent and the present efforts of that individual to enable other moral agents to acquire moral character. Moreover, a moral agent's teaching of moral character is relevant compensation for aid received in his or her teaching for a similar reason. Because the providers of the aid, being moral agents or a society of them, highly value moral character and thus the teaching of it to prospective moral agents, they logically have to regard an instance of this teaching as compensation for whatever help they have furnished to bring about this instance. Whether or not a given teacher's work in moral education will serve as full or only partial compensation for each of these two obligations would depend on various considerations, such as whether or not the work is that of a lifetime or something much less, whether or not the students involved are especially easy to teach, and whether or not the past or present helpers of the teacher suffered extraordinary burdens in providing assistance.

Besides duties associated with rights, however, there are those determined by the Criterion of Moral Duty, which holds that any moral agent is bound to secure and nurture freedom, knowledge, purposefulness, evaluativeness, and the other constituents of moral agency. So, regardless of their rights or those of their students, teachers of moral education, being moral agents, are obligated to maintain and encourage all features of moral agency. Two implications of this duty are obvious.

1. Teachers of moral education must strive to develop the traits of moral agency in their students. This means that such teachers must try to develop these traits not only through their teaching but also through intervention in situations involving their students that undermine their teaching. Thus, classroom teachers have the duty to intervene, directly or through liaison parties, in the home life of students when that life discourages their acquiring the features of moral agency. On the other hand, parents, church officials, and other nonschool teachers of moral character have the obligation to intervene in the school life of students when it prevents their growth as moral agents.

2. Teachers of moral education must oppose, in reasonable ways, decisions, policies, and conditions that threaten the elements of moral agency. Such decisions, policies, and conditions might bear directly on the academic freedom of the teachers. They might concern mainly the availability, amounts, and distribution of funds for moral education. But they also might relate to social and economic institutions; political, legal, and ecclesiastical practices; health care; and the public media. Targeted decisions and policies may be those of school administrators, school boards, church officials, legislators, judges, business leaders, or fellow teachers. Targeted conditions may be as complex and widespread as crime and poverty or as relatively simple and limited as the unavailability of measles inoculation in a given neighborhood.

Because these two directives are matters of duty, they must be followed. But that they have to be followed does not imply that they must be obeyed blindly. In intervening in the home life of students, for instance, neither teachers nor their representatives may violate the moral rights of students or parents. In opposing decisions and policies, they may not violate anyone's rights; they may be prudent as long as they do what is morally right; and they must do what is effective, at least, within the limits of morality. On the other hand, those who freely and knowingly prevent teachers of moral education from acting upon these directives or punish them for doing so violate the norms of moral agency and are liable to reproof not only from the teachers but from all other moral agents.

Duties of the Student

The students of moral education also are liable to correlative and reciprocal duties. Because the teachers of such students have pedagogical rights, the teachers impose on the students, insofar as the latter are morally responsible, any duties of noninterference and assistance that are correlative to the exercise of those rights. Thus, students must not disrupt the teaching of moral character either to themselves individually or to one another; and they must not deceive teachers as to their likes, desires, interests, and learning styles. Moreover, they might be bound to help their teachers not only in performing routine tasks, such as distributing and collecting materials, but also in maintaining a social order and climate in the classroom that are conducive to learning. Before students are mature enough to be morally responsible, they can learn, through training, to act according to prospective correlative duties. By becoming disposed early to act *according* to such duties, they will be prepared to act *from* them when they become old enough to understand the reasons for their obligations.

Because the students of moral education receive enormous assistance in the development of their moral character, they incur reciprocal duties. They might not be bound to execute some of these duties, such as any that may involve monetary compensation or extended public service, until they are finished with their moral education. Older students, however, can perform some reciprocal duties related to moral education. For instance, they can work with children who are morally "at risk," participate in charitable activities, and help keep the environment clean. Performing reciprocal duties during their student years might well increase the disposition of people to perform them later.

As long as, and in the respect that, the students of moral education are morally immature, they do not have duties to secure and nourish freedom, knowledge, purposefulness, deliberativeness, and the other features of moral agency. But as they develop in their capacities for moral action, they become increasingly responsible for maintaining and fostering the elements of moral agency. Hence, older students have a duty to stand up for the rational discussion of moral issues. This obligation holds whether the discussion is by the students, their teachers, or other moral agents. They have an obligation to oppose, in reasonable ways, unjustifiable censorship and indoctrination. Also, they have a duty to be concerned with the underlying conditions of moral life in their society. As students progress in their moral education, they supposedly will become disposed to appreciate the traits and supporting conditions of moral agency and, consequently, to act with respect to them. If they do, they will be substantially prepared to secure and encourage the characteristics of moral agency. Particular students, of course, are not logical entities; and they need not learn to appreciate these features fully. But the chances of students to learn to appreciate the elements of moral agency might increase by training students in their prereflective years to act with respect for those elements. Such training, we indicated in Chapters 4 and 5, will not violate the integrity of students as prospective voluntary agents as long as it involves attractive content and appropriate pedagogical methods.

VIRTUES IN MORAL EDUCATION

Because the teachers and students in moral education engage each other as moral agents, occurrent and prospective, they require dispositions that reflect the values, rights, and duties of moral agency appropriate to the respective levels of development of the teachers and students. Moreover, because these teachers and students engage each other in a special context, namely, that of moral education, they need moral virtues specific to it. Finally, because they have substantially different relationships to one another in that context, they respectively require different virtues in it. Accordingly, we will restrict the present discussion of virtues to those pertinent to moral agents as teachers of moral education and those appropriate to moral agents as students of moral education.

Teachers

Like all other moral agents, both those who are teachers and those who are not, the teachers of moral education are concerned with freedom, knowledge, purposefulness, deliberation, and the other features of moral agency. But unlike other teachers and other moral agents, the teachers of moral education are especially concerned with them. Because the teachers of moral education must conceive their purposes and select their contents and methods with respect to these traits, they have to be constantly attentive to the traits as qualities of their students and as theoretical principles. Other moral agents need not be attentive to them constantly. The teachers of moral education have to exemplify to their students, through habits and manners of action, the characteristics of moral agency. Other agents need not be exemplars of these traits. Also, the teachers of moral education regularly have to manifest to their students a high, abiding, and deep appreciation of moral agency. While other agents must value moral agency, they need not regularly display their esteem of it. Teachers of moral education can show their strong and vital appreciation in at least two ways: by pursuing and developing their interests in the features of such agency, and by fostering and defending them when opportunities and threats exist. Either way, they must be enthusiastic, if not passionate.

To be sure, teachers of moral education are not likely to be experts on all dimensions of moral agency; they will do well to be experts on the teaching of moral character. Nevertheless, they can have a general understanding of the conceptual features and the theoretical issues of moral agency and a general comprehension too of the moral problems in their respective societies and elsewhere. In their knowledge of teaching moral character, professional teachers are quite likely to differ from parents and other nonprofessionals. Because professional teachers of moral education have a large number of students, they must match content with a large variety of student likes, desires, and interests; and they have to match teaching manner with a rich diversity of learning styles. Hence, they must be cognizant of numerous contents and possess a wide repertoire of teaching methods. Because parents and other nonprofessionals have to deal with only a relatively few students, they do not necessarily require a wide familiarity with content nor do they have to be competent in numerous learning styles.

Whether professional or not, however, teachers of moral education are disposed to look after the rights of their students to such education. Because young students are not prepared to assert their rights, and because older ones sometimes are not prepared to assert theirs, students of moral education need advocates of their special rights. Where legislators, judges, police, and other·public officials fail, teachers of moral education must be inclined to assert and protect the claims of students to moral education. Where parents, clergy, and colleagues fail, too, teachers of moral education have to be inclined to advocate such claims. Teachers of moral education logically have advocacy as a quality of their character because they are specifically and directly concerned with the moral education of students. No one else is in a stronger position.

Students

Because students of moral education are to acquire the character of moral agents, they presumably will develop the virtues ingredient to that character. These, however, are not the virtues that pertain to them as students of moral education. Students in any subject area have to possess dispositions that enable them to learn what it is they are supposed to learn. Some of these might be natural, but many of them will be matters of habituation. Without these enabling dispositions, students presumably can learn only accidentally, through impulsive action on their part, or forcedly, through imposition on the part of someone else. Neither type of learning is desirable for voluntary agents. Enabling dispositions, however, make possible learning that is appropriate to voluntary agents. While natural inclinations cannot be freely or knowingly gained, habits may be. Even an enabling disposition, whether a natural one or a habit, acquired involuntarily might be desirable for a voluntary agent. It might help the agent to learn something that is important for his or her growth in freedom and knowledge but which he or she is not developmentally ready to learn voluntarily. The habits that enable students of moral education to acquire the character of moral agents are the excellences that mark such students.

To be certain, habits good for students of moral education might be good for other students, too, for instance: those of good health, moderation in pleasure, and hopefulness; an inclination to acquire and develop new interests; and a tendency to learn new styles of learning. Nevertheless, there are habits especially good for students of moral education. They may be grouped according to the virtues of moral agency.

With respect to the affective virtues, students of moral education need to be mannerly, friendly, willing to share interests, sympathetic, empathetic, charitable, and willing to sacrifice. Not only will these habits prepare students of moral education to gain other affective virtues, they also will help them to get along with one another as students and prospective moral agents and with their teachers and other adults as well. In addition, these habits will reinforce the other dispositions they need in order to learn the intellectual moral virtues. With respect to being able to learn moral reasoning, students must like being truthful; and they must like to gain knowledge. They need to be disposed to set goals for themselves individually and to understand them. They have to be inclined to identify and understand each other's purposes. They must have a tendency to identify and weigh different ways for attaining given goals. And they need to understand the superiority of the moral.

NOTES

1. For an analysis of the concept of teaching, see Robert D. Heslep, *The Mental in Education: A Philosophical Study* (University, AL: The University of Alabama Press, 1981), pp. 118–121.

2. Leon M. Lessinger, *Every Kid a Winner: Accountability in Education* (New York: Simon & Schuster, 1970).

3. Thomas F. Green, *The Activities of Teaching* (New York: McGraw-Hill, 1971).

4. Unfortunately, those who in the 1970s debated the choice between Knowledge-Based Teacher Education and Performance-Based Teacher Education did not understand this lesson. Both knowledge and performance are needed in preservice teacher education, but neither one by itself nor both together will abolish the gap between preparation and practice. See Stanley Elam, *Performance-Based Teacher Education: What Is the State of the Art?* (Washington, DC: American Association of Colleges for Teacher Education, 1972). See also Heslep, *The Mental in Education*, pp. 134–136.

5. Teresa M. Bey and Charles T. Holmes, eds., *Mentoring: Contemporary Principles and Issues* (Reston, VA: Association of Teacher Educators, 1992).

6. Mario D. Fantini and Gerald Weinstein, "Making Contact with the Disadvantaged," in *Radical School Reform*, edited by Ronald and Beatrice Gross (New York: Simon & Schuster, 1969), p. 173. See also Anthony S. Dallmann-Jones and the Black River Group, *The Expert Educator: A Reference Manual of Teaching Strategies for Quality Education* (Fond du Lac, WI: Three Blue Herons Publishing, Inc., 1993), Part II: Learning Styles.

7. Some views on the moral dimensions of effective teaching appear in F.K. Oser, A. Dick, and J. Patry, eds., *Effective and Responsible Teaching: The New*

Synthesis (San Francisco, CA: Jossey-Bass, 1992). Neglect of the moral dimension of effective teaching is found in David A. Squires, William G. Huitt, and John K. Segars, eds., *Effective Schools and Classrooms: A Research-Based Perspective* (Alexandria, VA: Association for Supervision and Curriculum Development, 1983). The neglect is found also in Madeline Hunter and Douglas Russell, "How Can I Plan More Effective Lessons," *Instructor* LXXXVII (September 1977), pp. 74–75, 88. The moral problems of the educational efficiency movement have been of concern to the movement's critics for several decades. See Raymond E. Callahan, *Education and the Cult of Efficiency* (Chicago, IL: The University of Chicago Press, 1962).

8. Robert Slavin, *Cooperative Learning* (New York: Longman, 1983). See also David C. Bricker, *Classroom Life as Civic Education: Individual Achievement and Student Cooperation in Schools* (New York: Teachers College Press, 1989).

9. To be sure, we sometimes say that people need or deserve to be successful. They might need to be successful for purposes of encouragement or for career advancement. They might merit success for the reason that they would have been successful if someone had not violated their right to try to succeed. The needs claim, I believe, does not justify a claim to success. Because ensured success is an oxymoron, success is not something that can be guaranteed through noninterference or assistance, even in needs programs where "every kid is a winner." Success can be made more or less easy to come by, of course. The desert claim does justify a claim to success as long as the "would have been successful" factor stands up. Thus, when Ben Johnson was found to have been using steroids, his Olympic gold medal was taken from him and awarded to Carl Lewis, who finished second to Johnson. But what if Johnson had not been on steroids and instead had deliberately tripped Lewis, who then did not finish? Should Lewis or a third runner have been declared the victor, or should Johnson be punished and no victor be declared?

10. This access, even though it is for the student's benefit, must not violate the student's moral right to privacy. Specifically, it must not make the student vulnerable to moral harm from others; it must respect the student's dignity as a moral being.

11. For an analysis of the importance of an actual case of teaching manner for moral instruction, see Philip W. Jackson, Robert E. Boostrom, and David T. Hansen, *The Moral Life of Schools* (San Francisco, CA: Jossey-Bass, 1993), pp. 101–115.

12. The recent increase of violence in schools has brought some school officials to focus on students' rights to physical safety. For instance, in Carter County, Kentucky, where a student shot and killed a class teacher on January 18, 1993, officials adopted a new disciplinary code "to hold sacred the rights of students who come to learn." Jerry Buckley, "The Tragedy in Room 108," *U.S. News & World Report* 115 (November 8, 1993), p. 46.

7 Moral Education for the United States

We have completed our task of constructing, on the basis of defensible norms, a theory of moral education suitable for Americans. The norms are those of moral agency; the theory contains the general end, content, and pedagogy of moral education. We do not know if we have made the theory clear enough to be comprehensible to all who might be interested in it. But even if we have made it transparent, we have done little, if anything at all, to show what moral education in the United States would be like if the theory were applied here. This we need to show. Americans can fully know whether or not to accept the theory only if they grasp what its application would entail. Moreover, policy makers, teachers, school administrators, community leaders, and others can follow the theory in practice only if they have some insight into what we intend in its application.

We will attempt to clarify the theory's application in different ways. In this chapter we will relate the theory to recent policies, proposed or implemented, that pertain to the end, content, and pedagogy of character education in America. In the next two chapters we will relate the theory to several fictional individuals from different social classes who require moral education. In the last chapter we will discuss the theory's implications for various types of institutions in America.

CORE VALUES AND THE END OF MORAL EDUCATION

Even though critics of current American education have often contended that the nation's schools need strong programs for character education, they have been somewhat divided over what type of character education is essential. Some commentators, such as Amy Gutmann[1] and Benjamin R. Barber,[2] have called for character development centered around the civic virtues of democracy. Others have insisted that America's youth sorely need education in moral character beyond citizenship. Thus, William K. Kilpatrick has described students as "morally illiterate."[3] William J. Bennett not only has argued that America suffers moral decline but also has published an anthology of readings to serve as materials for teaching moral virtues.[4] During the present decade, policies on character education have reflected this split over what sort of character should be developed.

Policies on the Ends of Character Education

In early 1991, the Bush administration presented its conception of six goals to be achieved in American public schools between then and the end of this century.[5] The conception had developed over a year's time and involved input from the nation's governors and some educators as well as members of the administration. Perusing the White House's statement of goals, one finds that neither the word "moral" nor any of its cognates appears. One does see, however, that "citizenship" appears in the title of Goal 3 and in the sentence setting forth Goal 5. According to the bill of objectives subsumed under Goal 3, "citizenship" refers to good citizenship, community service, personal responsibility, and knowledge about the diverse cultural heritage of this nation and about the world community. According to the list of objectives itemized under Goal 5, "citizenship" refers to an ability to think critically, communicate effectively, and solve problems. Three other goals may be seen as calling for conditions that will support the learning of citizenship and other matters in the schools: Goal 1 proposes that all children in America will start school ready to learn; Goal 2 calls for a major increase in the graduation rate of high school students; and Goal 6 calls for schools to be safe, disciplined, and drug-free.

Just as one does not discover any obvious mention of morality in the Bush administration's formulation of these six goals, one also does not detect any such mention in the remarks by which the President announced the goals to the public.[6] To be sure, the President described the nation as a force for good in the world; he also stated that classrooms "must cultivate values and good character, give real meaning to right and wrong." While this language has a moral cast, it remains obscure in meaning. Indeed, one has to look hard to find in the President's remarks any mention of citizenship education. There was none in the President's references to Goal 3; it is only in reference to Goal 5 that he talked about such education. On the other hand, he devoted a lot of attention to measures for fostering citizenship education along with the nation's position in global economic competition and technological competence. So, even if the Bush administration did have a slight impulse to call for education in moral character beyond citizenship, it restrained itself and recommended only that the schools develop civic character in its students. Hence, it sided in effect with Gutmann, Barber, and other Social Liberals.

The members of the Bush administration were not the only ones in the early 1990s making official proposals for character education: state officials also were. Unlike the members of the Bush administration, however, the state officials did not confine themselves to proposals for civic education.

For instance, the Georgia Board of Education recommended and eventually implemented a policy for the teaching of 37 "core values" by the state's schools.[7] The values fall into three categories: citizenship, respect for others, and respect for self. The values listed as promoting respect for others plainly are moral virtues: altruism, civility, compassion, courtesy, integrity, honesty, truth, and trustworthiness. Regardless of their categories, however, many of the values appear to be of moral significance. Thus, tolerance, classified as a citizenship value, and moderation, described as important for self-respect, prompted some public concern that they might be interpreted by the schools from a secular rather than a religious moral viewpoint. Indeed, one suspects that the Georgia Board of Education used the term "values education" rather than "character education" or "moral education" in order to minimize public disputes over its proposal.

The Virginia Department of Education included a list of character traits within its proposed common core of learning outcomes, which was oriented to outcomes-based education.[8] Some of these traits explicitly are civic virtues, for example, learning the responsibilities of citizenship within a democratic society. Others pertain to personal well being and to one's role as a worker and consumer. Still others are moral virtues in all but name. They are grouped as learning outcomes related to interpersonal relationships: friendship, truthfulness, respect, fairness, sensitivity to the needs and viewpoints of others, and cooperative conflict resolution. This list of character traits, however, was never made a part of the Virginia school curriculum. It was rejected, along with the rest of the recommended common core of learning, by Governor Wilder, who had strong backing from the Christian Coalition and other foes of outcomes-based education. Virginia, however, was not alone in trying to place comprehensive character education within the context of a common core of learning. Such education had already been advocated by other state departments of education, notably, in Connecticut, Maine, Minnesota, and Utah. In any event, the common core of learning approach to goals for character education has been broad enough to allow for moral character beyond its civic aspects as a goal. While Kilpatrick and Bennett oppose outcomes-based moral education, they have to give it credit for including a wide range of moral character as a goal.

The beginning of the 1990s also included character education policies at the local level. Perhaps the most famous of them was applied to the New York City schools. The policy may be read as promoting civic character for the reason that it aims at combating discrimination in students by teaching them to be respectful and appreciative of different life-styles. Specifically, the policy mandated schools, beginning at the first grade, to portray lesbians and gays as "real people to be respected and appreciated."[9] On the other hand, the policy may be seen as promoting moral character beyond its civic dimension in that its call for respect and appreciation goes beyond the conditions traditionally recognized as necessary for a pluralistic democracy. That is, the members of a pluralistic democracy traditionally are obligated to tolerate different life-styles that do not violate anybody's rights, diminish the public good, or endanger the public; but they are not traditionally required to respect and appreciate any particular life-style. Kilpatrick and Bennett surely would not approve this policy. However, because the policy appears to advocate the development of moral character beyond its civic aspects, it seems to fall on the side of Kilpatrick, Bennett, and all others who want the nation's schools to teach a wide range of moral virtues. Because the policy appears to transcend citizenship education, it does not seem to have the support of Social Liberalism. At any rate, the implementation of this policy met with stiff resistance, especially by the School Board of District 24 of the Borough of Queens. The clash over the policy between the Chancellor of the New York City schools and the Board of District 24 eventually led to the dismissal of the Chancellor.

Discussion of the Proposed Goals

While the Bush administration's statement of goals for this nation's schools dwells on education for the civic aspects of moral character, it is not necessarily and completely opposed to education for the whole range of moral character. Indeed, the civic character comprised by the administration's statement of goals appears to reflect some of the character virtues presented by our theory of moral education.

Moreover, the statement's idea of civic character education has features that are definitely favored by or at least consistent with the end of moral education contained in our theory of moral education. The concern of Goal 1 with the importance of preschool education and the role of parents in that education agrees with our recognition that the development of moral character begins in infancy. The insistence of Goal 3 that schools provide students with the intellectual skills needed to perform their roles as citizens is part and parcel of our stress on the need to learn to evaluate and deliberate. Also, this goal's contention that students must learn to participate in community service and accept personal responsibility is in keeping with the notion of a moral agent as well as with the Criterion of Moral Duty. Goal 5's declaration that adults must continue to learn in order to exercise the rights and responsibilities of citizenship closely compares with our theory's view that the intellectual virtues constituting moral character have to be developed throughout life. Also, Goal 6's proposal that the learning environment of schools must be supported by cooperative efforts of businesses and community organizations as well as parents goes along with our notion that moral character education is of vital interest to moral societies and communities.

Nevertheless, these goals suffer certain shortcomings from the perspective of the moral education purpose set forth by our theory. While the goals are concerned with a civic character that perhaps is morally acceptable to our theory, they are not significant for the whole range of moral character. They say nothing, for instance, about the character traits that should be learned for private life. Our theory, by contrast, aims at producing more than just a good citizen. It aims, rather, at producing a person with the general features of moral agency as well as any traits that are specifically relevant to America for the foreseeable future. Thus, in contrast with the Bush administration's proposal, the theory recommends that America's schools should not necessarily restrict their character education to the citizenship sides of moral education. It wants the schools, in coordination with other appropriate educational institutions, to be concerned with all facets of moral character.

It might be that the Bush administration would have preferred the nation's schools not to confine themselves to just civic education, but the administration might have believed that Individualists, Social Liberals, and Protestant fundamentalists collectively might have blocked an effort to make public school character education broader than civic education. This does not necessarily mean, however, that a wide spectrum of moral character is politically impossible as an end for public school character education. According to our theory, the mass of Americans, whether they are Individualists, Social Liberals, Protestant fundamentalists, or something else, are moral agents. Consequently, they esteem, implicitly or explicitly, the character of moral agents. And if they come to understand that the purpose of the moral education we have proposed for Americans is to produce people with a worthy character, they will have to favor that purpose. The way in which they can come to recognize their commitment to that purpose is through reflection, meditative or dialogical. Such reflection presumes that its participants will recognize that public schools can teach the character of moral agency without placing that character within a secular or religious framework. The frameworks with which our theory is apodictically incompatible are those rejecting the Principles of Identity and Noncontradiction or espousing hard determinism.

It should be noted that the Georgia Board of Education's plan to teach a wide range of core values gained public acceptance for at least two reasons. One was that almost all the values covered by the plan were, according to comments by educators, already being taught in the schools. Thus, the state's teachers felt comfortable with the plan. Even Individualists, who had not previously castigated the state's schools for destroying the autonomy of their students, could not oppose the plan without fear of self-contradiction. Virtually everyone agreed that the plan was simply focusing the schools' attention on the importance of teaching the core values. The second reason was that the state's Board of Education did not give these values any secular or religious slant. Hence, Social Liberals as well as Individualists could live with them. Protestant fundamentalists, who initially were wary of the Board's plan, soon recognized that they, along with everyone else, would be able to guard, at the local school district level, against any offensive interpretations of the concerned values.

The Virginia case stands in contrast with that of Georgia. The core values listed by the Virginia Board of Education were mostly familiar and unobjectionable. Nevertheless, because the Board placed the teaching of these values within the context of outcomes-based education and gave principals and teachers, not local school boards, ultimate authority over the interpretation and teaching of these values, the Board gave the state's Protestant fundamentalists a reason to fear that there would be no forum where they could challenge any secular humanist slant given to the values by principals and teachers. Accordingly, the Christian Coalition was able to raise the specter of secular humanism rampant in the schools, while Governor Wilder was able to gain political strength by seeking to protect the power of local school boards.[10] There is nothing necessarily righteous about local school boards, nor is there anything necessarily immoral about outcomes-based education. However, the exclusion of Americans from full public discussion of a proposal for moral character education appears to be a sure way to defeat even the most sensible recommendation.

Another lesson is manifest in the clash over the New York City school policy. The policy was plainly at variance with the moral beliefs of a significant number of citizens of the city. While those people might have been prepared for their children to learn to be tolerant of the homosexual way of life, they were not at all willing to let their children learn to respect and appreciate that life-style. The Chancellor subsequently sought to impose that policy in District 24 by a peremptory measure: He suspended the district's school board and assumed its powers. The point is that when a goal of moral education cannot receive a consensus established through public discussion, it can become operative only through methods threatening to voluntariness and other features of moral agency.

In sum, the whole of moral character can be generally accepted by Americans as an educational end if it is presented to them on the basis of the norms of moral agency. Probably most of the virtues constituting that character are already familiar and acceptable to most Americans. Who has not heard of altruism, moderation, politeness, justice, friendship, truthfulness, and moral reasoning? Who could be opposed to them? Moreover, because moral agency is a common sense notion, even being a constituent of both secular humanism and the vast majority of religious positions in the nation, the character of moral agency as an end of education should not be threatening to the mass of Americans.

That the Georgia plan for inculcating core values in the state's students was publicly acceptable does not mean that it totally concords with our theory of moral education. Actually, when the core values presented by the plan are viewed from the standpoint of the character of moral agency, they may be seen to contain several difficulties. First, the Georgia plan allows for certain inconsistencies. One of the stated values is frugality. Yet, at the same time that the Georgia Board of Education policy is advocating this character trait for the state's citizens, the state operates a lottery system whose expressed purpose is to raise funds to help support the state's schools. Thus, the schools are supposed to make the state's citizens frugal while the lottery's marketing agents are supposed to encourage them to risk, against great odds, their money on a game of chance. A point of possible inconsistency lies between the values of authority and liberty. In the course of history, authority and liberty have not always been in conflict with one another; but they often have. It is not evident, therefore, that schools can teach students to appreciate both authority and liberty without possibly creating division within them. The relationship between these two values can be coordinated within the framework of moral agency. Moral societies and communities do require persons in positions of authority for the beneficial operation of such groups for all members. Moral agents also require authorities in the sense of experts so that they can have full knowledge pertinent to their actions. Finally, each individual member of a moral group has liberty, or voluntariness, insofar as he or she honors the norms of moral agency.

Another difficulty is vagueness. The Georgia policy sets forth freedom of conscience and expression as a core value; and, as we have already mentioned, it also lists liberty. But it fails to explain the intended difference between freedom and liberty. According to our theory of moral education, the terms *freedom* and *liberty* are synonymous. The sort of freedom we want students to have as a part of their character is an informed freedom restrained by the norms of moral agency. The Georgia policy also mentions patriotism and civic loyalty as core values but, again, fails to clarify the intended difference between the two. For our theory, Americans are not to love their country simply from sentimental attachment; they are to love it mainly because they see it as a sustainer and nurturer of moral agency. Moreover, they are not to be loyal to their country in a blind way. They are to be faithful to it insofar as they have reason to believe that it upholds the norms of moral agency.

The final problem that we find in the Georgia policy is that it does not present moral reasoning as a virtue to be learned by students. In our discussion of the Criterion of Moral Virtue, we described moral reasoning as consisting of the knowledge, skills, appreciations, and psychical energy needed for making decisions consistent with the norms of moral agency. We also referred to it as being an especially important aspect of moral character. According to our theory of moral education, then, it is highly important that Americans be competent in moral reasoning. Perhaps the Georgia Board of Education assumed that if students learned its stated core values, they would automatically become adept in moral reasoning. Acquiring those values in a scattered way, however, will not lead students to engage in moral reasoning. In addition, to learn them in a way integral to moral character, they need to organize them around the principles of practical reasoning, of which moral reasoning is a part. In view of the absence of any mention of reasoning from the Georgia list of core values, one wonders if the state's Board of Education even recognized that morality involves thinking.

POLICIES ON THE CONTENT
OF CHARACTER EDUCATION

We mentioned in Chapter 5 that American schools and colleges used to have moral character as an educational goal and melded content relevant to that goal with academic subject areas. We also mentioned, however, that by the 1960s moral relativism and cultural pluralism undermined the nation's consensus on moral character and prompted schools and colleges to adopt, increasingly, "value-free" curricula. Instead of trying to develop the moral or even just the civic character of students, schools and colleges offered studies in values clarification,[11] in critical thinking,[12] and *about,* not *in,* different ethical approaches. While these studies sometimes were integral to other subject areas, they frequently were separate from them. During the 1970s and 1980s, there were strong criticisms of the value-free curriculum. A few social scientists insisted that citizenship education must involve character development, partly through national service.[13] Many educators turned to curricular studies centered around the developmental approach to moral education.[14] In addition, some critics charged that the so-called "value-free" curricula actually were not value-free.[15] Accordingly, the thinking behind the policies of the 1990s on the curricular content appropriate to character education did not arise from thin air; it has built on and benefited from policy thinking of the previous 20 years. With that background advantage, the policies of the 1990s have avoided some of the mistakes of their precedents. Nevertheless, from the standpoint of our theory of moral education, they have several weaknesses along with their strengths.

Proposed Content

The content policies of the Bush administration and the Virginia Department of Education overlap in places. Both call for studies that involve intellectual skills, such as reasoning, problem solving, knowledge application, and communication. They also want experience in community service and knowledge about cultural diversity in the United States and the rest of the world. Despite these overlaps, however, the two policies diverge on several points. The Bush administration emphasized a subject-centered curriculum in its frequent references, especially in Goals 3 and 4, to mathematics, science, English, and other academic disciplines, while the Virginia Department of Education explicitly expressed the need for interdisciplinary curricula in its suggestions for the restructuring of discipline-centered curricula.[16] The Bush administration's policy proposal was especially concerned with pre-school conditions that affect education, whereas the Virginia proposal made only allusions to them. Finally, the Bush administration called for a drug and alcohol component in the curriculum, while the Virginia Department recommended no curricular content related to any specific moral problem.

The Georgia policy contrasts with the Bush and Virginia proposals in that it, as already indicated, mandates a breadth of content commensurate with many moral virtues beyond those of civic life. Also, it differs from those proposals in the respect that it does not include moral reasoning or any other kind of intellectual skill as a curricular content. Finally, it departs from them in that it expresses no leaning toward any special type of curricular design. The Georgia policy, it may be noted, sides with the Virginia proposal in that it recommends no content related to any specific moral issue. By contrast, the New York City policy on the homosexual life-style sides with the Bush proposal in that it calls for a content dealing with a specific moral question.

Discussion of the Proposed Contents

According to our theory of moral education, the Bush and Virginia emphases on cognitive skills are positively important for the development of moral character. A moral agent is a person who reasons; more specifically, he or she evaluates purposes and deliberates about courses of action. Thus, such an agent has to be capable of gathering practical information, assessing it for its epistemic quality, analyzing and solving practical problems, carefully applying normative standards, forecasting and weighing consequences, seeing things from different points of view, and so on. But it is simply not enough for students to master cognitive skills if they are to acquire the character of moral agents. Consider the intellectual competences specified by the Bush administration: the ability to reason, solve problems, apply knowledge, and write and communicate effectively. All of these competences, one should remember, belonged to the vast majority of the high officials of the German government during Hitler's regime; but they plainly did not endow those officials with the kind of reasoning appropriate to moral agency. Cognitive skills are curricular matters suitable to moral character development only when they fall within the context of moral agency, when they are tempered by the awareness and appreciation of oneself and others as moral agents.

In other words, the abstract and deductive thinking in mathematics, the objective and inductive thinking in science, the problem solving in civics class and in automobile mechanics, and the critical thinking in literature are merely propaedeutic for acquiring the reason befitting a moral agent. If, therefore, genuine moral reasoning is to be learned by students, it must be learned in connection with curricular matters that specifically involve the concerns of moral agency. It follows that moral reasoning as a curricular content will consist of more than skills; it will contain as well morally relevant concepts, nonnormative principles, norms, and facts. If students do not approach cognitive skills as a part of their moral character development, they will come to see such education as simply learning nice feelings, rigid habits, or empty rules. As Barber has noted,[17] this point was made, early in this century, by John Dewey: "Moral education in school is practically hopeless when we set up the development of character as a supreme end, and at the same time treat the acquiring of knowledge and the development of understanding, which of necessity occupy the chief part of school time, as having nothing to do with character."[18]

Without question, there is much material of compelling moral interest that may be woven into various parts of a curriculum. The natural sciences can address the technical aspects of tobacco, drugs, alcohol, and sex as the latter relate to moral problems. The social sciences may speak to the cultural, economic, and political facets, including the historical origins, of the same matters. Literature may present materials in connection with moral problems involving the complexities of specific human characters and contexts. Thus, in Evelyn Waugh's *Brideshead Revisited,* there are treatments of alcoholism, homosexuality, and social inequality, among other moral issues, as they relate to individuals in the English upperclasses between the two world wars. Moreover, there are personages pertinent to various disciplines in whose characters students may see the embodiment of moral reason. In history, Henry David Thoreau and Abraham Lincoln show the thinking that led to their own responses to the issue of slavery. Martin Luther King, Jr., exhibits the reasoning that led to his response to the problem of racial discrimination. Ruth Bader Ginsberg displays the thinking that guided her responses to discrimination against women not only in the legal profession but also in all other work places in America. In natural science, moral concerns underlie the work of Lister, Pasteur, Koch, Einstein, and other eminent scientists. In mathematics, there is opportunity to note how the Euclidean method has been used by some philosophers, such as Spinoza, as the model of ethical theorizing and how quantitative calculation has been employed by others, such as Jeremy Bentham, as the method of moral decision making. There also is opportunity to explain, as in the case of Alan M. Turing, how theoretical genius by itself is not sufficient for getting along in practical life. Finally, literature enables students, as in the works of George Eliot and D.H. Lawrence, to experience characters inhabited by reason or marked by the tension between intellect and feeling.

Another morally important curricular content involved in the Bush administration's proposal is community service, but it too faces the separation problem suffered by the proposal's cognitive skills content. There is little doubt that the Bush proposal's mandate for community service is an improvement over earlier and present calls for national service. As usually conceived, national service, such as working in projects to clean up the environment or to build housing for the poor, is an activity in which youth engage after they have finished school. It is justified chiefly on the ground of reciprocal duty: Because youth received an education at the expense of society, they owe society something, which may be repaid in the form of national service. The problem with national service as an educational device is that if students have not acquired a sense of social obligation by the time they have finished school, they are not likely to perform any national service in a way that will develop their moral character. They are much more likely to do it grudgingly and of necessity. Thus, the Bush administration's recommendation for community service as a part of the public school curriculum makes it possible

MORAL EDUCATION FOR THE UNITED STATES

for students to embody a sense of social obligation as an element of their character.

Even so, the recommendation does not go far enough; for it leaves open the possibility that students will learn community service in a departmentalized way. If students do participate in community service in a strictly limited way, they are likely to learn to see it as being narrow in scope and importance rather than as something that might pervade all aspects of their moral life. If, for instance, a student's experience in such service is nothing more than participation in an extracurricular group devoted to a social project, that experience might lead the student to see social obligations as being neatly and formally pigeonholed and therefore to overlook or discount any moral obligations outside the project's category. To be fully meaningful to the student, community service has to appear in various areas of the curriculum. Science students can engage in socially useful activities of scientific relevance, for instance, analyzing the bacterial and chemical contents of streams or drinking water. Literature students can read to disadvantaged children and help them understand stories. Mathematics students can provide computational services for adults who are ignorant of arithmetic.

It is granted that the Bush administration's proposal does not rule out the interweaving of cognitive skills and community service into various segments of the curriculum. As a matter of fact, the proposal suggests, by explicitly saying that educators "must be given greater flexibility to devise challenging and inspiring strategies to serve the needs of a diverse body of students," [19] that curriculum designers may interject moral reasoning and community service into all curricular areas if they find such an arrangement desirable. But even if the proposal demanded an integration of moral reasoning and community service in the curriculum, it would fall short of being a satisfactory policy for education in moral character. As already explained, the recommendation is concerned with the virtues constituting the civic aspect of moral character; it is not interested in those involved in other facets of moral character. Accordingly, it does not indicate contents relevant to the development of moral character in all respects.

The Virginia Department of Education's proposal, it should be noted, does not involve the weaknesses just attributed to the Bush administration's. It makes clear that cognitive skills, including those of moral reasoning, should underlie many curricular areas. Also, because it is interested in the whole of moral character, it calls for curricular contents important for the development of a full moral character. So, how does the Virginia recommendation measure up to our theory of moral education beside the point that the former was impractically tied to the notion of outcomes-based education? The major fault of the proposal is that it tends to see moral education as something that occurs mainly within the school; it does not acknowledge that many forces affecting character formation are outside the school and must be coordinated with the school's endeavors if the latter are not to be negated. The recommendation does say that teachers must establish "links with businesses and the community to provide information and secure assistance."[20] But it never goes so far as even to intimate that curriculum designers, administrators, or teachers must work with parents, social workers, community organizations, churches, mass media, police, or other relevant nonschool agents to construct, through dialogue, a moral content for the school curriculum that coordinates with supportive and complementary contents outside the school. Indeed, one of the avowed guiding principles of the Virginia proposal is that "administrators and teachers are the best judges of how to use sound research and their own experience to turn the Common Core of Learning into effective curriculum, instruction, learning, and student performance."[21] While this principle might intend only that administrators and teachers, like doctors and lawyers, know best how to perform their work, it strikes one as saying also that contact between school and community on curricular content for moral education is to be a one-way street. There certainly are no statements elsewhere in the proposal that weaken this impression.

In maintaining that morality must be a content interlarded in the curriculum, our theory does not mean that schools should never have classes devoted to matters of special moral concern. There might be moral problems about which students can best learn in their schools and which are of such urgency that they should be treated in a concentrated way, perhaps in a course reserved for the study of such problems. Moreover, in holding that the content of moral education should occupy an extensive part of the school curriculum, our theory does not intend for moral education to replace or diminish academic education. The worry of some critics that the inclusion of moral education in the school curriculum will necessarily cheat academic education of its due share of the curriculum is simply unfounded.[22] Moral education, unlike driver education, is crucial for this nation. Nevertheless, how much of a school's curriculum it should occupy is not fixed; it depends on the background of students and on how well factors in the students' environment provide moral education. If students are morally deprived and community factors do very little to provide moral education, those students impose a heavy burden on their school's curriculum. If, however, students have well-developed moral characters, largely because of conscientious parents, attentive churches, and wholesome leisure activities, they pose nothing more than a minimum requirement on their school's curriculum. Those who insist that schools minimize moral education and maximize academics should figure out how to restructure America's institutions in such a way that the bulk of moral education may return to families, neighborhoods, churches, and government, where it principally dwelt once, long ago.

POLICIES ON THE PEDAGOGY OF MORAL EDUCATION

Most of the policies discussed above also make recommendations relevant to the pedagogical aspects of moral character development. Some of those recommendations are quite in keeping with our theory of moral education; others involve difficulties.

Proposals on Pedagogy

One thing on which the Bush and Virginia policies agree is that school teachers and administrators must be invested with authority to determine how students are to be taught citizenship and other aspects of moral character. As already noted, the Virginia position is to view educators as "the best judges" of how to use "sound research and their own experience" to use the guidelines of the Common Core of Learning for effective instruction. While the Bush proposal is mute on who is the best judge of matters pedagogical, it recommends, as previously mentioned, that educators "be given greater flexibility to devise challenging and inspiring strategies to serve the needs of a diverse body of students." The Georgia policy differs in that it delegates directly to local school boards, not school administrators and teachers, the authority to plan instructional methods and strategies. School boards, of course, can accord educators much leeway in how to instruct students; but, as suggested in the New York City case, a metropolitan board or superintendent's office might not delegate much authority to neighborhood boards or to school teachers and principals.

The Bush proposal is explicit in holding "professional educators" accountable for the results of their pedagogical efforts.[23] The Georgia policy also forthrightly requires local school boards to be responsible for writing instructional plans that meet state criteria. The Virginia proposal does not single out any group of agents as accountable for student learning. The closest that that proposal comes to saying anything on the matter is its declaration that support is sought "from all available sources (community, parents, students, and educators) that share in the responsibility for each student's success."[24] While this statement plainly says that various agents are responsible for any student's education, it does not say that any of them is accountable for what it does or fails to do for that education. This is somewhat puzzling for the reason that the Virginia proposal accords much authority to school teachers and administrators for designing curricula and planning instruction for students.

The Bush and Virginia recommendations also agree that the education of students cannot succeed with the efforts of just professional educators. The Bush proposal states that parents must become more involved in their children's education, that students must accept "the challenge for higher expectations for achievement," and that communities, business and civic groups, and the variou̇s levels of government have vital roles to play to ensure success in the achievement of the proposal's six goals.[25] In a similar vein, the Virginia proposal states that parents must play a key role in the education of their children, that students are responsible in large measure for their own learning, and that communities must support the state's educational efforts.[26] It must be noted, however, that neither the Bush nor the Virginia recommendations specify what contributions are to be made by parents, communities, business groups, or civic organizations. Nor does either of them indicate how cooperation between these agents and professional educators is to be secured.

Discussion of the Pedagogical Proposals

There are elements in the pedagogical recommendations described above that are in keeping with our theory of moral education. By relating those elements to our theory, we can explain what they would be like if they were conceived and implemented according to our theory.

First, the point that school teachers must have authority for planning instruction is a piece of our principle that teachers of moral education have the right to choose the content and methods to be used in teaching their students. As agents committed to being knowledgeable in their work, teachers of moral character are open to and seek information and advice from relevant parties, whether students, academic experts, community leaders, publishers, media specialists, or governmental officials. They also welcome thoughtful criticism. But they can have such deliberations only in a social context with organizational structures and institutional practices that encourage them. As long as school boards and superintendents continue to make decisions on instructional content and methods, they will not be supportive of the right of teachers of moral education to deliberate and decide upon content and methods. The same may be said of textbook and library committees dominated by nonprofessional teachers, however morally conscientious. The practice of legislative bodies to mandate specific educational contents, materials, and methods also undermines that right.[27] What are more likely to foster this right are representative groups with informational, advisory, and critical functions. In such groups, which may be local, regional, or national, representatives from the broadcast media, publishing houses, churches, government, the social sciences, and other concerned bodies can join with teachers in frank and comprehensive discussions of issues and problems related to the teachers' deliberations on content and methods without ever interfering with their right to choose the content and method.

Second, the point that school teachers and administrators should be accountable for their actions in trying to educate students in moral character closely relates to our theory's view of the teacher of moral education as a moral agent. Because a moral agent, according to that theory, acts voluntarily, such an agent is responsible for his or her actions, including the outcomes within his or her control. To the extent, therefore, that a school teacher or administrator fails, by voluntary action, to bring about the learning of moral character, that educator must be accountable for that shortcoming. Yet, as the Virginia proposal insists, professional educators are not the only agents who might be responsible for the success or failure of students in learning. Students themselves, their families, neighborhoods, peers, and others, too, might bear responsibility. Accordingly, if a free and competent teacher of moral education strives to develop the moral character of students, but works in an uncooperative neighborhood and with students with low motivation and unsupportive families, that teacher has little or no accountability for student failure. If, on the other hand, the teacher works in a cooperative community and with positively motivated students with supportive families, that teacher is likely to be answerable for student failure. In short, teacher accountability in moral education in America has to be decided on a case-by-case basis, not in a blanket approach.

Last, the Bush and the Virginia policy proposals are in keeping with our theory of moral education in the respect that they recognize that neighborhoods, civic and business groups, parents, and other extramural agents have a place in the moral education of students. Both recommendations declare that parents are their children's first teachers. In addition, the Bush proposal specifies that "every major American business will be involved in strengthening the connection between education and work" (Goal 5) and that "parents, businesses, and community organizations will work together to ensure that the schools are a safe haven for all children" (Goal 6). More vaguely, the Virginia proposal simply makes its declaration about seeking support from all available sources responsible for each student's success.

According to our theory, the moral agents teaching moral character may be not only school teachers but also parents, clergy, athletic instructors, TV personnel, authors, or any other moral agent trying to shape another's behavior or beliefs for the latter's benefit and by appealing ultimately to the latter's reason. Because students need the conditions that support and nurture the optimal development of their respective moral characters, they have a right to qualified teachers at home and in the community as well as at school. They have a right to an immediate environment and a public media expressive of the norms of moral agency and supportive of adequate nutrition, health care, and physical safety. Moreover, all agents who can reasonably provide these conditions for the development of the moral character of students are morally obligated to furnish them. What specific rights American students have to such conditions and what specific duties extramural agents in America have to provide those conditions depend on the availability of economic resources and talent and the differences among the situations of particular students.

While the Bush and Virginia calls for increasing the authority of professional educators are, on their face, compatible with our theory of moral education, they contain a major deficiency. They seem to intend that the authority for making decisions about school instruction will reside exclusively with school teachers and administrators. If they do mean this, they intend also that parents, clergy, business groups, and others are not to initiate or develop decisions about school instruction. The Bush proposal hints at this possibility when it places extramural agents in a passive role upon its saying that "community-based teams should be organized to provide students and teachers with needed support" for drug and alcohol prevention programs. The Virginia proposal strongly indicates the possibility when it says that "support is sought from all available sources," for instance, community and parents.

What the Bush and Virginia proposals actually intend here is not our concern. Our concern, rather, is what our theory holds that the structure of instructional decision-making authority should be for moral education in America. There are good historical reasons why the Bush and Virginia proposals insist that professional educators should have greater flexibility in designing, implementing, and evaluating instruction. School boards, legislators, parents' groups, and others have often attempted to micromanage instruction, treating school teachers and administrators as though they were unskilled hired hands. Nevertheless, the increase of the educator's pedagogical authority should not come at the price of excluding interested extramural agents from actively participating in the instructional decision-making process. While professional teachers and administrators logically have, because of what they are, pedagogical expertise that should be respected by lay people, they do not necessarily know all the facts they need to know for planning instruction for a particular group of students. They might not know, for instance, what the students' learning styles are. They might not know about the family backgrounds or personalities of the students. They also might not recognize that their instructional practices are perceived by extramural agents as being inadequate. Professional educators, then, can be prepared to know all that they need to know for developing the moral character of their students only if they are prepared to discuss instructional methods with parents, community groups, clergy, and others who have specific relevant information about those students.

How much decision-making authority for instruction in moral education the nation's public school educators should have is beside the point. Indeed, where that authority should officially reside is irrelevant, too. What counts is that Americans must learn to see instructional decision making in moral education as a collective process involving school educators and extramural moral agents with specific relevant information about the particular students of those educators. The educators have authority to participate in this process because of their professional expertise, whereas extramural agents have authority to participate because of their possession of needed information. Just as physicians may let patients choose among alternative procedures where the differences among them are not medically appreciable, educators also may let extramural agents choose among alternative methods where differences among them are neither pedagogically nor morally appreciable. Otherwise, educators are to make final decisions on the pedagogy of moral education. Extramural agents have to trust educators as well as hold them accountable.

There also is tension today between school teachers and administrators about pedagogical authority. Ever since the early decades of this century, when progressive reformers began trying, in the name of efficiency, to make the schools "teacher proof," superintendents and principals have accumulated much authority over pedagogical matters. Superintendents were to have such authority, according to progressive reform theory, because of their professional training and experience. For convenience, they were to and did delegate to their principals authority over pedagogy in the principals' respective schools. Since midcentury this line-staff model has given way. Principals often have been too occupied with public relations and other administrative affairs to have time for instructional supervision. More important, they sometimes have not had the expertise needed to make decisions in many instructional situations. As a result, pedagogical authority has been passed further down to assistant principals called "instructional supervisors" and even to some classroom teachers called "lead teachers." In the past 10 years there has been an effort by some professional educators to place pedagogical decision-making authority primarily in the hands of classroom teachers.

According to our theory of moral education, decision-making authority for moral instruction in schools resides mainly with teachers. This conclusion follows largely from the theory's contention that teachers of moral character have a justified claim to choose the content and methods to be used in their teaching of moral character. That contention in turn, it must be remembered, presupposes that school teachers of moral character are moral agents especially competent in moral instruction. Of course, few if any teachers are perfect; many need help in their teaching from time to time. When a competent teacher of moral education learns, through reflection or from input from students, parents, or colleagues, that he or she suffers an instructional deficiency, that teacher can seek advice from another classroom teacher or from a supervisor. This self-correcting model, however, will not work if classroom teachers are competing with each other for merit pay, if instructional supervisors have to spend their time doing the principals' donkey work, such as disciplining students and scheduling buses, and if instructional supervisors downgrade teachers simply because the latter seek help. But that primary authority for pedagogy in moral education in schools should lie with classroom teachers does not mean that school administrators do not have some pedagogical authority. According to our theory, the pedagogy of moral education requires support conditions, for example, equipment, physical facilities, food, health care, instructional materials, personnel, and monetary resources. The chief role of school administrators, whether superintendent or principal, is to serve the pedagogy of moral instruction by looking after such conditions. To perform their role, school administrators must have input from teachers and extramural agents; but they also, by virtue of their professional competence, have ultimate decision-making authority in performing their role.

Even if Americans agree that pedagogical authority must be integral to interactions between professional educators and extramural agents, they also must recognize that traditional arrangements for such interactions might not exist any longer or might not work. The shift in the nation's economy from an agricultural to a manufacturing and, most recently, to a service base has moved the nation's population from the rural areas to the cities and suburbs. This relocation has led to the disappearance of the extended family as well as to the decline in importance of small towns, neighborhoods, and other face-to-face communities that once served to inculcate and enforce codes of conduct. The shifts in labor markets and the expansion of labor pools through the increased hiring of women have greatly increased the number of two-working-parents families, thus reducing parental supervision of children. These shifts also have helped to undermine the nuclear family, which along with other face-to-face communities has long helped to provide moral education.[28] The vast increase of unwed mothers, most of whom were unsuccessful in school, means that educators will likely have a hard time gaining cooperation from the parents of numerous students. Court-ordered busing has eliminated most neighborhood schools, making school–community interaction very difficult in many instances. In addition, the expansion of the cultural diversity of American society has diffused, if not reduced, the practices and interests of churches in working with public schools. Thus, if professional educators and extramural agents are to make decisions on the pedagogy of moral education according to our theory, they must try to identify and develop new arrangements between school and society that will facilitate active and informed cooperation between the various parties. Until these parties have been able to determine which new arrangements are available and effective, they will have to work in an experimental and piecemeal way. What they might find is that different specific situations will require different institutions and practices. In the next two chapters we suggest institutions and practices that might work for each of the cases under consideration.

CONCLUSIONS

In view of the foregoing discussion of policy proposals, we may indicate several features of moral education for Americans if it were to result from the application of our theory. We do not know that these are the only features that would result from the application, but we believe that they are important ones.

1. Moral education for Americans would be much more extensive than the development of their civic character. As we have explained, the virtues of moral agency include civic virtues, such as justice and tolerance, but they also include other excellences of moral character, such as moderation, friendship, and the intellectual disciplines. While one, accordingly, may expect American moral education grounded on our theory to involve the virtues of civic life, one should further expect such education to include the virtues of the intellectual and social life beyond the limits of citizenship. Such education, therefore, would definitely differ from that advocated by Social Liberals, who tend to restrict moral education to civic education, and from that urged by Individualists, who avowedly want all character education to be a private affair. Such education also would significantly differ from that proposed by Communitarians and Virtuists. It would treat moral character as derivative from the values, rights, and duties of moral agency. By contrast, Communitarians would emphasize the duties of moral agency at the expense of its values and rights; and Virtuists would focus on the virtues of moral agency apart from their connection with its values and rights.

2. Moral education for Americans would pervade their schools. Depending upon the needs of a school's students, the development of the moral character of students would occupy a place, greater or lesser, in each school's mission. Rather than being concentrated in just special courses, moral education would be of serious concern in academic courses, vocational studies, and extracurricular activities.[29] It would be of serious concern in student conduct in the classrooms, at athletic

events, and at social events. Moreover, it would compel school administrators and teachers to conduct themselves in morally exemplary ways.
As a result of all these conditions, each school would have a climate
shaped by the norms of moral agency.

3. Moral education for Americans would entail vital and extensive cooperation between the educators of each and every school and the extramural moral agents with a close interest in the moral character education
of the respective students of each and every school. To prevent conflict
and needless duplication, classroom instructors, parents, clergy, and all
other relevant moral teachers must coordinate among themselves the
particular purposes they are to set for themselves. They have to devise
together the educational content, both formal and informal, that will
contribute to the attainment of their respective purposes. They also have
to plan together the methods and plans that will be most appropriate for
teaching. Finally, in order to identify and solve problems related to their
purposes, content, and pedagogy, professional educators and interested
extramural agents must work together in reviewing these matters.

This insistence upon cooperation between school educators and extramural agents is far from revolutionary. There are schools and communities in the nation today that work closely together in planning and car-
rying out the education of the involved students. Such schools and
communities, however, are the exception rather than the rule. Frequently, schools go their way with little input from the educational laity.
This situation exists partly because of logistics: The parents, clergy, social workers, and other parties with an interest in the students of a
school often live and work far from the school. But the situation exists
also because of a long-standing distrust between professional educators
and the educational laity: Some educators do not appreciate the judgment of laity, and vice versa; some laity are suspicious of the motives
of educators, and vice versa. If, then, there is to be cooperation between
schools and extramural agents in developing the moral character of the
nation's youth, there has to be a solution to the problem of logistics and
to that of distrust. A solution to the former might lie in the reconception
of certain institutions and practices, which will be discussed presently.
A solution to the latter might lie in a blend of staff development and
community relations oriented around the principle that professional and
lay educators have different tasks to perform in moral education and
that they must trust one another, as moral agents, to do their tasks well.

NOTES

1. Amy Gutmann, *Democratic Education* (Princeton, NJ; Princeton University Press, 1987).

2. Benjamin R. Barber, *An Aristocracy of Everyone: The Politics of Education and the Future of America* (New York: Ballantine Books, 1992).

3. William K. Kilpatrick, *Why Johnny Can't Tell Right from Wrong: Moral Illiteracy and the Case for Character Education* (New York: Simon & Schuster, 1993).

4. William J. Bennett, ed., *The Book of Virtues: A Treasury of Great Moral Stories* (New York: Simon & Schuster, 1993).

5. Lamar Alexander (comp.), *America 2000: An Education Strategy Sourcebook* (Washington, DC: U.S. Department of Education, 1991), pp. 45–58.

6. George Bush, "Remarks by the President at the Presentation of the National Education Strategy," in Alexander, *America 2000*, pp. 1–9.

7. "State Board Gives School Systems a List of 'Core Values' to be Taught," *The Atlanta Journal/Constitution* (March 14, 1991), pp. E2, E13.

8. Virginia Department of Education, "The Virginia Common Core of Learning," draft copy (October 20, 1992).

9. Alan Wolfe, "School Daze: How Politics Takes the Education Out of Schooling," *The New Republic* 208 (February 8, 1993), p. 25.

10. "Outcomes-Based Education Dies," *Newport News Daily Press* (September 16, 1993), pp. C1–C2.

11. Merrill Harmin, Howard Kirschenbaum, and Sidney Simon, *Clarifying Values through Subject Matter* (Minneapolis, MN: Winston Press, 1973).

12. See, for instance, Lawrence E. Metcalf, ed., *Values Education: Rationale, Strategies and Procedures* (Washington, DC: National Council for the Social Studies, 1971).

13. Morris Janowitz, *The Reconstruction of Patriotism: Education for Civic Consciousness* (Chicago, IL: The University of Chicago Press, 1983).

14. Lawrence Kohlberg, *The Concepts of Developmental Psychology as the Central Guide to Education: Examples from Cognitive, Moral, and Psychological Education* (Washington, DC: U.S. Office of Education, 1971).

15. For an overview of the point, see Elliot W. Eisner, *The Educational Imagination: On the Design and Evaluation of School Programs* (New York: Macmillan, 1981), pp. 74–92.

16. Virginia Department of Education, "The Virginia Common Core of Learning," p. 31.

17. Barber, *An Aristocracy for Everyone*, pp. 226–227.

18. John Dewey, *Democracy and Education: An Introduction to the Philosophy of Education* (New York: Macmillan, 1916, 1958), p. 411.

19. Alexander, *America 2000*, p. 45.

20. Virginia Department of Education, "The Virginia Common Core of Learning," p. 31.

21. Ibid., p. 3.

22. See, for example, Wolfe, "School Daze," p. 26.

23. Ibid., p. 46.

24. Virginia Board of Education, "The Virginia Common Core of Learning," p. 3.

25. Alexander, *America 2000*, p. 46.

26. Virginia Board of Education, "The Virginia Common Core of Learning," p. 3.

27. The so-called "state-initiated" school reforms of the 1980s were mandated by the legislatures of Tennessee, South Carolina, Georgia, and other states.

28. Frances Goldscheider and Linda Waite, *New Families, No Families? The Transformation of the American Family* (Berkeley, CA: The University of California Press, 1992).

29. Charles Bidwell and Anthony Bryk have classified high school teachers into four types: Rigorists, who emphasize school rules, knowledge of fundamentals, and student performance; Moral Agents, who focus on rules and discipline but also value student moral development; Pals, who form strong relationships with students; and Mentors, who focus on subject matter and teaching style. Charles Bidwell and Anthony Bryk, "How Teachers' Work Is Organized: The Content and Consequences of the Structure of the High School Workplace"; paper presented at the annual conference of the American Education Research Association (April 1994), New Orleans, LA.

From the standpoint of our theory of moral education, all teachers should have a strain of the Moral Agent. They might be Rigorists, Pals, or Mentors predominantly; but they each must be seriously concerned with the development of moral character in their students. A similar point may be made about school climate. A school may emphasize rigor, friendliness, or teaching; but it has to be attentive to the acquisition of moral character by its students. The ideal climate, perhaps, would be a mix of rigor, friendliness, teaching, and morality.

8 Moral Education for Natalene Turner

So far, our discussion of moral education for Americans has been rather general. It has identified a set of moral principles that may serve as a basis of the character education required by the members of this nation. It has clarified the kinds of goal, content, and pedagogy that are appropriate to this education. It also has compared and contrasted the latter with character education policies recently advocated in the United States. However, the inquiry has not shown what its proposed moral education would be like in particular situations of the United States today.

To help clarify this point, we will discuss two cases. One bears on members of the underclass; the other, on members of the middle class. This approach enables us to see just how differential, complex, and difficult moral education is likely to be for Americans. Each case is fictional; it is a composite drawn from the social sciences, journalism, personal experience, and imagination. Not only is there no need to risk violating the privacy of any actual person for the sake of this investigation, there is no pressing need to use actual cases. Fictional cases, it is widely recognized, may bear resemblances to actual ones. In this chapter we will consider the case of Natalene Turner, a child of the underclass. The next chapter will take up the case of a small group of male adolescents from a lower-middle-class suburb.

THE CASE OF NATALENE TURNER

Characteristics of the American underclass have become commonly agreed upon during recent decades:[1] poverty, urban ghetto, Appalachia,[2] no work ethic, public welfare, poor education, unmarried mothers, irresponsible fathers, neglected children, poor personal health habits, drug and alcohol abuse, theft, violence, and much television watching. In view of these traits, many social commentators might contend that, at least at this time, moral education for the American underclass would be a futile, if not irrelevant, enterprise. Such education would be beside the point because the members of this social-economic class are not voluntary agents: They are not capable of acting freely and wittingly; they are driven to do what they do in reaction to the social structure of American society, which imposes upon them severe constraints and a negligible range of opportunities.[3] Also, such education would be ineffectual because the members of the underclass, whose culture sanctions dysfunctional conduct, tend to reject schooling and social responsibility.[4]

Of the commentators who might take this position, some argue that the present policy of social maintenance and containment should be replaced with measures that offer underclass people genuine economic opportunity.[5] Others insist that the American underclass ought to be drastically reduced in size through the imposition of disincentives to be in it. Two disincentives that have been proposed are limits on the time a person may receive public welfare and the outright elimination of public welfare.[6]

Whether present measures for dealing with the underclass in the United States should be continued or new ones ought to be adopted is certainly a morally important question, but it is not an urgent one for the problem at hand. The one that does demand attention here is whether or not moral education for this group is useless or irrelevant. How one answers the question depends on whether or not one sees it as asking about the moral education of the American underclass in general or about particular members of the group. If the question is given the former interpretation, it might be properly answered in the affirmative. One should recognize, however, that any possible futility and irrelevance of moral education for the underclass in general might be due to something other than the characteristics of this class. It might be due to the kind of moral education one has in mind. Hence, on its face the failure of present modes of moral education to improve the American underclass in general does not necessarily mean that there is something incorrigible about that social-economic group. It might mean that the established kinds of moral education are hopeless and inappropriate.

But even with acknowledgment of this possibility, it is rather doubtful that we should focus on the American underclass in general. We are committed here to showing as specifically as possible how to apply our theory of moral education to the United States as it actually is today. The way to do this is to deal with individuals in particular situations.

Therefore, we take the issue of concern to be if the moral education of this or that underclass member in this or that situation is futile or irrelevant. A focus on the moral education of particular members of a social-economic group does not mean that generalizations cannot be made about the members of the American underclass or any other social-economic class, but it does mean that such generalizations will have their limitations in relation to particular members. Let us proceed by considering what, if anything, should be done for the moral education of Natalene Turner.

Description of the Case

Natalene Turner lives in a black public housing project with her mother. While she is in the third grade of a public school with a racial balance, obtained through busing, she is absent more times than school personnel deem advisable. And when she is in school, she engages in occasional scuffles with other students and often pays little attention to class instruction.

Earlier in the year, while her mother, single[7] and a school dropout, served a sentence for drug possession, Natalene and her pre-school brother lived in a nearby apartment with Grandmother Turner, also a school dropout. The grandmother once had a husband and a job as a nurse's aid. The husband deserted her, and she left her job to look after her four children. Even though the grandmother always opposed drugs, she lost her influence over her son as well as over Natalene's mother. Of the other two daughters, one managed to finish high school and has a job as a clerk in a retail store. The other has a job in a food processing plant. Both occasionally visit their mother at her apartment.

Several weeks after leaving jail and its rehabilitation program, Ms. Turner returned to her crack habit, which she had begun shortly before becoming pregnant with Natalene's brother.[8] She sometimes has received the drug gratis from a boyfriend, but she occasionally has practiced prostitution to obtain it. Shortly after being born, her son went through a period of suspected withdrawal from the drug; he still suffers some behavioral disorder. Since his mother's return home and at her request, the boy has continued living with Grandmother Turner. When the weather is right, the grandmother takes the child outside to play while she talks with neighbors on a front stoop, a sidewalk, or the playground.

On those school-day mornings when Natalene awakes and finds her mother still asleep, she usually continues wearing the dirty clothes in which she slept and spends the morning watching TV cartoons while eating potato chips and drinking a cola. She has few toys and no books. Neither Grandmother Turner nor anyone else sees to it that she goes to school. Natalene has never suffered immediate physical danger, but she has heard of beatings, stabbings, and shootings in the housing project where she lives. In the afternoon she often plays with other children from the project and sometimes visits with Grandmother Turner and her brother. She finds her grandmother comforting and her brother fun. The Turners do not go to church except for an occasional funeral and Easter services. Despite personal requests from school officials, Ms. Turner has never visited Natalene's teacher to talk about her daughter's school problems.

Analysis of the Case

Despite her grim situation, Natalene shows signs of being a prospective moral agent. Those are the features of moral agency that she has in some degree and traits she has that will help her acquire features of moral agency. There also, however, are factors in Natalene's environment that threaten her development as a moral agent. These include people and cultural matters.

Without question, Natalene enjoys much freedom. She often gets up only when she likes, does not always have to go to school, passes her mornings at home as she wants to, spends her afternoons as she pleases, and does not have to change clothes. While Natalene likes her everyday liberties, she is not the only child in her neighborhood who has and enjoys them. They are a part of the culture of the people who live there. To be sure, Natalene has not considered many other ways in which she might be free or that freedom logically has value for all people; but she has recognized that her playmates and the adults she knows have freedoms and that they like to act freely.

Knowledge too is a feature of Natalene. She is aware of who she is and who her mother, grandmother, and brother are. She knows where she lives and goes to school. She knows what cartoons are on TV in the morning and what the rules of her games are. She knows how to operate the TV set, how to feed herself, and how to use the bathroom. She also has concepts, such as mother, grandmother, brother, residence, playmate, school, sleep, night, morning, afternoon, TV, food, danger, safety, play, and fairness.

Even though Natalene is not purposeful in a full-blown sense of the term, she does express a degree of purposiveness in what she does. Her actions are guided by likes and desires whose objects are the members of her family, junk food, TV cartoons, games, playmates, fun, and security. In that Natalene does what she does because she is trying to attain something that she likes or desires, she acts with purpose. Some of Natalene's goals quite likely are whimsical, reflecting no sense of worth on her part. Those we have specified, however, implicitly involve norma-tive principles, namely, pleasure and security. She eats junk food, watches TV cartoons, and plays games with neighborhood children be-cause they all are fun. There is nothing at school that she finds to be pleasant; there is very little about it that she likes. Occasionally, Nata-lene's mother is fun to be with; visits with her grandmother and brother usually are pleasant. Her mother and grandmother, however, also are desirable for the security they provide. They furnish Natalene food, clothing, and a warm place to sleep. They make her feel safe from the unknown dangers of the outside world. She knows to whom she would flee if the violence of which she has occasionally heard became immi-nent. No doubt, desires for things pleasurable and safe have a natural base. But what specific things are pleasurable and secure, as well as what hardships and risks are acceptable, are often learned from one's social environment. Thus, that Natalene does not like school is partly cultural; that she feels secure without her father living with her is cul-tural, too. In any event, her choosing things on the basis of pleasure and security indicates that she has become somewhat evaluative.

Natalene has assumed some of the rudiments of deliberation, too. Be-cause she does not yet clearly understand what a means or an end is, or that some actions might be better or worse means to a given end, she is not prepared to weigh actions with respect to the pleasure or safety that they will bring. Because, however, she learned that some are fun in themselves and some are inherently dangerous, she does not have to deliberate in order to engage in pleasurable activities and to avoid dan-gerous ones. Moreover, most of the activities that she takes to be inher-ently pleasurable or dangerous she learned about from her mother, grandmother, other adults, playmates, and TV. There are, nevertheless, occasions when she does something like deliberation. From time to time, she and her playmates become bored with the games they are playing and try out new ones. Every once in a while, Natalene becomes tired of watching the same cartoons and switches to other programming. Occa-sionally, she drinks a different cola to see if it is better than what she usually drinks. Because she learned from her grandmother that meat and vegetables, not candy, would make her strong, she sometimes eats meat and vegetables with the idea of growing up strong.

Besides possessing major features of voluntary agency in some mea-sure, Natalene also has other traits that can support her development as ·a moral agent. Getting up in the mornings on her own and spending the day as she pleases are signs of self-reliance. This can serve as a basis for the autonomy that she will need to acquire as a moral agent. More-over, the fact that Natalene likes to be with the members of her family and play with friends suggests that she is sociable. This will help her learn to identify with other people and, thus, to recognize the equality between herself and others as moral agents. Finally, her concerns with security and growing up strong can constitute groundwork for learning to maintain and foster other auxiliary conditions of moral agency.

Because Natalene has major characteristics of moral agency to some degree and has other traits that can help her develop as a moral agent, she appears capable of acquiring moral character. Nevertheless, there obviously are factors in her life that strongly oppose her moral growth. Her mother is a glaring factor. Whether or not she first took addictive drugs voluntarily we do not know. Whether or not she regretted her drug habit while she underwent rehabilitation during her jail sentence we also do not know. Whether or not she knew or cared that using crack during pregnancy might make her fetus addicted to the drug we do not know either. But while we are uncertain about the mother's blameworthiness, we are confident that her drug life involves conditions that can easily have deleterious effects on Natalene. Most importantly, Natalene is susceptible to absorbing maxims embedded in her mother's behavior, such as: immediate pleasure and escape from reality are preferable to freedom, and it is acceptable to trade one's body for money in order to gain immediate pleasure and escape from reality. That Grandmother Turner's disapproval of drugs failed to keep the mother from using drugs does not indicate that it necessarily will counteract the mother's negative influence on Natalene. Moreover, the widespread use of drugs by people in the periphery of Natalene's environment is liable to suggest that her mother's life is normal and that her grandmother is just cranky.

Another negative influence is the meager cognitive stimulus in Natalene's environment. Books, newspapers, and magazines are absent; so is discussion. Being told stories and being read to are not a part of her experience either. Play, talk about everyday events, and TV cartoons provide the bulk of her cognitive stimulation. A related obstacle is the mother's indifference toward Natalene's performance in school. There is nothing magical about Natalene's school. Nevertheless, it is an institution that tries hard to help minority children. Also, besides the church that Natalene and her mother occasionally attend, the school is the only institution available to Natalene that can help her acquire facts, concepts, skills, and appreciations important for developing her moral character as much as it might be. Finally, the culture of the people living in Natalene's neighborhood is an additional difficulty. According to that culture, communication with governmental institutions is to take place only when necessary;[9] and public schools serve mainly the interests of white people.[10] The prevalence of these attitudes not only reinforces sentiments in Natalene's family, but also reduces her chances of having friends with different outlooks.

NATALENE'S NEEDS

By describing the aspects in which Natalene has become a moral agent and gives promise of developing as one, we have provided a basis for determining some of what needs to be done for her moral education. By describing the environmental factors that threaten her growth as a moral agent, we have furnished a ground for determining what else has to be done for her moral education.

Her Moral Education Needs

Natalene, we have pointed out, has and enjoys definite liberties. Yet, even though these freedoms suggest some growth on her part toward moral agency, they certainly do not constitute the freedom that marks such agency. Moral agents, who act voluntarily, accept responsibility for what they do. While Natalene might have a sense of responsibility for what she does in playing games, she does not even recognize what she is freely doing to herself in some important ways. For instance, she is not aware that staying home from school as much as she does will severely limit her development as a moral agent. She also is not aware that passing her mornings regularly in TV cartoon watching might eventually make her intellectually passive and restricted.

Moreover, what one does freely as a moral agent has to be justifiable. Moral agents, who are rational, cannot do just whatever they want to do; they can do only what they can defend by appeals, ultimately, to the values, rights, duties, and virtues of moral agency. While Natalene has begun learning to defend her actions to her mother and grandmother, she has not started to learn to appeal to the norms of moral agency in any extensive way. Finally, moral freedom is a fundamental value of moral agents; it is something that they can never forsake. While Natalene likes the liberties she has, she does not grasp that there are many other freedoms she might have. She does not perceive, either, that freedom is generally estimable. Certainly, her mother does not show her that freedom is a basic value.

Even though Natalene's store of knowledge is relevant to her everyday life, it is quite limited: It does not contain the facts, concepts, and intellectual skills and appreciations that will prepare her to comprehend and act in the wider world in which she lives. Much of what she is missing are the familiar school subjects of reading, arithmetic, science, social studies, history, drawing, and singing. Something else she could learn at school is to interact with and appreciate students outside her neighborhood.[11] Something else absent is the concept of a task. That concept could be learned at school through class assignments and at home through the assignment of chores. Regardless, her learning about tasks could eventually help her understand what full social membership entails and what a moral duty is.

Natalene's purposefulness, which is sporadic and related mainly to fun and security, seems typical of a child her age. Nevertheless, it requires much development in order to approach that of a moral agent. The plainest need is for Natalene to become interested in attaining goals other than fun and security. For instance, she needs to become concerned with developing her game skills, with gaining knowledge, and with drawing pictures. A less obvious need is for Natalene to increase her tendency to think of distant goals, which she can do only when she expands her capacity to understand that actions have results beyond the present. That she has a notion of growing up strong indicates she has at least a rudimentary idea of a remote goal. It would help further if she had an opportunity to form a notion of what she wants to do when she grows up, such as, being a nurse like Grandmother Turner. But there are closer goals to think about, such as birthdays, Easter egg hunts, going to bed with the idea of getting up to go to school, doing a homework assignment today so that it can be turned in tomorrow, and thinking of something to do on the weekend after the school week is ended.

Other purpose-related qualities that Natalene should acquire are delayed gratification and hopefulness. These qualities make sense only with respect to a distant goal. In addition, delayed gratification makes sense only with reference to means for attaining such a goal that are unpleasant in themselves; and hope makes sense only with respect to obstacles to be overcome in attaining such a goal. Accordingly, Natalene can learn to delay gratification and to become hopeful only as she learns to conceive and act toward remote goals. At the same time, her gaining the capacity to delay gratification and to be hopeful will support her disposition to formulate and work toward such goals. Who would be interested in distant goals if we were always disposed to seek immediate satisfaction or if we had no hope of attaining them?

Natalene's sense of evaluation is limited, relying principally on fun and security for its tests of value. So far, no conflict between these criteria has arisen for her, but one eventually might. Security is sometimes dull or unpleasant, and fun is sometimes dangerous. When she does encounter a conflict of this sort, she will have to have an underlying standard by which she can resolve it. That standard, we submit, should be a norm of moral agency. Meanwhile, there are principles that she needs to be cultivating now.

Fairness, we have pointed out, is a concept she has learned in her game playing. With pedagogical guidance, she could expand the concept to cover all other areas of rule-governed interpersonal activity. In developing the concept of fairness, she would be in a position to begin acquiring also a sense of justification as a value. To appeal to fairness means to be prepared to cite a rule; and to cite a rule to support a claim is to provide a reason, or justification, for the claim.

Other principles that have connections with play and other areas of Natalene's life are friendliness, politeness, and truthfulness. Friendliness is appropriate for governing the relationship she has with her regular playmates and classmates. Politeness is relevant for regulating her relationship with new playmates and adults outside her family. Truthfulness is certainly germane to settling disputes in play and elsewhere. In resolving a charge of unfairness, one not only has to appeal to a relevant rule but also to relevant facts. Stating the facts entails truthfulness. This quality also is involved in a child's learning to be responsible for actions. Children can become voluntary agents only if they recognize that their actions have consequences. That voluntary agents know that their actions have consequences means that they are accountable for those outcomes. Thus, children learn to be fully accountable for their actions by owning up to any actions of theirs that have brought about unpleasant results.

While industriousness is a quality often associated with just the work place, it may be seen as a standard appropriate to moral agents. Being autonomous doers, moral agents are not industrious in the sense of busily and tirelessly performing tasks at the behest of others. They are industrious, rather, in the sense that they opportunely and energetically do things of moral worth by their own initiative. For Natalene and other children, the seed of industriousness lies in play, not in chores. Children naturally are busy and energetic in their games and other ludic activities. They usually learn to do tasks and other chores, however, under the direction of others. Teaching Natalene to perform tasks industriously might profitably start, then, by assigning activities that might be fun. Like other students, however, Natalene will start performing onerous activities energetically only when she perceives them as activities which for moral reasons she wants to perform. When she begins to perform chores and other tasks for reasons of her own, she will no longer be performing them as tasks except in name only. Moral industry might help provide Natalene with a sense of confidence and dignity as a moral agent. These qualities in turn might strengthen the value that she places on freedom, knowledge, and the other factors of moral agency.

That Natalene has not yet assumed the quality of deliberativeness should not be surprising. It is more difficult to learn than evaluativeness. Deliberation presupposes a puzzlement about how to attain an end in view: One does not know any way to reach the end, or one does know what is the right way to attain it. Moreover, deliberation entails that an agent be acquainted with the facts of the situation of concern, for example, identifications of other agents, obstacles, and opportunities. Deliberation also requires an awareness of alternative courses of action for achieving the entertained goal. It further involves one's being able to forecast consequences likely to occur by taking one or another of these courses of action. In addition, deliberation presupposes that an agent possesses a set of norms suitable for evaluating the various courses of action being entertained. Finally, it requires that an agent be able to weigh these courses of action according to the norms used in view of the end to be attained, the facts of the situation, and projected consequences.

In her present situation Natalene lives largely by routine, following established actions. Thus, she has few if any perplexities about achieving her purposes. Until she becomes puzzled about how to achieve some aims, she will not be interested in the other aspects of deliberation. Indeed, her intellect is not developmentally ready to engage in the forecasting of consequences and the weighing of alternatives in any full-blown way. She can begin feeling perplexed if she entertains ends that she does not know how to reach. They might be as immediate and insignificant as new games and TV cartoons. They might be as remote but important as wondering how she can get rich and be a nurse. They might be as urgent and important as wondering how she can have clean clothes and do better in school.

Meanwhile, there are facts that Natalene needs to understand about her situation. Her mother is a drug addict. Her mother's addiction possibly caused irreparable damage to her young brother. Her mother and other women in the area have never held jobs, but her grandmother once worked and most other women outside the project have jobs. While her mother and some others in the neighborhood have never been married, her grandmother and some others in the area have been. Indeed, most mothers outside the project are married. School is a place where she can learn new and interesting things. In absorbing the facts mentioned about her mother and grandmother, Natalene will be in a position to think of them as they relate to her as possible courses of action. One consequence of drug addiction by a woman is that it can damage the life chances of her offspring. Work is something that women do. Unmarried mothers usually do not work for a living and must live on public welfare. In perceiving school as a place for new and attractive experiences, Natalene will be better prepared to acquire additional facts, concepts, skills, and norms that will contribute to her growth in deliberation.

Her Environmental Educational Needs

It is not enough, however, to consider just the shortcomings in Natalene that must be remedied if she is to gain the character of a moral agent. It is also necessary to determine what needs to be done about the environmental elements influencing her as a prospective moral agent.

If Ms. Turner ceased to be a negative, albeit passive, role model for her daughter and actively encouraged her daughter's moral education, she would improve the chances of that education's success. As far as one can tell, however, she presently is in no position to direct her daughter in any endeavor. One reason is that she has largely abandoned the responsibility of caring for her children: She has left her son under the care of her mother; she frequently does not awake to look after Natalene; and she has not made an effort to see what can be done about Natalene's school problems. Another reason is that she has centered her interest on a crack-induced fantasy world, seeking escape from her dreary everyday world. If Ms. Turner is to make a positive contribution to Natalene's moral education, she too will have to develop morally. She will need to overcome her drug addiction, gain control of her life, and accept her parental responsibilities. Meanwhile, there is some solace in the fact that Ms. Turner will not provide her daughter with any active guidance; for she will not seek to prevent Natalene from acquiring the virtues of moral agency.

This lack of interference will help Natalene to be open to whatever support her grandmother might be able to furnish.[12] As suggested by the drug addiction of two of her children, Grandmother Turner's record of success in moral guidance is mixed. This record, however, might not be due decisively to any pedagogical deficiencies on her part. Peer influence and cultural milieu might have overwhelmed any impact that she might have had on her errant children. Regardless, the grandmother is the person best qualified to give Natalene definite moral guidance. She knows Natalene well, likes her, lives near her, and has the time to take care of her. Also, Natalene likes and trusts her grandmother. Yet, no matter how well qualified Grandmother Turner is, she needs help to be as effective as she might be. She requires authority, formal or informal, as well as increased financial assistance to become the guardian of Natalene and her brother. She has to have direction from Natalene's school on what to do about her granddaughter's school problems. Also, she should seek insight and comfort through shared experience with other mothers and grandmothers in the neighborhood who are concerned about the moral plight of their children and grandchildren.

While the violence and drug trade on the fringe of Natalene's environment cannot soon be eliminated, they might not engulf the child if certain steps are presently taken by Natalene's aunts and by the morally concerned adults living in her neighborhood.[13] The aunts, both of whom have jobs, need to visit their mother not only to see her, but also to encourage Natalene to work hard in school, to stay away from drugs, to get a job when she finishes, and not to have children until she is married to a responsible man. Frequent, not just occasional, visits by the aunts will help give Natalene the impression that members of her family can retain control of their lives. Also, the morally concerned parents and grandparents of Natalene's playmates have to persuade their children and grandchildren to be responsible students and to look forward to self-sustaining lives. Aunts and uncles who have assumed responsible lives outside the neighborhood need to reinforce the urgings of the parents and grandparents. By being determined that their young family members will grow up and lead decent lives, these people will jointly create cultural and peer pressure that will favor the neighborhood children's moral development, Natalene's included.

Family and neighborhood members are not the only environmental agents that must help promote Natalene's moral education. If Grandmother Turner is to receive additional money and authorization to be Natalene's guardian, she has to be aided by the social welfare agency that deals with her neighborhood. To help her, that agency might have to relax some of its rules. Natalene's grandmother and other morally responsible adults in the neighborhood often talk with each other on front stoops, sidewalks, and playgrounds; thus, they can employ such informal arrangements for discussing the neighborhood children's moral problems. Nevertheless, there will be times when these people will need a facility for more or less formal gatherings. For economy's sake, it should be a multiuse hall, serving as a social and recreation center as well as a room for formal meetings. To obtain that facility, the neighborhood members will need the cooperation of the agency in charge of their housing project. Also, after getting the hall, they will have to have assistance from that agency and perhaps the police to ensure that the facility does not become a gang hangout.

While it is possible that the morally responsible adults in Natalene's neighborhood will spontaneously come together and work on the moral problems facing their children and grandchildren, it is much more likely that they will interact regularly about these problems only if they have leadership. One of their own members who comprehends the problems, who recognizes the need for neighborhood action, who is not afraid to talk with city officials, and who has the trust of the other members should provide the leadership. If it does not come from within the neighborhood, it will have to come from a church, a politician, a charitable foundation, a school, or even a professional neighborhood organizer.

So far, in discussing what needs to be done by Natalene's family members, by her neighbors, and by institutional agencies, we have had very little to say about Natalene's school. While this silence does not intend that the school should not undergo adjustments, it does emphasize that the school is not the only factor in Natalene's environment that has to change to enhance the prospects of her moral education. To be sure, what needs to be done by the school is vital; it just is not all that is important. An additional point about needed changes in the school is that they cannot be made in isolation from other elements in Natalene's environment.

One thing that school officials have to do is find out who is to function as Natalene's guardian. They can learn about Grandmother Turner from the appropriate welfare agency. Next, the school should establish close contact with Grandmother Turner and work regularly with her on Natalene's class difficulties. This means that the school will have to be personable and friendly toward her, trying to build the trust and confidence that the grandmother, a school dropout, must have to assume responsibility for looking after her granddaughter's academic work. Moreover, the school should attempt to work with the parents and grandparents of other underclass students. Because other underclass students in the school are quite likely to influence Natalene, they should be responsible students, valuing academic work and appropriate conduct.[14] Those students from her neighborhood, we have proposed, will come under the guidance of the morally concerned adults there. Those from other underclass neighborhoods will probably require neighborhood guidance, too. How such guidance is to emerge and what procedures it is to follow will depend on the circumstances of the particular neighborhoods. This uncertainty, however, does not obscure the point that Natalene's moral education poses needs not only for her family, neighborhood, and school, but also for other neighborhoods. In any event, her school must work closely with the parents and grandparents of the other neighborhoods on the academic problems of their children and grandchildren. Finally, the school needs to ensure that the objectives, content, and pedagogical methods it proposes for Natalene and other underclass students are relevant to their developmental levels, interests, and learning styles.

PROPOSED PROGRAM OF MORAL EDUCATION

For Natalene Turner, moral education is neither irrelevant nor hopeless. It is not beside the point because she has qualities as a prospective moral agent, and it is not futile because what needs to be done for her moral education can, practically speaking, be done. What has to be done presupposes neither a utopian society nor a political revolution; it requires only manageable changes in the lives of involved moral agents and in the practices of related agencies. That these changes are manageable does not mean that they can be made with great confidence or with ease. Indeed, the measures that we are about to propose for Natalene's moral education are intricate and demanding, thereby involving uncertainty and difficulty. As far as I can tell, however, there is no sure and simple way to deal with Natalene Turner's situation.

While we believe that the proposals to be presented will amply illustrate an application of our moral education theory to a particular situation in the United States today, we do not intend that they are the only measures which might connect that theory with that situation. The application of a normative theory to a particular situation depends largely on one's understanding of the theory, one's knowledge of the facts of the situation, and one's forecast of the possible outcomes of alternative courses of action. In relating our theory of moral education to Natalene Turner's case, we assume that neither our understanding of the theory nor our awareness of the facts of her situation is at stake. What is open to question is our estimate of the consequences that should occur from the implementation of the recommendations that we make. We might be wrong in our predictions of what ought to happen; we might have failed to recognize some possible results suggested by our proposals. Accordingly, different recommendations could be made in view of a different reading of the possible consequences of competing courses of action. Despite this point, we shall present our recommendations for Natalene's moral education without considering alternatives that come to mind. This procedure provides convenience, but it also keeps us from saying that our proposals are the best conceivable. Our objective, however, is not to find the best or even one of the best solutions to Natalene's case; it is only to help show how our idea of moral education might operate in the real world of the United States.

The proposals we have in mind are very limited in scope: They constitute a short-range program aiming to do nothing more than head Natalene toward optimal moral development. An attempt to formulate an extended program would not only be cumbersome but also would be of dubious value. It would presume that the events and circumstances for the next 10 years of Natalene's life would be predictable, which they likely would not be. It would make more sense to develop Natalene's program of moral education as she undergoes change and foreseeable conditions appear. At any rate, the recommendations constituting our program for Natalene's moral education fall in two categories. Category I consists of those measures intended to remedy deficiencies in Natalene's environment; Category II consists of those meant to remedy Natalene's own deficiencies.

Category I Recommendations

For Natalene's sake, her mother should undergo moral education. This education will take a relatively long time and should be coordinated with other measures to be implemented. Earlier, we said that Ms. Turner needs to overcome her drug addiction, to gain control of her life, and to accept her parental responsibilities. Because she can neither gain control of her life nor assume her parental responsibilities until she has defeated her addiction, she must begin her moral education by eliminating this impediment to her freedom of action. Hence, she has to enter, again, a drug rehabilitation program. Like the one she experienced in jail, this one too has to be publicly financed; but unlike the former, this one is to last as long as it takes for her to be rid of her addiction. Much is involved in an effective drug rehabilitation program. But whatever else is involved in the one for Ms. Turner, it must help her see that the freedom she regains through treatment is to be cherished and preserved by her and not to be used by her as a means for returning to crack and thus losing that freedom. We do not imagine that Ms. Turner all by herself will arise one morning and decide to take the cure. We do think it conceivable, however, that her two responsible sisters, her mother, some sympathetic neighbors, a social worker, and perhaps a minister might persuade her to enroll in a program. To be successful, they will have to overcome any opposition from Ms. Turner's current boyfriend; or they will have to deal with her between boyfriends.

But even if Natalene's mother enrolls in and successfully completes an effective drug rehabilitation program, she still will not be in control of her life. She will not have a sense of specific purpose for her life, nor will she have an environment in which to live on her own other than a public housing project, where the temptations to return to drugs will be strong for her. She can obtain this sense of purpose and an appropriate place to live if she acquires a job. Before she can take a job, however, she will need to enter a public vocational education program. This program should include not only vocational counseling and job training, but also instruction in adult literacy, inculcation in a work ethic, and job placement. While she is still in drug rehabilitation and then when she is in vocational education, she ought to live with one of her employed sisters. In the evenings and on weekends she should have regular visits from her daughter, son, and mother; but she also should receive parental education. This may be provided by a social welfare agency or by a public school. It should include instruction not only in the daily routine of caring for one's children, but also in the moral aspects of sexual conduct, including forecasts of its consequences and acceptance of responsibility for those consequences.

When Grandmother Turner assumes authority as Natalene's guardian, she must have an attitude of hopefulness: She must believe that what she and others do for Natalene's moral education will be effective. She can acquire this attitude if she understands that she will have help from neighbors and governmental agencies and thus will not be working alone with her granddaughter, as she did with her children. But she can gain this understanding only if she develops an attitude of trust toward governmental agencies, especially the housing authority and Natalene's school. As will soon be explained, there are steps that these agencies can take to help build this trust. It will help also if Grandmother Turner remembers that one of her children finished high school and has a steady job. In addition, it will help if the grandmother learns from other neighborhood adults about school successes of any of their children.

Once Grandmother Turner has developed this trust, she should make a practice of visiting Natalene's school to observe the milieu in which Natalene is taught and to keep in touch with Natalene's teacher about her granddaughter's academic problems. At home, Grandmother Turner must see to it that there are some books and magazines for herself, Natalene, and Natalene's brother to look at and read. She has to encourage Natalene and her brother to watch educational programming on television, not just cartoons. She should make a practice of telling and reading stories to Natalene and her brother at bedtime. She ought to give Natalene some suitable chores to do about the apartment. Finally, she has to see to it that Natalene and her brother develop habits of personal cleanliness, have clean changes of clothing, and eat nutritional foods.

Grandmother Turner is not the only one in the neighborhood who has to develop attitudes of hopefulness and trust. All the other morally responsible adults have to acquire these dispositions, too. Furthermore, they all have to work with their respective children and grandchildren in ways similar to those just recommended for Grandmother Turner. Nevertheless, there also are things that all the concerned adults, including Grandmother Turner, have to learn to do as a group. Most obviously, they need to learn to work as a group. To do this, they have to perceive themselves as sharing problems of moral education for the children of the neighborhood. They have to establish regular means for communicating their concerns with one another. They should be able to recognize some party as their leader or leaders. They need to be able to develop an agenda of action. Finally, they must be prepared, intellectually as well as emotionally, to discuss the agenda with appropriate governmental officials.

Moreover, they have to learn to organize themselves for implementing whatever measures they and officials agree upon. They should know how to develop a talent bank among themselves that is relevant to the measures to be implemented. If, for instance, they accept responsibility for operating and maintaining a neighborhood meeting hall, they need be able to identify those members fit and willing to take care of this responsibility. If they decide that the neighborhood meeting hall is to be reserved at certain times as a place of study with tutors available, they need to identify, without causing embarrassment for anyone, those members who can and would serve as tutors. If they decide that there should be regular trips by the children to the community library or that there ought to be a book and magazine exchange among the children and adults, they have to be able to enlist those members who know about the library or who are interested in operating such an exchange. Lastly, the concerned adults as a group have to learn to monitor the effectiveness of the measures they implement, seeking remedies where difficulties are found and finding alternatives for failed measures. They also have to review with one another and school officials the progress and problems their children and grandchildren are experiencing in school. Thereby, they will be able to present their individual concerns with the thrust of an articulated group interest.

Even though the housing, welfare, and school agencies dealing with Natalene's neighborhood have sincerely tried, through outreach programs, to help the people there with their problems, they have found the people to be somewhat unresponsive, noncommittal, and skeptical. To remove these barriers, these agencies must make sure that they do not intimidate the neighborhood inhabitants, that they gain their confidence, and that they demonstrate, not just explain, to the inhabitants what they can do for them.

To do these things in working with the neighborhood's responsible adults about the moral development of its children, the agencies must take several steps. First, the agencies must adopt the attitude that this group of people, despite their many social shortcomings, possess much knowledge about their neighborhood and that they also have a sense of what will and will not work in their neighborhood and for their children. Second, the agencies should be disposed to work with the neighborhood group and not try to manipulate it into adopting some preconceived plan of the agencies. Third, the agencies have to learn to let this group of adults take the initiative in calling meetings and drawing up an agenda of action. Fourth, the agencies ought to know how to offer, not impose, their expertise. In discussions with the group, for instance, they should point out what they perceive as logical problems, likely outcomes, and the feasibility of proposed measures. They may suggest alternative measures when such are needed and the neighborhood group can think of none. They also may indicate problematic areas not covered by the proposed measures under discussion. But they must solicit critical comments from the group on their proffered expertise and be willing to modify their recommendations in view of justified criticism. Fifth, the agencies must be ready to follow through on their commitments to the group. If they encounter unanticipated insuperable obstacles, they should report that fact to the group and then help find an alternative course. Finally, the agencies must cooperate with the group in evaluating the measures that they have implemented for the moral education of the neighborhood children. This not only will enable the agencies to share with the group what they see as strengths and weaknesses in the measures, but it also will enable the group to share with the agencies what it sees as strengths and weaknesses. As a result, the group and the agencies will have a basis for considering revisions.

Category II Measures

Natalene, we pointed out, has numerous deficiencies as a prospective moral agent. Her school can do much to overcome them as long as it receives reinforcement from her home and neighborhood. The Category I proposals, we believe, will provide the support her school requires.

To develop the freedom appropriate to a moral agent, Natalene needs to learn to accept responsibility for her actions, to act for good reasons, and to respect freedom as a basic moral value. Acceptance of moral responsibility for an action is acknowledgment of oneself as the voluntary cause of the action, including its immediate consequences, and thus as accountable for the action. If, therefore, one accepts responsibility for an action that is morally right, one is open to praise as a moral agent; and if one accepts responsibility for an action that is morally wrong, one is liable to rebuke as a moral agent.

At school Natalene can learn to accept responsibility as a moral agent in informal as well as formal ways. On the school grounds or in the classroom, her teacher may put relevant questions to her about problematic conduct: Did she do such and such? Did somebody else make her do it? Did she know what she was doing? Why did she do it? The teacher may also put suitable questions to her about the failure to do assignments: Did she do the given assignment? Why not? Does she know why it is important to her to do the assignment? Regardless of the informal context, the point of the questioning is not to discourage, embarrass, or intimidate Natalene; it is, rather, to guide her into reflecting on the connection between herself and her actions. Natalene's teacher, therefore, should make her questioning brief, timely, and constructive. Some circumstances might warrant humor and gentleness; others might warrant seriousness and firmness. At all times, however, the teacher must convey her concern about Natalene's need to accept responsibility for her actions. In the respect that the questioning will stimulate Natalene to think of reasons for her actions, it will introduce her to the process of justifying her actions.

The formal way in which Natalene can learn to accept responsibility is her study of academic subjects, especially reading and history. In Aesop's fable of the ants and the grasshopper, for instance, Natalene can easily recognize that the ants are hard working and prudent but not much fun, while the grasshopper is lazy, imprudent, but fun loving, a trait with which she is likely to sympathize. But after some discussion of the story she soon might see also that the ants and the grasshopper

are responsible for their respective activities and thus that the grasshopper later has no one to blame but himself for being hungry. Natalene or
some other student, however, might ask if the grasshopper should starve
to death just because he is responsible for his hunger. Would not the
ants be mean if they did not share some of their food with the grasshopper? But, another student might ask, what if the ants do not have enough
to share? Even if they do, what about next year, and the year after that?
Is it right for the ants to have to care for the grasshopper the rest of his
life when he could look after himself? Yet, what if the grasshopper
played music that the ants liked while they were working? Should not
they give him food for the enjoyment that he gives them? Maybe the
ants and the grasshopper could make an agreement based on their respective responsibilities: The ants store enough food for the grasshopper
as well as themselves, and the grasshopper plays music that the ants
like.

History offers Natalene opportunities to see responsibility in different
aspects. It enables her to see which personages did what things. It helps
her to identify people who admit to their misdeeds and those who deny
them. It gives her a chance to learn about the making and keeping of
promises. And it enables her to distinguish between individual and group
responsibility. Simple biographies of George Washington, Harriet Tub-
man, Abraham Lincoln, Booker T. Washington, Harry S. Truman, Martin Luther King, Jr., and other historical figures can supply lessons in
the acceptance of individual responsibility. Stories of wars, the struggle
for civil rights, and other national events can furnish lessons in the acceptance of group responsibility.

In studying about responsibility in reading and history, Natalene can
learn about the justification of actions, too. More specifically, she will
be able to see that people frequently have reasons for the things that
they do, and that some of these reasons are good and some are not. Did
the ants have good reasons for withholding food from the grasshopper?
Assuming that George Washington did cut down his father's favorite
cherry tree, should he have confessed to the deed? Why should Abraham Lincoln have walked 24 miles to repay a debt of just a few pennies?
Should anyone, such as Martin Luther King, Jr., place his or her life in
danger for the sake of other people?

Before Natalene can perceive freedom as a fundamental value of her
and other moral agents' lives, she needs to understand several points
about it. First, freedom has enormous instrumental worth. It enables
Natalene and other people to pursue and develop their respective interests. Also, it helps them acquire new interests. Second, neither Natalene
nor others are morally free to do just anything she or they might want
to do. People ought to do only things that they can justify. Because they
share freedom as a basic value, they must not interfere with one an-

other's justifiable freedoms and should help each other secure and foster those freedoms on occasion. In other words, Natalene and her classmates must acquire a rudimentary understanding of the Criterion of Moral Rights. The third, and last, point for Natalene to learn is that freedom is reflexive. An action done freely might enable the repetition of similar actions done freely; it might lead to a different sort of action done freely; or it might lead to action done forcedly. Accordingly, Natalene has to realize that free action must be rational if it is to be preserved.

Literature and history can tell Natalene about the struggle of individuals and groups to be free in their lives. Science, even at an elementary level, can help her sense the importance of intellectual freedom but also the opportunities and problems for freedom posed by scientific technology. In addition, science can help her grasp that there are physical consequences for human actions. The enforcement of rules of conduct can enable Natalene to experience the negative as well as the positive reflexivity of free conduct. Moreover, if Natalene's teacher attends to her students's respective interests and learning styles in selecting content and method, she will make it possible for Natalene and the other students to appreciate freedom because of what they do in class.

Other aspects of moral agency where Natalene suffers deficiencies are knowledge, purposefulness, evaluativeness, and deliberativeness. The difficulty with the knowledge she possesses is not just that it lacks the concepts, facts, and skills that she needs to succeed in school, but also that it lacks information and skills relating to life beyond her family, neighborhood, and TV world. Knowledge about this extended range of life is crucial for the growth of her capacity to make free choices. The study of language arts, social studies, and art can help expand her perspective of life opportunities. Field trips by her class can help. Also, interaction with classmates from middle- and upperclass neighborhoods can help. Yet, no knowledge that Natalene has of life opportunities beyond her everyday world will serve her to take advantage of any of those opportunities if it does not prepare her to choose an opportunity in which she is interested. While the fact that a black woman legally can have a career as a business executive or physician, even become President of the United States, might suggest a life opportunity to Natalene, it alone will not enable her to seize that opportunity if she ever wants to. It is important, therefore, that what Natalene learns in school about the extended world increases in tandem with changes in her interests and abilities.

Following from her desires for fun and security, Natalene can learn to seek new purposes, for example, friendship, physical and intellectual skills, knowledge, and aesthetic expression. For instance, she probably will make friends initially with classmates who are fun or protective.

After a while, however, she might learn to cherish these people in their own right when she recognizes that they share some of her interests. Also, she likely will acquire and improve physical skills, knowledge, and aesthetic expression if she finds it fun or comforting to do so. But she might come to see these as matters to be had for their own sakes if, eventually, she recognizes that the attainment of these objects increases and becomes a part of her control of herself as an agent. It is vital for the growth of a sense of hopefulness in Natalene that some of her goals in school are proximate and attainable without unusual difficulty, but it is also important for the development of her purposefulness that she learn to conceive and attain goals more or less distant. To help Natalene in this regard, her teacher might start by giving assignments to be turned in a day later and continue subsequently by making assignments to be finished at the end of a week. Her teacher can help further by encouraging Natalene occasionally to think of a project on her own and to name a day when she will have it finished.

Natalene, we have explained, is not totally bereft of the power of evaluation; for she does seem to make at least prudential judgments, however dimly and unsystematically, by appealing to fun, security, and fairness. Freedom, we have indicated, is something that Natalene can learn in school to hold as a moral criterion. But there are other qualities, too, we have suggested, that she can and should acquire in school as moral standards. She can learn to see fairness as worthy not just because it might be to her advantage, but also because it applies to all students, teachers, and citizens committed to interacting with one another under certain rules. She might come to value rationality not only in academic subjects but also in games, other play activities, and class conduct, where appeals to rules by students as well as teachers are common. She can cultivate friendliness when interacting with students who appear to have interests similar to hers, whereas she might learn politeness when interacting with students who do not seem to have interests in common with hers. She can acquire truthfulness initially under the supervision of her teacher and grandmother, who are in positions to know when she is telling the truth. She can learn subsequently, through interactions with students and through stories, that people have to be truthful with one another if they are to get along. Much later she can learn about the conditions under which it is acceptable to lie. Industriousness, being a quality of habits, is not something she can learn as a special habit. Natalene, accordingly, can learn to be industrious only by seizing opportunities promptly and by working diligently to attain purposes undertaken. Her teacher can help here by providing Natalene with opportunities in academic assignments, in class discussions, and in recreation that excites her interest and allows the flow of energized action. Her teacher can help further by monitoring Natalene's progress, seeing to it that she does not daydream or act impulsively, that she understands what she is to do, and that she does not get hung up on snags.

CONCLUSIONS

By themselves, the recommendations that we have made for Natalene Turner's moral education are far from adequate for the optimal development of her moral character. Being focused mainly on what needs to be done for the next 2 years at most, they are sufficient for nothing more than starting Natalene in the direction of full moral growth. Natalene has about 9 more years of schooling to undergo. During that time there probably will be changes affecting her moral education which will require measures other than the ones we have put forth but which cannot be presently anticipated.

It is well known that students performing below grade level early in school will probably continue having academic difficulties in school. So, even if Natalene began to like school and to work hard at her studies, she would likely perform below normal academic levels; and she might slip further behind in another year or two. If she did, should she be put in remedial classes, separating her and other sublevel students from those performing satisfactorily? Should she and all other students have classes together without opportunities for remediation? Should remedial studies be done in the evenings at neighborhood centers and all classes at school be in common? That any of these or some other alternative should be followed would depend on presently unforeseeable circumstances. Would separate classes in Natalene's school engender invidious distinctions in the eyes of the students? Would separate remedial classes be effective for Natalene and the other students? Would those classes tend to hurt Natalene's or other students' life chances? Would Natalene's neighborhood center be effective for overcoming her particular shortcomings?

Another eventuality that presently is obscure is the outcome of the drug rehabilitation and vocational training of Natalene's mother. Will Ms. Turner give up drugs once and for all and get a job? If she does, should she resume responsibility for Natalene and her son? If she does not, what ought to be done for her; and are Natalene and her brother to live indefinitely with Grandmother Turner? Also, it is impossible to tell now whether or not the morally responsible members of Natalene's neighborhood will persist in their efforts to maintain and encourage conditions supportive of the moral education of the neighborhood's children. Will they maintain a necessary level of motivation? Will they decrease their efforts because of ennui? Will they become overwhelmed by an increase in neighborhood gang activity? Moreover, we cannot presently foresee what specific moral educational measures would be required to deal with problems posed by Natalene's entry into pubescence and puberty. Some sort of sex education presumably would be appropriate, but whether it should take place at school, at home, at the neighborhood center, or at all would have something to do with the likely effectiveness of sex education at each of these institutions. In addition, the specific content and methods of that education would bear on what Natalene and other students already know and feel about sex. We know, generally speaking, that we want them to delay an active sexual life until they, unlike Natalene's mother, are in a position to control it, that is, until they are largely in control of themselves. But what specific content and methods would serve that purpose cannot be projected 4 or 5 years into the future.

Finally, it is unclear what the job market will be for Natalene when she is preparing for an occupation. In the United States today, the rate of unemployment for blacks is the worst for any racial employee group; it is, for instance, more than twice as great as that for whites.[15] Under present job-market conditions, therefore, one has reason to believe that Natalene would have an unusually difficult time in securing a job. If, therefore, Natalene is to find employment, she must do all that she can to make herself attractive to the job market. But what sort of vocational studies would effectively prepare her for an occupation of interest to her, even if it were not her first choice? Yet, knowing the answer to this question would not be the same thing as knowing if a job would be available for Natalene when she finished school. Will there be some way to link vocational training with the labor market in such a way that successful trainees would likely find jobs? There probably could be a way, and it probably would require policy cooperation among government and industry at local and national levels. But if educators, politicians, and business executives could not or would not work out a more sensible relationship between vocational training and the job market than what we now have, they would consign Natalene to a life where work is uncertain and poverty a strong likelihood. We then would face a dreadful question for her moral education: Just what moral virtues should be taught to prepare her for a life with minimal economic opportunity? A better question, however, would be, what moral virtues should be taught so that the nation's leaders would be sure to devise policies that would provide Natalene with a fair economic opportunity?

Even though the moral education program described above pertains to Natalene Turner in particular, it has significance for other people in the underclass. It makes recommendations for the other children in Natalene's neighborhood and for classmates from other underclass neighborhoods. It sets forth proposals relating to all responsible adults in the neighborhoods directly and indirectly affecting Natalene's moral development. It includes measures for Natalene's mother that would probably speak to other mothers like her. Finally, it recommends actions for public agencies of welfare, housing, and schooling that ought to be pursued by such agencies in attempts to improve conditions for the moral education of many other children of the underclass. Nevertheless, the program is no panacea. It has little to say for Natalene's brother and other underclass children with behavioral disorders. It is silent on the possibilities of moral education for underclass gang members. Also, while it speaks to moral education for underclass students at public schools, which the vast majority of underclass students attend, it is concerned only with a racially and socially integrated school. Many underclass students attend schools without racial and social integration. Accordingly, applications of our moral education theory to cases involving these other conditions would likely lead to proposals different, at least in part, from those that we have advanced for Natalene Turner.

NOTES

1. Ken Auletta, *The Underclass* (New York: Random House, 1983). Christopher Jencks, "Is the American Underclass Growing?" in *The Urban Underclass*, edited by Christopher Jencks and Paul E. Peterson (Washington, DC: The Brookings Institution, 1991), pp. 28–100. William Julius Wilson, "Public Policy Research and The Truly Disadvantaged," in Jencks and Peterson, *The Urban Underclass*, esp. pp. 474–476.

2. Between 1960 and 1990, the rate of illegitimacy among white births went from 5 to 22%. During the 1980s, according to one study, 44% of the births to poor white women in that decade were illegitimate. Some analysts maintain that this increase not only signifies an enlargement of the number of underclass whites but portends as well an increase in the distribution of their numbers beyond Appalachia. Charles Murray, "The Coming White Underclass," *The Wall Street Journal* (October 23, 1993), p. A14.

3. J. David Greenstone attributes this position to William Julius Wilson as well as to Ulf Hannerz. Wilson, however, maintains that he does not subscribe to the view. J. David Greenstone, "Culture, Rationality, and the Underclass," in Jencks and Peterson, *The Urban Underclass*, esp. pp. 401–404. William Julius Wilson, "Public Policy Research and The Truly Disadvantaged," esp. pp. 474–476.

4. Charles Murray, *Losing Ground: American Social Policy, 1950–1980* (New York: Basic Books, 1984).

5. Whether those measures should be targeted at the underclass or should apply to people of all social-economic classes is an issue strongly contested among social policy analysts. See Theda Skocpol, "Targeting within Universalism: Politically Viable Policies to Combat Poverty in the United States," in Jencks and Peterson, *The Urban Underclass*, pp. 411–435. Robert Greenstein, "Universal and Alternative Approaches to Relieving Poverty: An Alternative View," in Jencks and Peterson, *The Urban Underclass*, pp. 437–459.

6. Time limitation has been suggested by President Clinton.

Abolition of public assistance has been proposed by Charles Murray, "The Coming White Underclass," *op. cit.*

7. In 1959, the illegitimacy rate of black births was 15%; in 1964, the rate was 24%; in 1982, 57%. In 1990, the rate had climbed to 68%. William Julius Wilson, *The Truly Disadvantaged: The Inner City, the Underclass, and Public Policy* (Chicago, IL: The University of Chicago Press, 1987), p. 87. Murray, "The Coming White Underclass," p. A14.

8. According to one account, the present frequency of the infants born each year in the United States who were exposed to illegal drugs in the womb is 9%. Michael Ruby, "The Children's Crusade," *U.S. News & World Report* 115 (December 13, 1993), p. 112.

9. Following Paolo Freire, Brian Fay speaks of "the culture of silence" among oppressed people. Brian Fay, "How People Change Themselves: The Relationship Between Critical Theory and Its Audience," in *Critical Theory and Praxis*, edited by Terence Ball (Minneapolis, MN: The University of Minnesota Press, 1977), p. 220. Paolo Freire, *Pedagogy of the Oppressed* (New York: Herder & Herder, 1972).

10. John U. Ogbu, "Understanding Cultural Diversity and Learning," *Educational Researcher* 21 (November 1992), p. 10.

11. Wilson, *The Truly Disadvantaged*, pp. 56–58.

12. For an account of the moral strength and guidance of one actual grandmother of black urban ghetto children, see Alex Kotlowitz, *There Are No Children Here* (New York: Anchor Books, 1991).

13. See Ogbu, "Understanding Cultural Diversity and Learning," esp. pp. 12–13.

14. Jonathan Crane, "Effects of Neighborhoods on Dropping Out of School and Teenage Childbearing," in Jencks and Peterson, *The Urban Underclass*, pp. 299–320. Susan E. Meyer, "How Much Does a High School's Racial and Socioeconomic Mix Affect Graduation and Teenage Fertility Rates?", in Jencks and Peterson, *The Urban Underclass*, pp. 321–341.

15. The figures for November 1993 were 12.2% for blacks and 5.6% for whites. Department of Labor statistics as reported on "The Morning Edition," National Public Radio, December 20, 1993.

9 Moral Education for The Force

The American middle class is widely recognized as having positive features.[1] Its members are law abiding and pay a significant portion of the taxes supporting the nation's social institutions and programs. While the people from middle-class America strive for social-economic advancement, they live modestly and respect everyone's right to equal opportunity. Thus, they are not rich, not even wealthy. Although some are comfortably well off, most contend with strained budgets, brought on by increases in housing costs, medical expenses, and consumer spending.[2] Their occupations range from skilled mechanical trades to sales, school teaching, bank telling, midlevel management, and small business enterprise. All that they insist upon for anyone's social-economic advancement is fairness, including merit. While middle-class Americans are family-oriented, they also are altruistic to an extent. In times of crisis, they make sacrifices for the nation and help the less fortunate although they are reluctant to help the able-bodied who do not try to help themselves. In normal times, they participate in public service organizations, such as the PTA, the Rotary Club, and the Lions. Even though middle-class people rarely are leaders of the United States or adders to the value of the nation's economy, they perhaps are the ones who, by dint of their hard work, prudence, and social responsibility, make it possible for the society to function as well as it does. In the parlance of politicians and pundits, the American middle class is the mainstay of the nation.

To be sure, this group is also well known for its faults. First, it has suffered a streak of selfishness.[3] It has escaped urban problems by fleeing to the suburbs but keeping its jobs in the cities. While it has been willing to help the unfortunate in prosperous times, it has in hard times looked out largely for its own interests, for example, Social Security, Medicare, real estate taxes, and tax deductions on residential mortgage interest. Second, it has tended to be socially intolerant, being adamantly opposed to homosexuality, atheism, minority immigration, and eccentricity, to name only a few objects of its disapproval. Third, it has fostered a rather limited culture, never producing anything of excellence, being content with romances and thrillers in literature, being appreciative of nothing more aesthetic than electronic gadgets, automobiles, and sentimental art, watching mainly sports, game shows, and situation comedies on television, and pondering nothing deeper than how to lose weight and have a comfortable retirement.

Regardless of its faults, the American middle class appears to be a group for which moral education is not likely to be a crucial problem. The members of this group generally esteem in some respect freedom, knowledge, purposefulness, and the other features of moral agency; and they usually assume responsibility for passing on these values to their children. However, even if moral education is not a festering problem for middle-class people as a group, it certainly can be a profound problem for some middle-class individuals. Actual middle-class Americans are far from being perfect moral agents; nor do they always teach their children all the moral virtues. In addition, it is simply a fact that the incidence of moral anarchy has increased among people from middle-class America, especially among its adolescents.[4]

THE CASE OF THE FORCE

Description of the Case

All of the students at Ramstock High School lived in Stonewood, a modest white suburb. Besides its schools, Stonewood contained tract housing, churches, shopping centers, and a recreation complex. Nearby were a vocational institute and a community college, where Ramstock students frequently sought postsecondary education. A majority of Stonewood families had two working parents, with many fathers commuting to skilled jobs at outlying manufacturing plants and mothers driving various distances to employment as nurses, school teachers, secretaries, and clerks. A few of the parents had grown up in the suburb; many planned to retire there.

Irrespective of their occupations, the parents tended to value a pleasant home life as their overarching goal. They took pride in ownership of their houses and in maintenance of their lawns. Fathers and sons shot baskets on parking-pad courts; mothers and daughters took sunbaths on patios. While the parents were not strict in religious observances, they all agreed that church was important. Also, they saved money for annual family vacations and furnished their homes with entertainment facilities, especially audio-video centers. They pampered their children with bicycles, clothes in the latest fads, and cars, usually second hand. They regularly attended Ramstock High's football and basketball games. Despite disagreements, quarrels, and occasional acts of unfaithfulness, the Stonewood divorce rate was below the national average. Reports about increased crime in the nearby metropolis and about loss of business by the local manufacturing plants slightly chilled the feeling of security that the parents had about their way of life, but those stories did not erode the parents' conviction that that way was good. While the parents did not have specific goals for their children as prospective adults, they generally assumed that their children would pursue a way of life similar to Stonewood's. All parents belonged to the suburb's community association, which supervised the recreation complex, watched for zoning violations, and sponsored semi-annual picnics for its members.

Joe, Chris, Ken, Gary, and a few other male students at Ramstock High made up a clique known as "The Force." Most members of this group were good looking; all were seniors, athletic, and disinterested in academics. Ever since coming together, The Force had earned a reputation for excitement and popularity with female students, still called "coeds" by the adults of Stonewood. Indeed, many male students spoke enviously of this pack's members; and some female students longed to have dates with them. During the past year, however, The Force began to be more than smooth operators with female students. They started to engage in aggressive sexual activity, bragging to one another and other students about their conquests. In hallway gossip some of these conquests were sometimes described, accurately, as date rape and gang action. Two girls were even said, also accurately, to have invited The Force over to their houses when their parents were away for the night. Upon hearing some of this talk, Ramstock's guidance counselors informed the school's principal of it. The principal, however, decided that even if the rumored events had occurred, they had taken place off grounds and therefore were of no responsibility to the school.

The parents of the involved female students were not acquainted with the parents of The Force's members, but the former knew one another well enough to discuss what to do jointly about these boys. At their parents' urging, several coeds filed complaints with the district attorney against the members of The Force. Much to the dismay of most Stonewood parents, these charges resulted in indictments for sexual misconduct.

Local news media covered the case closely and extensively. While waiting to stand trial, the members of The Force accepted several invitations to appear on local TV talk shows and discuss their situation. Some of the accusing female students also accepted invitations to appear on programs with The Force. Each of the female students on the programs said she felt worthless because of what had happened to her. Each member of The Force, however, denied he had done anything wrong. Some insisted that their accusers were eager to have sex with them. The mothers of the boys berated the character of the girls, and the fathers tended to refer to their sons as real men. When asked by the media to discuss The Force case, Ramstock's principal declined to comment except to say that the school had no responsibility for what had happened. Shortly afterwards, upon receiving complaints from some parents and an expression of concern from his superintendent, the principal initiated a sex education program at the school. Of the indictments, only two went to trial; both, for lack of decisive evidence, ended in acquittal, just before the new school year began.

Analysis of the Case

Whether or not the members of The Force acted immorally is one question; whether or not they were wanting in moral development is another. Our concern is much more with the latter issue. However appalled we are by the clique's behavior, we are mainly interested in determining what the moral education of the group's members should be. To that end, we do not have to concentrate on their moral culpability; we just have to consider the respect in which moral agency pertains to them.

When one thinks about the members of The Force as moral agents, one wonders just how free they were. It is well established that the biochemical makeup of adolescent youths sometimes involves extraordinarily strong sexual impulses. One wonders, then, if what the members of The Force did ultimately was caused by biochemical interactions. Social scientists have long held that peer pressure is a powerful factor in teenage behavior. Hence, one must wonder if each member acted as he did because of pressure exerted on him by the others. Moreover, psychologists have traditionally distinguished between group and individual psychology, noting that because of group associations people might do things that they would not do as individuals. Thus, one has to wonder if Joe, Chris, Ken, Gary, and the others did what they did because of the dynamics of group membership. Finally, it should be remembered that the boys' fathers regarded them as acting like real men. After all, social scientists have generally agreed that in nuclear families mothers and fathers function as role models respectively for their adolescent daughters and sons. One has to wonder, accordingly, if the members of The Force behaved as they did because of what their fathers had indicated to them about manliness.

While these points evoke some doubt about the freedom of the members of The Force, they surely do not compel the conclusion that these boys were not free. There is no doubt that they had strong sexual drives, but there is no evidence in the case that they were not in control of themselves because of those drives. Perhaps a large majority of teenagers are bedeviled by sexual urges, but most of those who are keep such urges within acceptable bounds. Moreover, there is no reason to think that the peer pressure working on the members of The Force drove any of them to engage in sexual misconduct. The Ramstock male student body did not apply any such pressure on them; if anything, The Force was on the cutting edge of male behavior at the school. Also, there is no evidence that any of the members of The Force was made by other members to participate in sexual assaults. A similar point may be applied to the argument that they were not individually responsible because they were severally acting as elements of a group. Maybe in their gang assaults they did lose control of themselves as individuals. Nevertheless, they were acting as individuals when they arranged their nocturnal visits. Also, not all of their sexual assaults were group efforts; some were performed by the members as individuals. While the boys might have gotten the impression from their fathers that sexual conquest is a mark of masculinity, they quite possibly were acting on their own when they engaged in their assaults. It is one thing to say that a role model encourages a person to act in a certain way; it is quite another thing to say that such a model causes the person to act in that way. So, even if the fathers encouraged their sons to seek sexual conquests, they did not for just that reason make their sons commit sexual assaults.

It is possible, however, that a combination of two or more of the factors described above exerted an influence on these youths that was so powerful that it practically determined what they did. In other words, the influence of these factors might have been so strong that the members of The Force could not have acted otherwise and still be who they were in the situation of concern. Yet, even if this possibility had been an actuality, it would not have eliminated the question of freedom for these youths. If they had committed any or all of their sexual assaults only after they had struggled against whatever influences might have overwhelmed them eventually, they could have argued that they did not act freely. Both on television and in court, however, they allowed that they freely did what they did, which strongly suggests that they had never tried not to do what they did. That they appear not to have resisted their tendency toward sexual assault does allow that they might have been acting freely, but it does not necessarily mean that they were. They might have been so influenced by conditions beyond their control that they never entertained resistance as an option.

But what is to be made of the fact that The Force's members did not express any remorse for what they had done? Does this lack of ruefulness mean they freely would have done what they did even if at the time they were not in a position to act freely? Maybe, but not necessarily; for the lack might indicate that they were sociopathic. That is, it might be that these teenagers were shaped by environmental influences in such a way that they suffered extraordinary hostility and acted it out, with great satisfaction, in their aggressive sexual behavior. There never was, however, either during their earlier lives or during the district attorney's investigation of them, a clinical judgment that any of them was sociopathic.

What we find, then, is that the freedom of The Force was problematic. There are reasons for thinking that the pack's members were not made to do what they did, but there also are reasons for thinking that they were under influences beyond their control. Perhaps their actions were a mixture of freedom and force, which is often the lot of actual people. Yet, even if the members of The Force had acted under compulsion and thus without moral culpability, they were agents for whom freedom was a pertinent quality; for they would not have suffered such conditions, maybe, if their familial, school, and neighborhood environmental influences had been different. Different influences could have promoted freedom extensively in the lives of Joe, Chris, Ken, Gary, and the others. Indeed, they could have encouraged a freedom that would not have opposed moral rectitude in the sexual life of this clique. We shall return to this point later.

Knowledge is another moral quality relating to the members of The Force in a mixed way. While they were, at best, mediocre students in their classes, they were not cognitively subnormal: They were capable of having the knowledge needed to function as moral agents in their everyday lives. The difficulty is that they lacked some important understanding and cognitive skills.

What they knew best were sports. Along with having good skills in football, basketball, and baseball, they could recite the rules of these sports and they had some grasp of the strategies employed in playing them. They also knew something about automobiles. They could identify them by styles and describe them by engine power and configuration. On the other hand, they could not explain how engine power is measured or why some engines had an in-line configuration while others had a V or slant configuration. Nor could they explain engine combustion according to Boyle's law of gasses. In their class life they knew how to pass courses with minimal effort and inconvenience. They signed up for courses and teachers regarded as undemanding. They got female students to help them with homework and to study for tests, and they relied on crib sheets from time to time. Finally, they knew how to attract, impress, and excite coeds. Besides their good looks and well-formed physiques, they had trendy haircuts, clothes, and cars. They also took their dates to rock concerts as well as to restaurants popular with Ramstock students.

One major cognitive shortcoming The Force had was its egocentric perspective. This clique's members understood their actions mainly from the standpoint of what they liked and valued; they did not consider that their perspective might not be shared by other people, especially by the victims of their sexual assaults. Another serious cognitive failing was that these boys were not given to asking moral questions. A possible explanation for this was that they were not aware of what morality is in its ordinary descriptive sense. Certainly, they did not think it notable that they or others might be voluntary and interpersonal agents. They did not regard voluntary and interpersonal actions as suitable for special consideration. Also, they did not allow, in their minds or in their statements, that there might be regulations of voluntary and interpersonal conduct that are superior to all other sorts, including their code of fun and excitement. Finally, The Force's members were ignorant of the norms of moral agency; they were either oblivious to or misinformed about them. If they had been simply aware of these norms, they might not have followed them; but if they had understood them correctly, they would have recognized and accepted the idea that the female students at Ramstock High had rights which had to be respected.

There is no question that these boys were purposeful. They pursued physical fun and excitement, and they tried to avoid or minimize activities that interfered with their pursuit of those objects. Yet, although their purposefulness was relevant to them as moral agents, it certainly was not all that there might be to the purposefulness of moral agency.

First, even while allowing for physical fun and excitement, the concept of moral agency excludes them as ends of action. Agents may have fun and excitement, as we all know; but they do not, as philosophers have explained, have them as attained ends. They have fun and excitement, rather, *in* the doing of things, that is, as qualities supervening upon consummatory actions. When moral agents take fun and excitement as ends of action, they suffer an intellectual confusion. This in turn can have morally dreadful outcomes. For instance, it might lead moral agents to treat one another as mere means for attaining fun and excitement. Moreover, when moral agents do regard each other simply as tools for attaining goals, they fail to see one another as intrinsically worthwhile. Rape, prostitution, and sadism are famous as practices where moral agents have treated others simply as instruments of pleasure. Thus, the pursuit of fun and excitement by the members of The Force not only led them to treat coeds merely as means for attaining these goals, but also left them unprepared to act toward female students as people worthy in their own right. As Immanuel Kant might have expressed the point, they were unfit to dwell within the Kingdom of Ends.

Second, the fun and excitement sought by The Force were largely physical; that is, they mainly were sensual, superficial, and intense qualities of physical activities, such as sex and fast driving. But there are fun and excitement also in friendships, altruism, academic studies, travel, camping, hiking, and the comprehension of art works, to name only a few alternatives for teenagers. Third, while fun and excitement are especially appealing to high schoolers, they surely are not all that such students might consider as goals. There also are college educations, careers, summer jobs, and future ways of life. If the members of The Force continue to neglect other purposes for their lives, they will become arrested in the development of their moral characters; they will remain dependent upon their parents for food, clothing, shelter, cars, and television. In short, they will never grow up, not even in their fathers' eyes.

The fact that the members of The Force preferred ends with physical fun and excitement indicates that they were evaluative: They tended to employ physical fun and excitement as the norms by which they judged something, whether an end, an action, or a feeling, as good, bad, or indifferent. These standards, however, involve a very specific notion of physical fun and excitement. They do not involve what is physically fun and exciting for all moral agents; they include what is physically fun and exciting for the members of The Force, regardless of others. Accordingly, they are egocentric, not moral, criteria. Also, they are not prudential, either. Whatever is physically fun and exciting for me might be what I intend by "good." But that something is good in this sense does not logically entail that it is good for me. The road of physical hedonism is littered with early death, disease, boredom, and regret. Prudential standards logically presume rationality, whereas egocentric ones do not. Because teenagers in the pursuit of physical fun and excitement tend to be unreflective, they rarely wonder if such objects are good for themselves.

That The Force's norms are egocentric helps to explain its members' perceptions of the feelings of their sexual partners and victims. Understanding that whatever is physically fun and exciting is whatever is physically fun and exciting for himself, a member presumed that any sexual act that was fun and exciting for himself would be fun and exciting for his partner or victim. If the act was not enjoyable to her, then there was something wrong with her. This egocentricity also helps to explain why the members of The Force psychologically could treat the female students at Ramstock as mere means. By regarding themselves as the measures of goodness, they perceived these girls as inferior to themselves and thus as fit for their personal use. It follows that they psychologically were in no position to see the Ramstock girls as their moral equals and thus as bearers of rights to be respected by them.

Like the purposefulness and the evaluativeness of The Force's members, the deliberativeness of these students was quite limited. In sum, they deliberated only when they had to in order to have fun and excitement. When they received, infrequently, an invitation from a coed to engage in gang action with her, they had the means for a good time laid out for them; they did not have to think any up. They certainly never hesitated to weigh the pros and cons of accepting the invitation, nor did they pause to wonder if there might be a better way for having fun and excitement. Those boys looked at alternatives only when they had to figure out which dating routines would impress which girls sufficiently enough that the latter would become compliant. In considering such alternatives, they never asked what consequences any course of action might have beyond attaining a pleasure of the moment. Hence, they never even entertained the idea that their seductions might cause at least some girls to feel ashamed of themselves. Also, they never considered that their reckless driving on dates might lead to wrecks and death. We need only to mention that those in the clique did not wonder about the long-term consequences of their neglect of academic studies and their preoccupation with fun and excitement.

The members of The Force were not the only ones whose features as moral agents were seriously lacking. While we are sympathetic with the female students, especially the victims, who were the objects of the members' actions, we have to question some aspects of their conduct. These girls knew The Force's reputation. So, in consorting with the pack's members, they too must have been quite interested in the prospect for physical fun and excitement. This is not to say that any of these students looked forward to being raped; it is not even to say that they looked forward to nothing but a fast ride and hot sex. Some of these girls might have been after peer approval as well; indeed, in the back of their minds they might have seen having thrills and chills with The Force as something that they would do en route to establishing a wonderful romantic relationship. Nevertheless, if they acted for peer approval, they were deficient in freedom, purposefulness, evaluativeness, and deliberativeness. If they acted with the idea of establishing romantic relationships, they acted naively, that is, without comprehending much of what The Force's members were up to.

In addition, the conduct of the peers of these girls and The Force was troublesome. While those peers were not on the leading edge of physical fun and excitement at Ramstock, they certainly valued such qualities; they also encouraged, gossiped about, and vicariously enjoyed the experiences of the risk takers. One has serious doubts, then, about the moral development of more than just a handful of Ramstock students. Moreover, the peremptory denial by Ramstock's principal that the school might have been in some way responsible for the behavior of The Force makes one wonder if he was responding with regard to his job security rather than from concern for the strengths and weaknesses of the school as an environment favorable to the development of moral character in its students. His ad hoc instigation of a sex education program certainly looked like an attempt at a bureaucratic quick fix.

The behavior of the immediately involved parents reflected, in one dimension, a disposition for self-preservation but showed, in another dimension, serious gaps in moral character. The comments by the boys' parents that their sons were just acting like men and that the wronged girls must have had character defects may be seen as defensive rationalizations. The self-respect and social standing of the parents were in jeopardy by what their sons had done. To preserve that respect and standing, the parents could not blame the Stonewood way of life, with which they identified. But they could claim, as the fathers did, that the boys' behavior was natural for a healthy male and thus something to which all other males in Stonewood were susceptible. Also, they could claim, as the mothers did, that the boys' behavior was partly, if not entirely, the girls' fault, and thus blame had to be parcelled out to other Stonewood families. Nevertheless, the parents' responses indicated serious gaps in moral character. First, these parents were concerned exclusively with preserving their own way of life, not with what values, rights, and duties of moral agency had been violated. Second, they were not attempting to recognize any flaws of moral character in their sons or themselves. Third, they were not prepared for moral reflection. Specifically, they were not prepared to sit down with the girls and their parents and try to discover what had happened, what character weaknesses were involved, and what needed to be done to help ensure that these weaknesses would be remedied.

The actions by The Force involved, indirectly as well as directly, enough residents of Stonewood to be of community concern. Thus, one is struck by the fact that the community made no effort to come to grips with what had happened beyond implicitly allowing the principal of Ramstock to start the sex education program. One is further struck by the fact that the community possessed no institutions, besides table talk, gossip, and sermons, by which it could address the actions. The neighborhood association, which was the only community agency, confined itself to enforcing zoning restrictions, encouraging attractive lawns, and promoting community spirit through its semi-annual picnics. By default, then, public talk about the case fell to newspapers and TV talk shows. While these media presented some facts and conflicting points of view on the case, they also emphasized the sensational and fostered a strange kind of celebrity by featuring The Force's members and their accusers on talk shows. In any event, this public talk did nothing to improve the moral life of Ramstock students, Stonewood residents in general, or the people of surrounding communities.

MORAL EDUCATION NEEDS IN THE CASE

In discussing what needs to be done to develop the moral character of The Force's members and other involved parties, we might be tempted to take up the issue of what should have been done earlier in the lives of these people to have kept them from getting into the moral mess in which they got themselves; but we do not want to dwell on what ought to have been done. While discussing what was needed in the past might enable others to avoid the mistakes in this case, it alone will not serve anyone suffering such difficulties to overcome them. To help that person, we must discuss what should be done presently for those involved in the case of The Force.

Joe, Chris, Ken, Gary, and their associates need to acquire the freedom that is integral to moral agency. Their gaining such freedom depends on several conditions. One condition is their learning to restrain and moderate their sexual urges. While there is no doubt that these boys were aware of their sexual feelings, it is not clear that they ever considered that such feelings can be controlled. Maybe their talk about fun, excitement, and manhood was just a cover for a perception on their part that they suffered a profound weakness, namely, an incapacity to control their sexual feelings. In any event, if they are to develop the virtue of moderation, they have to change that perception by recognizing that sexual desires can be controlled by the vast majority of people.

The Force's members will require more than this new outlook, however; they will have to have immediate help from their fathers and from one another. If the fathers persist in proclaiming that sexual prowess is essential to manliness and thus that sexual moderation is for sissies, they of course will hinder efforts to encourage such moderation in their sons. It is necessary, therefore, that those fathers rethink their notion of an adult human male so as to recognize that, at least from the standpoint of moral agency, grown men are in control of themselves and respect the moral dignity of human females.

If The Force's members find that they simply cannot associate with one another without returning to their previous ways, they will have to dissolve their clique, maybe stay away from each other entirely. It might be, however, that they will not aggravate their situation; they might lose interest in one another and drift apart. On the other hand, if they learn to see each other as friends and thus as individuals whom they are especially committed to help as moral agents, they might be able to benefit from their interactions with one another. They could commiserate with one another, keep each other out of trouble, share new ways of enjoying themselves, and talk about opportunities for the future. They also could help each other accept a reduced status among their peers at Ramstock.

But even if these boys knew that their sexual impulses were controllable and had support from their fathers and from one another, they still would likely have sexual itches and urges with which to struggle. Most late adolescents suffer such feelings under the best of circumstances. During the past half-century, various practices have served American teenage males as ways of dealing with intense sexual feelings.[5] Such practices have ranged from suppression, prayer, cold showers, and hard physical exercise to masturbation, pornography, prostitution, petting, concupiscent love, and romantic love. While suppression and prayer might serve some teenagers, they do not seem suitable to The Force's members. Cold showers and arduous exercise seem fitting for them, but only as palliatives. The same may be said of masturbation and pornography. Even though prostitution is necessarily immoral for the reason that it involves two moral agents willfully treating each other strictly as means, it does have the advantage of being morally better than rape. Petting might prove too aggravating for the members of The Force. While concupiscent love, which involves mutually consenting sexual partners, is not necessarily wrong by the norms of moral agency, it poses the risk of people learning to engage in sex for no other reason than lust and thus without respect for one another's moral good. Romantic love entails both mutual consent and mutual respect for one another's moral good, but by the same token it tends to concentrate one's interest uncritically on a single individual, thereby limiting the development of oneself as a moral agent. Presumably, then, there is no given right way for the members of The Force to deal with their nagging sexual feelings. What they need to do is to discover what is workable for themselves individually and at the same time is morally correct. A practice that is morally correct, we should remember, might be morally good or simply the least of evils.

Another condition for acquisition of moral freedom by the members of The Force is their perception of other students, especially females. If Joe, Chris, Ken, Gary, and the others are to act with the freedom of moral agency, they must respect the rights of all other moral agents. But if they continue interpreting and valuing things in an egotistical way, they will fail to grasp that they are no better as moral agents than other students, including females. Hence, they will not see that they must respect the moral rights of coeds let alone that they might have a moral duty to help them on occasion. Accordingly, the members of The Force need to understand and appreciate the moral equality that they share with the other students at Ramstock.

Finally, The Force's members are not likely to become morally free unless they, in addition to satisfying the conditions already described, alter their standards of value. Physical fun and excitement, we have explained, were their foremost values; they were the principles by which these boys had chosen their purposes. While there is nothing essentially immoral about these qualities, there is serious doubt that they can serve as standards of the highest moral worth. We have seen in the case of The Force that fun and excitement, when functioning as premium standards, can lead to immoral acts. Moreover, we have already established (Chapter 2) that, according to the theory of moral agency, the principal moral values are the major features of moral agency. If The Force's members steadfastly cling to physical fun and excitement as their prime values, they will find it quite difficult, if not practically impossible, to moderate their sexual desires. But if they, through talk among themselves, with their fathers, and with their peers, reflect upon what the traits of moral agency are, they might see that physical fun and excitement are not the most important things in life. It will not do, however, for them just to lower these qualities on their scale of values. They also need to reorder them with respect to the norms of moral agency. That is, they have to learn that these qualities are morally acceptable only when experiencing them concords with the values, rights, and duties of all concerned moral agents.

Knowledge is another feature of moral agency that was problematic for the members of The Force. They saw the world from an egocentric perspective. They did not understand what it means for something to be of moral relevance. They were not aware of the norms of moral agency.

The educational needs posed by these failings begin with the problem of egocentric perspective. If Joe, Chris, Ken, Gary, and the others are to get away from their egocentric view of the world, they will have to realize that other people also have their own views of it, that the latter perspectives may or may not agree with theirs, and that there are facts in the world which supposedly are independent of any individual's outlook. To realize that other people have their own perspectives of life, The Force's members need to become acquainted with people beyond their clique and their imitators. These may be other students at Ramstock High or people outside the pale of Stonewood. They may be historical or fictional persons, too. But being acquainted with different people is not sufficient for realizing that they have views other than one's own. Thus, it is also necessary that The Force's members interact with the other people whether in reality or in imagination. Communication and shared activities are one condition for interaction with real people; sympathy and empathy are another condition. A foundation for interactions in the realm of reality or imagination is practical analysis, which seeks to understand what people's purposes are, what standards of evaluation they employ, and what courses of deliberation they follow.

A part of learning that other people have viewpoints of their own is recognizing how these outlooks compare and contrast with one's own. Accordingly, if The Force's members do grasp the perspectives of other people, they will quite likely see that at least some of these perspectives differ from their own. This in turn will put them in the position of seeking to determine which, if any, perspective is true and thus seeking standards of truth.

Another cognitive shortcoming of The Force was that its members did not raise moral questions, which indicates that these youths had little or no conception of what morality is even in its descriptive sense. To acquire a notion of morality in this sense, they have to become aware of themselves and the people with whom they interact as voluntary agents engaged in interpersonal conduct. Besides gaining this awareness, they have to learn that in the respect that they and the others are capable of controlling their behavior toward one another, each is responsible for his or her actions. Moreover, they have to come to see that insofar as they and the people towards whom they act share the same traits as interpersonal voluntary agents, none is superior to the other; they and the others are equal to one another. In addition, they have to recognize that they and all other moral agents are committed to performing only actions that are rationally defensible. Thus, they must learn that when they and others disagree over which actions are right or wrong, they should try to settle their differences through rational discussion.

It will further help The Force's members to become disposed to raise moral questions once they grasp that moral actions are special. First, because any moral action is voluntary, it could have been other than it is. Hence, Joe, Chris, Ken, Gary, and the others have to learn to ask of their moral actions not just whether they *want* to perform them but also whether they *should* do so. Second, any moral action, having a recipient, has a consequence for some moral agent other than that action's agent. Hence, The Force's members have to learn to consider the influences of their moral actions on other moral agents. Third, because the correctness of a moral action depends on nothing more than moral reasoning, it depends on no official authority; it is subject to challenge and defense by any interested moral agent. Thus, the members of The Force have to become concerned with finding the kind of reasons for their actions that any moral agent would regard as acceptable.

Also, it will help The Force's members to entertain moral questions if they learn that moral directives are supreme for them. This they can grasp upon seeing that moral agents logically are bound only by action guides that are appropriate to such agents. Hence, the clique's members have to recognize at the same time that moral agents must spurn any and all directives opposing moral ones. Once these teenagers have comprehended the logic of the superiority of moral norms, they will be prepared to wonder about the moral acceptability of the precepts and rules to which they are subject, whether those norms are personal, parental, peer, scholastic, neighborhood, political, or legal.

Finally, The Force's members were oblivious to the norms of moral agency. Students at Ramstock High tended to regard values as relative, either to individuals or to cultures; largely agreed that all individuals have some rights in common but disagreed over what some of those rights are; and generally did not consider whether or not people have duties to one another beyond those of telling the truth and keeping promises. Joe, Chris, Ken, Gary, and the other members of The Force, however, thought of values as relative to themselves primarily, never considered that students besides themselves might have rights, and regarded obligations only as holding among themselves. Thus, they were a long ways from recognizing that there are values, rights, and duties relevant to themselves and other students and people as moral agents. To become understanding of the norms of moral agency, this clique's members have to realize that they are logically committed to prizing their features as moral agents and thus recognizing that they share these values with other people who are moral agents. They must grasp that they and other people have rights to things belonging to themselves as individual moral agents and thus are bound to respect one another's rights to these matters. Moreover, these teenagers must realize that they, along with all other moral agents, are obligated to help maintain and engender social conditions favorable to moral agency.

There are several educational needs pertinent to The Force's members' purposefulness. To realize that physical fun and excitement are qualities of, not separate from, action, they have to recognize that purely instrumental actions may be pleasant in themselves. They also have to understand that actions performed just for the pleasure in them are performed not because these actions are instruments for obtaining something apart from the actions, but because they are actions in which pleasure inheres. To recognize that there are nonphysical pleasures to be had, the clique's members have to learn to engage in intellectual activities, aesthetic activities, and physical activities that de-emphasize the sensual. To see that there are matters to be interested in besides fun and excitement, physical or not, they have to learn to project themselves from their present life to the future, asking themselves what kind of life they want and whether or not their present activities will help them achieve it.

In learning to think about their future lives, Joe, Chris, Ken, Gary, et al., will be in a position to become prudential, that is, will have occasion to reflect upon what is good for themselves. They will be able to see, by looking about their community and considering life elsewhere, that physical fun and excitement usually are not primary values of adults and that there is a wide variety of possible careers and ways of life from which to choose. Thus, without their principles of physical fun and excitement, they will not know, at least from their own perspectives, what is good for themselves. Their prudential considerations, as already indicated, will not be moral ones; but they will be an improvement over the ego-centric considerations that the group presently employs. By their ego-centric stance, the clique's members assumed that they themselves set the standards of all values. By a prudential stance, however, these youths will have to recognize that they themselves are not the only source of norms. Being compelled to choose their futures on some basis other than the potential for physical fun and excitement, they will have to search beyond themselves for a new set of norms. They can look to their fathers, to peer acquaintances, to the Stonewood culture, to the media, and elsewhere; but wherever they look, they will be seeking something beyond their particular selves as a source of action guides. Thus, they will have to acknowledge that there might be standards independent of themselves by which to assess what is good for themselves. Moreover, by allowing that there might be such criteria, The Force's members will have to concede that these criteria might apply equally to other people, too. Hence, they will be better prepared to engage in the interpersonal considerations involved in moral evaluations and deliberations.

As we have previously suggested, The Force's members are not the only ones at Ramstock High with moral education needs. The female students who engaged, as victims or as willing partners, in sexual activity with these boys also have to moderate their interests in physical fun and excitement. They have to cease being subservient to peer approval and to start looking for norms that they can rationally defend. Moreover, to avoid being further gullible in their relationships with boys and other people, they have to become analytical about actions, questioning purposes, evaluations, and deliberations. Other persons at the school with moral education needs are the student body at large and the principal. While the students at Ramstock generally had not followed the lead of The Force, many of them regarded the pack admiringly. Others simply groped about in a mental fog without any definite action guides. Accordingly, the student body at large requires some sort of moral education at school. It was clearly a responsibility of the principal to help meet this need. His institution of a sex education program in reaction to the legal charges against The Force was not only late but woefully ad hoc. While sex education is a need of the school's students, it is only one of their needs. Also, it is symptomatic rather than causal. The root problem is that the students at Ramstock had been set adrift by their families, community, and school without having absorbed a definite body of guides for their conduct. Consequently, the principal has to learn to assume leadership for moral education at his school.

The parents of The Force's members were decent parents by present-day American standards. They provided their children with a stable home life. They took care of the food, clothing, and shelter of their children. They provided them with recreation and entertainment. And they saw to it that their children went to school. Nevertheless, these parents have several significant moral education needs. While they took pride in the athletic achievements and popularity of their sons, they did not pay serious attention to the development of their moral beliefs and attitudes. Hence, the reaction of these parents to the legal charges against their sons consisted of shock, denial, and accusation. Because these parents have responsibility for the development of the moral character of their sons, they must learn to help the latter embody the norms of moral agency and plan for the future. If the parents are to be able to do this, they will have to understand what these criteria are and how they apply to their own lives. This means in turn that the parents will have to forego their presumption that the Stonewood way of life is necessarily the marker of morality and the kind of life to which their sons should aspire.

But if these parents should learn to help their sons develop morally, the parents of the girls involved with these boys should also help their daughters develop morally. They too must comprehend the norms of moral agency and how they apply to their lives as well as their daughters' lives. They too must become prepared to help their daughters choose careers and future ways of life that may or may not be similar to those of Stonewood. Moreover, both the parents of these girls and those of The Force's members need to learn to deal, at least initially, with moral problems involving members of their own community[6] not by litigation or defensive posturing, but by joint moral inquiry involving all concerned parties. These parents should have been primarily concerned with discovering what needed to be done for their respective children's moral character and only secondarily interested in discovering who was guilty and punishable for what acts. The litigation and the defensive reactions distracted everybody from what was most important. If moral dialogue had proved impossible, ineffective in changing the attitudes and behavior of The Force, or inappropriate for determining and administering just punishment, then the filing of legal complaints would have been appropriate.

Perhaps the parents would readily have engaged in a joint moral inquiry if they had lived in a neighborhood where such inquiry was a common practice and where there were institutions that facilitated it. Joint moral inquiry, however, was not a widespread practice in the suburb; and no institution there fostered inquiry of the sort. Even Ramstock

High, as indicated by the principal's denial of responsibility, did not function to bring together the parents involved in the case of The Force. Plainly, Stonewood has to initiate practices and develop institutions that will enable it to function as a real moral community.

PROPOSED PROGRAM OF MORAL EDUCATION

We sometimes talk as though our lives can be started over brand new, as though our bad actions and consequences can be erased and replaced by good ones. Strictly speaking, however, there is no starting over in practical affairs. We might check actions in midcourse; we might contain their consequences; we might reform our characters; we might pretend that nothing has ever happened; we might forgive and forget. But we cannot do away with actions and their consequences and begin again without those actions and consequences having ever existed. The best we can do is start over in the sense that we can make adjustments so as to act differently from how we have been acting. Just as springtime does not mean that there was no winter, redemption does not mean that there was no sin; nor does deliverance mean that there was no captivity.

If we could assume that Joe, Chris, Ken, Gary, and the others could start over as though they had never perpetrated any sexual assaults, as though the dispositions leading to those actions had never existed, as though the consequences of their actions were totally gone, we might have a strong reason for discussing mainly what the moral education of typical male late adolescents at Ramstock High should be. But because we cannot make this assumption, we must set forth moral education proposals with reference to how The Force's members and other related persons presently are and how they got to where they are. The proposals will center around discussion groups, academic courses, and community institutions.

Discussion Groups

To develop their moral character, we have insisted, The Force's members require encouragement from their parents; they must have help from one another; and they have to have support from their peers at Ramstock. The girls who were involved with these boys also need encouragement from their parents and their school peers. In addition, the parents of these girls and those of The Force's members should all have understanding and support from one another.

These various parties can help each other in an optimal way only if they come together for sustained and focused discussions about their intermeshed problems. A son or daughter and his or her parents might benefit from intense discussions on their own. If they cannot, they should seek counseling from an outside agent, who might be a staff member of their church or an independent family counselor. A school counselor might work especially with the members of The Force as a group on how they might best serve one another. In any event, the principal should see to it that counseling groups are organized for all students at Ramstock who want to learn to cope with their sexual feelings or who want to discuss the values, rights, and duties involved in sexual and loving relationships. Moreover, the principal, working in conjunction with his counseling staff, should take the lead in bringing together the parents of The Force's members and of the involved female students so as to bring about a mutual understanding and reconciliation of these parents and their children.

In discussions between sons and parents, the individual parties have to entertain certain questions. The fathers must consider if they truly think that men, including themselves, should view women, including their wives, mainly as sex objects. The mothers have to ask themselves if they really want their sons to think of themselves as not being responsible for their behavior toward women. The sons must consider if they want their fathers regarding their mothers and other women chiefly as sex objects. Such reflection will help the various family members to recognize the moral indignity that the boys had inflicted on the girls with whom they had been involved. It also will enable them to see the equality that exists between males and females as voluntary interpersonal agents. Because the sons and their parents no longer are threatened by legal charges, they no longer have to be defensive about what they admit to themselves as well as to others; they can afford to be honest and open with themselves. Some might enter into self-reflection from force of conscience; others might require cue questions from one another or family counselors to do so. Daughters and parents also will have to engage in self-reflection. The daughters have to wonder if they want to continue being naive and passive or become knowledgeable and assertive. Their parents must consider what they have done to render their daughters vulnerable in the practical world and what they might do to help them gain control of themselves.

Once the parents of The Force's members have become more or less cognizant of their and their sons' commitments as moral agents, they need to begin talking with their sons about the direction the latter's recent conduct has been taking and what better alternatives there might be. They also should discuss with their sons what changes in the latter's attitudes and behavior are entailed by whatever better alternatives might be chosen. Likewise, the parents of the concerned coeds have to talk with their daughters about their futures and what changes they need to undergo in order to be in charge of their lives and to attain morally worthy life purposes.

In the meetings of The Force's members and their parents with the involved girls and their parents, the different participants have to learn to perceive the situation from each other's viewpoint. For instance, the boys must learn to understand what it is like to be taken as nothing more than a sexual target. The girls ought to learn to see how they might have acted toward the boys other than as they did. The parents of the boys should learn to grasp what it would be like to be told by one's daughter that she has been sexually assaulted. The parents of the coeds have to learn to understand that the boys' parents might be willing to engage in reflective dialogue as long as they are not put in an adversarial position. The consummatory sign of success for this dialogue is that The Force's members would apologize to the girls and the latter's parents, the girls and their parents would accept the apologies, and the two sets of parents would apologize for having been hostile and distrusting toward each other.

After the formerly adversarial parties have made significant progress toward an accord, school counselors could start student discussion groups with a reduced risk of the latter's being hopelessly polarized between adamant defenders and harsh critics of The Force. In organizing the student groups, the counselors should include, when feasible, some of The Force's members or the involved female students in the meetings. The latter students can help the others by explaining what they should have done differently. They also can tell about the process of moral dialogue. By no means should the counselors regard these discussion groups as temporary measures. They should see them, rather, as the origin of the practice of student moral dialogue at Ramstock High School. Moreover, they should view such dialogue as concerned not with just sexual problems but with all moral problems of student concern. The groups can meet more or less frequently as circumstances demand. Moreover, by meeting in afternoons or during evenings, they will not have to cut into academic class time.

How these various groups are to get together initially is a difficult problem. After all, The Force's members and the involved female students have been legal adversaries; the two sets of parents have been critical and distrusting of each other; and the principal has denied any responsibility for the situation. Despite the uncertainty here, several facts in the situation are apparent. Ramstock High School is the locus of the case; the principal is the presumed leader of the school; and the sex education program instigated at his behest has not made any significant changes in students' attitudes and conduct. Accordingly, it is appropriate for the opening move to come from within Ramstock; moreover, it is appropriate for the principal to make that gambit. Before he can make it, he has to understand that his sex education program has not been effective. He also has to recognize that the situation at the school cries out for affective and cognitive changes that can occur only through face-to-face discussions among all parties. To see these points, he should have the sex education program evaluated; and he ought to seek input from staff counselors, teachers, students, parents, and community leaders. Finally, the principal has to face up to the fact that he has responsibilities for the moral education problems at his school and that denying these responsibilities in order to protect his job is immoral. Some reminders from parents, community leaders, or his superintendent might help him acknowledge this fact.

But even if the principal leads the effort to get all the right people talking to one another, he will not ensure thereby that these people will use the norms of moral agency to guide their discussions. He has no clear or extensive conception of these standards, nor does any of the students or parents. While some of the counselors working with the various groups might have a stronger grasp of the criteria, none of them consciously employs them systematically in the counseling process. If, then, the dialogues involving all the groups will contain no person who is an articulate advocate of the norms of moral agency, how can the dialogues alter beliefs and feelings according to those norms? Indeed, how will anyone know if anybody's feelings or beliefs have been changed with respect to these criteria? If we had assumed that the people to participate in the discussions were nonrational or were oblivious to any feature of moral agency, we would have to concede that the discussions would be pointless. But we did not make this assumption. We took the participants, rather, to be imperfect moral agents, meaning that they individually have at least a modicum of competence in practical reason and have at least a dim comprehension of some of the features of moral agency. The possibility that these people will modify their beliefs and feelings according to the norms of moral agency will depend upon nothing more than their clarifying their consciousness of the features of moral agency and increasing their esteem of those features.[7]

It is not begging the question to presume that all or at least the large majority of the participants individually like to act voluntarily and expect each other to do the same. Let us presume also that they expect people to have reasons for their actions and that they reject inconsistencies when they see them. With this mental set students, parents, and school officials will be in a position, through self-reflection and the multiple perspectives and active interchanges of discussion, to recognize freedom, knowledge, purposefulness, evaluativeness, and deliberativeness as values and rights that they mutually share and should respect. They also will be able to see that they are obligated to help sustain and develop the traits of moral agency in themselves as individuals, in Ramstock High School as an institution, and in Stonewood as a community. There is no guarantee, of course, that these dialogues will succeed even if our assumptions about the makeup of the participants are granted. Passions, argumentativeness, and talking in circles might break off talk. A failure to see inconsistencies might direct a dialogue away from the norms of moral agency. On the other hand, the practical world does not ensure successful outcomes.

Academic Classes

The members of The Force, as mentioned, have never had a positive interest in academic matters. Moreover, by the time the trials for sexual assault had ended, there was only one year of course work at Ramstock High School left for the clique's members. Accordingly, their prospects for gaining any moral insights or sensitivity through academic study might not initially appear hopeful. There are reasons, nevertheless, for thinking that such study might be morally beneficial to them. Despite their publicly declared innocence and the jury acquittals, they enter their senior year with less ground for confidence in their past ways. They cannot be sure that they will continue to be popular with the female students, who now might regard dates with The Force's members as overly risky. They cannot be sure that they will keep the envy of male students, who now might think that The Force carried things too far. They also are to begin the intense and extended discussions, described above, that will concern not only what they have done but also what worthy life goals they might pursue. It is more than barely possible, then, that these boys will be open to the moral content of academic studies.

There certainly are topics and issues relevant to the group's members and many other Ramstock seniors that may be covered by academic courses. In history, these students can come to understand that, while male domination of society has been traditional, there have been outstanding women leaders, such as Joan of Arc, Elizabeth I, Catherine of Russia, Indira Gandhi, and Margaret Thatcher. In anthropology and sociology, they can learn about gender biases built into cultures and social institutions and how these biases influence people's perceptions of the world. In social philosophy, psychology, and biology, they can examine the issue of equality between males and females. In literature, they can take up the questions of what it means to be a man, what it means to be a woman, and what love is. They also can pursue these questions from a multiplicity of perspectives, platonic, romantic, naturalistic, and so on, comparing and contrasting works by both male and female writers, contemporary as well as past.

Yet, even if the academic courses offered to the Ramstock seniors are related to the latter's moral concerns, they will not necessarily be of interest to these students. Teachers might approach the courses as repositories of knowledge to be learned for its own sake. Readings might be so abstract or complex that they obscure their relevance. The students might tune out the classes as a way of protecting themselves from shame and embarrassment. It is important, therefore, that the teachers of the courses recognize that some, if not most, of their students face moral problems to which the courses should speak. It is equally important that the teachers relate the courses to the learning styles of the students.

Despite their pertinence to male–female issues, much of Plato's *Republic* and Aristotle's *Politics* is too difficult for most high school students; but a few short selections from these works need not be.[8] Franco Zeffirelli's and Leonard Bernstein's versions of *Romeo and Juliet* are more likely than is Shakespeare's play to communicate to American adolescents. *The Scarlet Letter* is straightforward enough to convey its message about a male-dominated society's injustice toward women. Carson McCullers' story, "A Tree. A Rock. A Cloud," is a treatment of love, youth, and wisdom that can be grasped on several levels. Andrew Marvell's poem, "To His Coy Mistress," affords students a comical approach to the male viewpoint of sexual relations. By contrast, Edna St. Vincent Millay's sonnet, "What Lips My Lips Have Kissed," offers an aged woman's observations on physical pleasure that should touch most late adolescents, male as well as female. While Thornton Wilder's drama, *Our Town,* suffers a sentimental view of small town America, it provides students with an accessible holistic treatment of some of life's major problems.

Regardless of texts used, however, teachers must approach them as vehicles for moral reflection by students, not as opportunities for preaching or for exhibition of scholarship. The reflection can express itself in essays, journals, small group discussions, and hallway conversations, to name only a few possibilities.

Community Institutions

The suburb of Stonewood, we have indicated, lacks institutions that facilitate public moral discussion. While the community's schools, as exemplified by Ramstock High, have looked after academics, athletics, and extracurriculars, they have usually dealt with morality only as a matter of particular cases occurring on premises. Even though the churches in the neighborhood have advocated moral principles and rules to their congregations, they have not directly addressed the moral quality of the Stonewood way of life; nor have they attempted to present a moral point of view to more than their respective congregations. The suburb's community association looks after the property and public recreational interests of its members and occasionally brings these people together for picnics, but it makes no effort to provide programs dealing with moral problems. Also, it does not facilitate a network among its members for the discussion of moral questions. While the news and talk shows on Stonewood's television screens report events of moral concern, they emphasize the sensational aspects of the events and rarely attempt to clarify standards of moral conduct. Plainly, if these institutions are to support moral education in Stonewood as a matter of genuine public interest, they must undergo change. The change, however, does not have to be drastic.

What has to happen to the schools of Stonewood is for their leaders to reconceive them as institutions with responsibilities for developing all aspects of the moral character of their students. In other words, Stonewood's school leaders must commit their institutions to instilling in the community's youth the character virtues of moral agency. It matters not if the origin of a moral virtue or vice is off school grounds; what counts is that Stonewood's schools do what they can to help their students acquire the virtue or ward off the vice. It matters not that the schools have a special mission to instruct their students in academic subjects; what counts is that the schools regulate student conduct according to the norms of moral agency and teach those norms where they are integral to academic subjects. It matters not that other institutions engage in moral education activities that affect, directly or indirectly, the character of Stonewood's youth. What does matter is that these other institutions and the community's schools coordinate their efforts with one another so that they do not conflict with each other and so that they reinforce each other. In sum, all that the leaders of the schools have to do is to take seriously the moral education of the youth of Stonewood.

Because the churches of Stonewood, like its schools, have been largely inward looking in moral education, they, like the schools, must become interactive with the community's other institutions in undertaking moral education. To do this, the churches do not necessarily have to compromise their ecclesiastical beliefs. They and the other institutions simply have to identify values, rights, and duties of moral agency whereon they all can find agreement. Insofar as the ecclesiastical beliefs special to the various churches cohere with the norms of moral agency, they can serve the churches' members as special reinforcers of those norms. If there is a church in the community that rejects voluntary action as an illusion or rejects the normative criteria of moral agency as false moral principles, it is not likely to join other institutions in moral education programs. If it does not, it will hinder Stonewood from becoming a solid community for moral education. But as long as the church does not threaten the moral agency of the rest of the community and does not fundamentally harm its members as moral agents, it is to be tolerated. Those churches that do cooperate with other community institutions on moral education will be in a position to establish a public fund of knowledge on community moral problems, to exchange with the other institutions ideas on the pedagogy of moral education, to see what the other institutions are doing in their programs, and to plan with the other institutions how they all can complement each other.

In altering itself to become an institution supporting moral education, the Stonewood community association need not, and must not, become a moral police agency, spying on people and enforcing moral rules. What the association should do, without radically altering itself, is to assume responsibility for identifying moral problems of significance for the Stonewood community in general and supporting educational programs relevant to those problems. The problems might be as immediate as a marked tendency of disrespect for authority by the community's youth or as abstract as the question of whether or not there is more to life than a comfortable home, an accumulation of material goods, and a secure retirement. To fulfill this new responsibility, the association should help the parents of Stonewood to establish a network among themselves, provide forums on moral problems, serve as a clearing center for counselors who might be able to help families and individuals with moral problems, and help coordinate moral education programs among schools, churches, and other community institutions.

NOTES

1. Harold M. Hodges, Jr., "Peninsula People: Social Stratification in a Metropolitan Complex," in Robert J. Havighurst, Bernice L. Neugarten, and Jacqueline M. Falk, eds., *Society and Education: A Book of Readings* (Boston: Allyn and Bacon, 1967), pp. 3–19.

2. See William Severini Kowinski, "The Squeeze on the Middle Class," *The New York Times Magazine* (July 13, 1980), p. 28.

3. Norman Goodman and Gary T. Marx, *Society Today*, 4th ed. (New York: Random House, 1982), pp. 479–480.

4. See, for instance, Joan Didion, "Trouble in Lakewood," *The New Yorker* 64 (July 26, 1993), pp. 46–65.

5. The problem, of course, is not special to Americans nor to this century. Consider the plight of the fictional novice monk, Adso, seeking guidance from the writings of the medieval Christian philosopher, Thomas Aquinas, and the medieval Arabic philosopher, Avicenna, on how to deal with sexual urges. See Umberto Eco, *The Name of the Rose*, translated by William Weaver (New York: Warner Books, 1984), pp. 334–336, 390–392.

6. In principle there is no reason why moral agents not members of one another's communities should not initially try to solve their moral problems through joint moral inquiry. Practical difficulties, however, tend to prevent them from employing such inquiry. One is that distant parties are unacquainted with one another's competence as moral agents. Another is that structures through which distant parties might communicate with one another are often lacking. As

cumbersome as it is, judicial inquiry is the vehicle that distant moral agents practically have to use to settle their problems.

7. There lies in the background of this discussion something like Meno's paradox: We cannot learn that which we already know; but we also cannot learn that of which we are ignorant for the reason that we will not recognize it when we come upon it. Our resolution of the paradox, which is that an incomplete knowledge of the norms of moral agency will enable people to learn more about those norms, is similar to Plato's resolution. See Plato, *Meno*, 80A–100A.

8. For instance, Plato, *Republic*, 451C–62E. Aristotle, *Politics*, 1259a36–1260b20.

10 Implications

Before closing our inquiry, we have to address two more issues: What are the implications of our proposed moral education for Americans for their nonmoral character education? And what changes in American institutions does our moral education entail? Prior to taking up these questions, however, let us review the course of our investigation.

SUMMARY

To provide a framework for shaping the character of Americans, we have established a theory of moral education that sets forth the end, content, and pedagogy of character education grounded on the normative principles of moral agency.

The norms are based on freedom, knowledge, purposefulness, evaluation, deliberation, and the other features of a moral being, mainly, a voluntary agent acting in relation to another voluntary agent. Consequently, the standards pertain to Americans insofar as the latter are moral agents, thus being the tie that at least implicitly binds Americans in moral fellowship. Moreover, the norms appear to be feasible as moral principles for Americans. We could think of no substantial reason why the members of this nation should reject the standards; in addition, the standards seem to be consistent with traditional American principles.

The aim of moral education, our theory holds, is to produce a person with a character consisting of dispositions structured according to the criteria of moral agency. These dispositions, or moral virtues, are cognitive and affective. The chief intellectual disposition is moral reasoning, which embodies the knowledge, skills, appreciations, and psychical energy needed for making decisions consistent with the norms of moral agency. Other intellectual habits of moral character might relate to science, technology, and aesthetics. The affective virtues are self-regarding and other-regarding. The former are such habits as hopefulness, moderation in pleasure, and self-esteem. The latter are such habits as empathy, charity, politeness, justice, and friendship.

The content of moral education may reside in several areas: in the commonplace world of the student, in academic subjects, and in career preparation for the world of service and production. Because conditions in play, recreation, family relations, peer associations, and neighborhood life significantly influence any individual's acquisition of freedom, knowledge, and the other features of moral agency, they have to be structured so that they will contribute to, not hinder, the moral character of students. Because a school's moral education that is kept separate from academic areas tends to departmentalize and discount morality, it should be an integral part of the school's academic subjects. Because the services, products, and processes making up the world of commerce and art involve moral agents, they are subject to the norms of moral agency. Thus, the values, rules, and decisions specific to the utilitarian or aesthetic life must agree with the precepts of moral agency; and concern with the learning of moral character is appropriate to career preparation in these two areas.

Being moral agents, both teachers and students of moral education are subject to the norms of moral agency. Teachers, whether school teachers, parents, ministers, or some other sort, logically value the purposefulness, evaluativeness, content, methods, and other factors involved in their teaching. Teachers morally have the right to determine the specific moral character to be acquired by their respective students and to choose the content and methods to be used in their teaching. Also, it is the moral duty of teachers of moral education not only to develop the moral character of their students, but also to oppose hindrances to the moral education of their students. As developing moral agents, students should become positively interested in the major features of moral agency. They have the right to the opportunity to acquire the character of a moral agent, to study whatever relevant subject matter appeals to themselves, to teaching that matches their learning styles, and to the conditions that support and nurture the optimal development of their respective moral characters. As students grow in their capacity for moral action, they become increasingly responsible for respecting the rights of their teachers, one another, and other moral agents, and for maintaining and promoting the major traits of moral agency. Consonant with their respective values, rights, and duties, both teachers and students of moral education should acquire the virtues specific to their respective roles. Teachers, for instance, must exemplify to their students the characteristics of moral agency. Students have to possess the dispositions that enable them to learn to be moral agents, for example, empathy, charity, self-denial, truthfulness, and a love of knowledge.

In trying to clarify our theory of moral education, we pointed out that the theory would make moral education pervasive in the lives of students. Hence, unlike the Bush administration's statement of goals, *America 2000,* the theory would not confine moral education to just the civic sphere of the student's life. We also stated that the theory would call for active collaboration between school personnel and extramural agents in identifying the specific moral education needs of students and in developing programs to remedy those needs. Thus, in contrast with "The Virginia Common Core of Learning," the theory would encourage a distribution of leadership in moral education between school officials and extramural agents.

In further efforts at clarification, we related the theory to cases of fictional individuals, namely, Natalene Turner and members of a clique called The Force. Even though we depicted these cases as involving individuals from the underclass and the middle class, respectively, we explained that moral education is ultimately to pertain to individuals, not social classes. While the members of a social class do share certain characteristics, they have their individual differences. Hence, the moral education appropriate to one member of a given social class might not be proper for other members of the same class. Also in examining these cases, we noted that the moral education of individuals must address the latter as they are. This means that moral education for Americans has to deal with imperfect moral beings in imperfect situations. It must begin by identifying their desirable and undesirable circumstances as well as their moral strengths and weaknesses. It then must build on their desirable circumstances and moral strengths and rectify their undesirable circumstances and moral weaknesses. Consequently, efforts to make this education successful sometimes will be tedious, frustrating, and unsure; they will require persistence and resolve from Americans; they will rarely, if ever, have perfect results. These, nevertheless, will be efforts that Americans as moral agents will see as worthy and to which they are committed.

NONMORAL CHARACTER EDUCATIONS

Moral education alone, we have mentioned, is not sufficient to overcome the difficulties in the normative structure of American society. It has to be complemented by other types of character education; it also has to be supported by certain kinds of social, civil, and economic institutions. Our theory of moral education contains suggestions for such types of character education and for such institutions.

Prudential

The other kinds of character education that must accompany moral education are prudential, cultural, social, and civic. People sometimes refer to prudence as "looking out for Number One," thereby setting it up as the art of selfishness. They conceive it as such presumably because they tend to view it and morality as being necessarily opposed to one another. The norms of moral agency, however, do not logically stand opposed to a person's caring for his or her own good. While they do presuppose that no voluntary agent is more or less valuable as a voluntary agent than any other, and while they do prescribe occasional sacrifices, they do not ask that one should neglect one's own good. They simply ask that people should care for their own interests only while respecting the moral interests of others. Indeed, they specify that one should make sacrifices only when the moral good to be gained by the latter is greater than the sacrifices. Perhaps people see prudence and morality as inevitably opposed to one another because they learn prudence apart from morality, making morality a matter of open talk and behavior and making prudence a matter of secret talk and behavior. Even so, prudential education for Americans must go on alongside and in harmony with their moral education. In this way students will be in a position to learn that even though their personal interests do have moral limits, those limits are reasonable. Also, students will learn to care for their individual goods without moral hypocrisy and thus without undercutting morality in American society. If Americans were to learn to be prudent in conjunction with their learning to be moral, they would not have to cope with the resurgence of another "Me" generation.

Cultural

The groups in which people live frequently have their own cultures, but they also might contain a manifold of them. While the United States has always had different cultures, it has become quite culturally diverse this century. Indeed, this trend toward multiculturalism has become so vigorous that it has sorely diminished, if not overwhelmed, the historical dominance of the nation's British cultural inheritance. The result is that cultural education in the United States has become problematic. Inevitably, the beliefs, values, and practices of some groups oppose those of other groups. When, therefore, cultural groups pass on their respective ways of life to their young, they sometimes contribute to conflict within the nation. But if antagonistic cultural groups are not to pass on opposing ways of life, what are they to do?

Of the responses to this question during the past two decades, two are familiar. One is that each cultural group must adopt tolerance as a practice. Thus, in enculturating its young, each group would help ensure that the numerous cultural groups in the United States would coexist with one another. The other answer is that each group must subordinate itself to the principles of democratic society and respect the nation's other cultural groups. Hence, in imparting its way of life to its young, each group will place its beliefs, values, and practices within a democratic framework and provide understanding and appreciation of other cultural groups.

Neither of these responses, unfortunately, is satisfactory. Some cultural groups cannot infuse themselves with tolerance without eliminating some of their most distinctive values, beliefs, and practices. Consequently, they cannot accept the principle of tolerance unless they have a convincing reason for wanting to modify their ways of life significantly. As recent events in the Balkans, the Middle East, Northern Ireland, and central Africa demonstrate, coexistence alone might not be a good enough reason for some groups. Moreover, there are cultural groups that cannot accept the principles of democratic society without seriously modifying their ways of life. If, therefore, they are to trim their features to fit a democratic framework, they must have a strong reason for so doing. Cultures that are essentially authoritarian would have reasons for not accommodating themselves to democracy. To be sure, an intolerant or antidemocratic group might be prepared to suppress its hostility toward others in order to avoid legal sanctions or to gain a tactical advantage. But while a lull in the cultural wars might be better than a resumption of hostilities, it is no substitute for cultural peace.

The members of antagonistic cultures will have a convincing reason for comporting themselves toward each other in morally correct ways once they recognize that they are moral agents and that their commitments as moral agents are superior to their commitments as members of any cultural group. Upon comprehending the superiority of the norms of moral agency, they would see that they are logically committed to adjusting their ways of life to those norms. Hence, they would change their ways not because they would want to avoid legal sanctions or gain a tactical advantage, but because they would grasp the implications of moral agency.

It follows that the cultural education of Americans must be coordinated with their moral education. If a student's cultural and moral educations are kept separate, they might be in conflict with each other, perhaps making the student divided and confused and rendering the moral education ineffective. School teachers, parents, and others responsible for the moral education of students must work with one another and all others responsible for the students' cultural education to ensure that all parties mutually understand the logical demands of moral agency on the involved cultures, and that all mutually grasp the respects in which the cultures relate to the values, rights, duties, and virtues of moral agency. Where conflicts are found, they must be thoroughly discussed so as to reduce the possibility of mistaken interpretations. Confirmed conflicts will point toward changes that must be made in the given cultural education, including changes that will have to be made in cultural beliefs, values, and practices. It is practically necessary, therefore, that the leaders of cultural groups be actively involved in the coordination of their members' cultural education with the latter's moral education. The reason for their participation will be, of course, not to frustrate, for political reasons, the moral education of Americans, but to help ensure that the relations of their respective cultures to the norms of moral agency are correctly understood.

Social

Social education aims at the members of a society learning the social roles and manners existing in that society. A social role consists of the rights and duties attached to a position within a society, for example, mother, brother, employer, employee, soldier, lawyer, legislator, and neighbor. Social manners are the formal ways in which the members of a society should act toward each other in public settings. Even though the manners of a society are largely arbitrary, they are the conventions of that society whereby its members publicly express their respect to one another as members of that society. As far as a society is concerned, its roles and manners are good or bad only in that they enable its institutions to function properly and enable their members to publicly express their respect to one another. But even if the roles and manners of a society are good for that society, that does not necessarily mean that they are morally good or correct. The roles of master and slave in the ante bellum South plainly opposed the norms of moral agency, as did the manners expected of master and slave in their relations to each other. Also, the roles assigned to and the manners expected of American women since the Civil War have often been opposed to these standards. It is quite possible, therefore, for the social education of Americans to conflict with their moral education.

Many roles and manners in the United States today are in turmoil. Because the nation's social institutions have suffered accelerating and deep changes this century, they are largely unsettled. So, while some traditional roles are still intact, many are uncertain and fragmented. Upheavals in family structure, for instance, have left open the question of what are the rights and duties of fathers, mothers, social workers, judges, and teachers. Because the nation's traditional manners have their origins in the Victorian era, many of them today are meaningless; some of them even suggest disrespect. Moreover, replacements for our traditional manners have not been generally accepted. The result is that Americans are often unsure how to behave toward one another in public places or have come to regard manners in America as irrelevant. It is ironic that a locus of one of the most acute concerns about manners is juvenile gangs, which have developed codes for expressing respect or disrespect through eye contact, ways of wearing caps, hair style, and other behaviors.

That Americans will generally agree on new social roles and manners in the foreseeable future is doubtful. Our institutions show little sign of settling enough that one might be able to tell what roles are appropriate to them, and our normative structure is so uncertain that people are not apt to reach even a consensus on what things ought to be respected let alone a consensus on what behaviors will count as signs of respect. Nevertheless, some sort of socialization of the nation's members must go on; otherwise, there will be social chaos, not just conflict.

It is doubly important, therefore, that the socialization of Americans take place in conjunction with their moral education. If their social training occurs independently of their moral education, it is likely to be opposed to and thus obstructive to the latter. On the other hand, if their social training proceeds in connection with their moral education, it will be able to rely on the norms of moral agency, thus becoming an extension of the moral education of Americans. As such an extension, the socialization of Americans will reinforce moral education dealing with matters other than social roles and manners; but it also will have a basis for reaching agreement or at least minimizing disagreement over roles and manners. Because Americans as moral agents are committed to the norms of moral agency, they logically must consent only to social roles and manners that accord to those norms. They must reject, for instance, any parental claim that authorizes a father or mother to thwart the development of the moral autonomy of an offspring. They also must reject any manners that do not express respect for one another's moral equality. In being grounded on the norms of moral agency, the socialization of Americans does not necessarily involve a common consensus upon what their roles and manners specifically are. It can allow for differences from group to group, region to region. Those differences, however, will all be consistent with each other in that they all are compatible with the standards of moral agency. Moreover, a socialization based on these standards can and should instruct Americans to recognize that any specific differences among their roles and manners are to be respected as morally correct.

Civic

Civic education in the United States might run counter to the moral education that we have proposed for Americans. Statutory laws sometimes violate, for instance, one's moral rights to knowledge, equal opportunity, and health. Constitutional law occasionally allows arrangements that are logically absurd, such as the federally mandated racial integration of schools that has resulted in the actual resegregation of many urban schools. The nation's ideals, whose meanings are rather ambiguous, occasionally receive interpretations that oppose some of those ideals to the norms of moral agency. Thus, freedom is sometimes taken to mean rugged individualism, which emphasizes the independence of individuals at the expense of their cooperativeness. When, therefore, civic education instructs Americans to know and appreciate the nation's laws and ideals, it is liable to encourage them to follow legal rules and principles opposed to the standards of moral agency, thereby undercutting their moral education.

To eliminate the possibility that the civic education of Americans will conflict with their moral education, we recommend that the former be grounded on the values, rights, duties, and virtues of moral agency. We are not thereby proposing, however, that Americans are to learn to disobey whatever laws they regard as violating the criteria of moral agency. To be sure, there is a morally worthy tradition of civil disobedience in the United States, exemplified by Henry David Thoreau and Martin Luther King, Jr. But civil disobedience as a reasoned political strategy for effecting legal change is one thing; as a general response to all immoral laws, it is something else. Such a response would likely lead to more social turmoil than there already is. Moreover, such a response is not necessary. The American legal system, despite its being cumbersome, is self-correcting. Legislators can write new statutes. Federal judges can reinterpret the Constitution from time to time. The nation's ideals are open to reconsideration.

So, rather than learning in their civic education to be disobedient to each and every immoral law, Americans need to learn to understand American law from the standpoint of moral agency and how to bring about changes in statutes and judicial decisions that will align the nation's law with such agency. Teaching Americans to do these things presumes that legislators and judges will be receptive to arguments implicitly based on the norms of moral agency. Incumbent legislators and judges can be encouraged, directly or indirectly, to reflect on the point that, because law is to guide interpersonal actions, especially those among voluntary agents, it has a conceptual connection with moral agency. Prospective legislators and judges who have developed, through moral education, the character of moral agents will be sensitive to the moral framework of American law when they do assume office.

INSTITUTIONS

Moral education takes place in a social setting, not a vacuum. Integral to that setting are established practices, or institutions. Of the institutions required by moral education, some are pedagogical while others may be legal, economic, religious, and political. The sorts of institutions specific to a given society depend on the latter's history and its given conditions. Thus, to understand what our theory of moral education implies for institutions relevant to the moral education of Americans, we must consider not only the types of institutions required for their education, but also the limitations that existing conditions in the United States are likely to place on those institutions.

Few, if any, of the institutional changes entailed by our theory are novel; most of them have appeared as policy recommendations by various social analysts during the past decade or so. But while novelty might be fascinating, it is not necessarily justifiable. In any event, our purpose here is not to justify the institutional modifications called for by our conception of moral education for Americans. It is simply to show what those changes are.

Family

In the course of our inquiry we had numerous occasions to refer to the importance of the family and the school as pedagogical institutions in moral education. Indeed, we insisted that families are key institutions for developing their children's character. They have the earliest impact upon that character, and they can weaken the moral education efforts of other institutions, including schools. Not all familial arrangements, however, are equally suitable for a given type of moral education. The extended family, for example, might be especially effective in providing the moral education advocated by Communitarianism; whereas the two-working-parents family might be especially effective in furnishing the moral education urged by Individualism. Regardless, an implementation of any kind of moral education must make do with the familial structures that are feasible where the education is to occur.

The extended family began to lose its dominance in the United States to the one-working-parent nuclear family during the early part of this century. The prevalence of the latter started to give way to the two-working-parents nuclear family around the middle of this century. During the past three decades, the single-parent family has gained in number and influence as a family form and shows no sign of abating. These changes in familial structure were not the results of social planning; they were, rather, the outcomes of changes in historical conditions, for instance, industrialization, the migration of people from rural to urban areas, the mobility of the work force, the women's rights movement, and the welfare rights movement. Thus, any hopes of making large use of the extended family or the one-working-parent nuclear family in American moral education appear to be unrealistic. For the foreseeable future, it seems, such education must rely mainly on two-working-parents nuclear families and single-parent families.

As noted earlier in our investigation, each of the last two types of families has actually presented difficulties for moral education. In two-working-parents families, some children have had no after-school supervision, thereby picking up indiscriminately whatever values and habits they might encounter through television or acquaintances. Even children of such families who attend after-school centers often have received very little supervision. The problems associated with single-parent families have included mothers unfit to provide moral guidance; a dependency on welfare agencies; a negative attitude toward schooling; a lack of cognitive stimulation; living amidst gangs, violence, and crime; and a deep and abiding sense of being separate from the rest of society. If, therefore, these sorts of families are to contribute to and not obstruct the moral education of Americans, they and conditions related to them must undergo changes.

In two-working-parents families, the main modification to be made is in priorities. One possible reason why both parents of a family work is to have a larger income than they otherwise would have. Other reasons are the satisfaction that each parent finds in a career and the enriched experience that two careers bring to a family. The fulfillment of any of these motives can be beneficial to a family's children. Larger incomes obviously can help with the material needs of children. When both parents have jobs, they show their children that work is suitable for both men and women; in addition, children can be proud of their parents for their career achievements. Moreover, the enrichment of experience between employed parents opens up possibilities and understandings of experience for their children. Whether singly or collectively, however, these benefits could never justify a neglect of the moral education of children. Parents have it wrong when they adjust their children's moral education to fit occupations; they have the moral duty to accommodate their working lives to their children's moral education as much as they practically can. What is the point of being a hard-working lawyer if your children are learning to violate the law? What is the point of being a devoted psychiatrist if your children feel unloved? What is the point of accumulating material goods for the family when the family is never together to share them? When both parents work, they are especially obligated to be conscientious about the moral quality of day-care centers and after-school programs. They also are especially bound to devote the energy and time to overseeing their children's moral education on a day-to-day basis. Some parents might be able to perform these tasks without much difficulty. Others might have to stagger their work schedules. Still others might have to reduce their job hours.

With respect to single-parent families, various changes need to occur. At-risk students have to gain moral maturity before they become parents. This they might learn to do through programs that encourage them to delay parenthood, finish school, get jobs, and marry. Single parents have to strive for economic independence, which they might do with incentives to enter the work force. Policies on impoverished neighborhoods and related governmental agencies have to be reconstructed so as to eliminate gangs, violence, and crime. Sensibly designed day-care centers and responsible relatives not only can look after the children of unmarried mothers while the latter work, but they also can provide an educationally stimulating environment for those children, thereby enhancing their chances for succeeding in school. Extended school days can benefit older children from single-parent families as well as those from two-working-parents families. Unmarried parents should be inclined to work with school teachers and counselors to be aware of their children's moral education needs and to help meet those needs. Also, such parents should be willing to receive help for their own moral education needs from relatives, schools, churches, and other social agencies.

Schools

The changes just suggested for two-working-parents and single-parent families have much importance for American public schools. Beginning in the nineteenth century, the nation's schools assumed the goals of instructing the mass of youth in academic subjects, citizenship, and culture. Around the time of World War I, the schools began to expand their instruction in nonacademic areas, for instance, home economics, vocational training, health, and athletics. By the 1980s, however, the schools had taken on even more nonacademic responsibilities, for example, racial integration, nutrition programs for poor students, drug education, sex education, and parenting education for student mothers. The suggestions that we have made to improve American families as moral education institutions would add even more nonacademic responsibilities to public schools: day-care service, extended-day custodial service, collaboration with parents and social agencies, and so on.

Some commentators have held that America's public schools have severely de-emphasized their academic function, thereby threatening the nation's position in scientific, economic, and political leadership. These critics, consequently, have maintained that the schools should not accept any more nonacademic responsibilities and divest themselves of many of those they already have. In truth, a few commentators have argued that schools should accept only a passive role in moral education: Rather than taking the initiative in providing such education, they should simply reinforce the moral education provided by other institutions. The problem with these critics is that they see public schools as existing in a social context other than the one the nation now has and probably will have for a long time to come. America's traditional institutions, as we have explained, are in flux; churches, families, and others that used to lead in moral education no longer do so and seem incapable of doing so. The reason why public schools have had to accept more and more nonacademic functions is that they appear to be the only institution available to perform them. Thus, where families, churches, and other institutions of moral education have left a vacuum, the schools must enter. There is no alternative on the horizon.

If the schools are to become actively engaged in moral education, they must organize themselves especially for this task. This assignment, we should remember, is not the simple one of the McGuffey reader days when schools merely instructed students in values that the rest of society generally upheld and enforced. The assignment, rather, not only involves the teaching of morality in all aspects of the scholastic curriculum, but also includes regularly working with parents, community leaders, and social agencies; furnishing day-care and extended-day programs; and dealing with social conditions that support or undermine the moral development of students. To fulfill these various responsibilities, the schools must relax the departmentalization of their curricular offerings, especially in high schools, so that they can enable students to learn about morality as it interpenetrates all areas of intellectual life. But the schools have to do more: They need to organize themselves as the coordinators of moral education in America. More specifically, they have to work jointly with families, churches, social agencies, and other relevant institutions to determine together which pedagogical roles the various institutions are prepared to play, what moral development needs students have, and what social conditions need support or elimination.

In saying that public schools should become coordinators of American moral education, we do not mean that they should view moral education as theirs primarily and that other institutions should have only secondary interests in it. The moral education of Americans is of general interest; it is not the business of just one institution or another. All relevant parties must contribute to it where they can; all must help in shaping its policies and programs. What we are proposing is that each public school coordinate the construction and implementation of the moral education policies and programs for its students. Other parties may lead in policy and program construction. Policies and programs might be national as well as local in scope. Who is to lead and how specific to a given school policies and programs should be will depend on local circumstances. In some situations, schools might be unprepared to provide leadership; some communities might be so different as to require particular policies and programs. It is important, nevertheless, for public schools and their personnel to guard against treating other institutions and people as outsiders, as parties whose views and efforts are to be tolerated but not as informed or adept for the design and implementation of moral education. It is important also, of course, for nonscholastic institutions and people not to view public schools and their personnel as incompetent if not morally evil. The moral education of Americans must begin with mutual respect among those who are to be responsible for it.

Schools customarily invite parents to special school performances and to involve them in special fund-raising activities, such as carnivals, bake sales, and raffles. The goal of this practice, which is the major way that many schools relate informally to parents, is twofold: to give parents an opportunity to learn about the schools and to help support the schools. While this goal is admirable, it would have some unfortunate features for moral education. By putting parents in the role of invitees, the practice would treat them as passive. Also, by looking to parents primarily for monetary support, the practice would encourage them to think that they have no other ways to contribute to moral education programs. These imbalances could be remedied rather simply. If parents invited teachers and administrators to meet with them in, for instance, community centers to discuss problems, urgent and routine, of the moral development of students, parents not only would become active in their concern about moral education but also would recognize that they can support schools by contributing to the understanding that teachers have of their students' moral education needs and by learning how to coordinate their efforts at developing their children's moral character with the efforts of teachers.

The administration of America's public schools also would have to be adjusted. The traditional top-down leadership structure of school districts would hinder the application of our theory of moral education in the nation. According to that structure, local school boards, usually elected by the people, formulate policies for the purposes, curriculum, and pedagogy of the schools of local districts. The boards then hire superintendents to implement and administer these policies. The superintendents typically delegate authority to school principals to implement and administer the policies in individual schools. The reason why this arrangement would probably interfere with the moral education we have advanced is that it would enable school boards and administrators to impose specific purposes, curricula, and pedagogical methods and content on teachers and students, thereby violating the rights and duties of teachers and students in moral education. We do not recommend the elimination of district school boards, but we do maintain that their policy making should be at a general level, producing general guidelines. We also recommend that each school should have its own policy-making council consisting of teachers, the principal, parents, and other extramural agents. Superintendents, then, would coordinate the moral education programs of their respective district boards. While school boards should retain authority to review programs in relation to established moral education guidelines, they should work with school councils in resolving identified problems. Indeed, school councils should have the authority to call for changes in guidelines. Discussions of guidelines and programs, it must be noted, are to rest on appeals to relevant facts and norms of moral agency, not to political agendas.

Political Institutions

School boards, legislative bodies, courts, governors, the presidency, and popular elections are the political institutions that are likely to have the most serious influence on the implementation of any program for the moral education of Americans. Most of these institutions are the official channels for stimulating and organizing public sentiment on American moral education. Each of them has some authority for permitting or forbidding such education. Altogether, they can fund such education adequately or poorly. Regardless of their importance, however, none of these institutions has to undergo any changes for the application of our theory of moral education. This is not to say that some of these institutions do not have serious faults. School boards, for instance, are no longer just the instrument by which the public holds schools accountable for their performance; they have become a tool by which social issue factions attempt to thwart public policy. We mean only that these institutions do not require alteration especially for the application of our theory.

Nevertheless, if the nation's political institutions are to support the moral education that we have recommended, they must satisfy several conditions. The occupants of positions in each of the institutions must respect the norms of moral agency, for without that respect they will favor the moral education we have proposed only as long as it is to their political advantage to do so. It might seem utopian to expect not even all but just most public officials to appreciate the norms of moral agency. Such a criticism, however, would ignore important considerations. Because, as we have argued, the norms of moral agency are consistent with American ideals, they probably will be operative, at least weakly, in the moral thinking of most public officials as well as many other

Americans. Moreover, discussion about these norms in the media, during campaigns, and during official sessions should provide incumbents and aspiring office holders with adequate opportunity to reflect on and recognize the relevance of the values, rights, and duties of moral agents to American life.

Another condition is that the public must take seriously the moral character of those who seek public office. Officials whose character involves stupidity, prurience, greed, expediency, love of power, or other major vices will support moral education only haltingly or in the short run. In addition, if such officials have immoral characters, they will make a mockery of moral education.

The final condition to be mentioned concerns the moral character of the electorate. Voters are not likely to be especially concerned with the moral character of those seeking office if voters themselves do not possess the character of moral agents. This point poses a dilemma. If voters do not already have the character of moral agents, how will they get it? As far as we know, a program for developing such character in Americans is sorely lacking. Yet, if the mass of voters already have the virtues of moral agency, why have we insisted that there is an acute need for moral education in America? After all, if the nation's members already possess the character of moral agents, they have already undergone a satisfactory moral education, thus rendering otiose any application of our theory of moral education to American society. This difficulty, which was anticipated by Plato in his dialogues *Protagoras* and *Meno,* starts to dissolve when we remember that people implicitly respect the norms of moral agency. Through discussion of the moral situation in the United States, the members of the public will be in a position to recognize and esteem the features of moral agency and the dispositions required by such agency. While that awareness and valuation will not automatically stamp Americans with the character of moral agency, it will enable them to prize and seek the development of such character in themselves and their children. It also will enable them to want such character in their officials. Accordingly, our belief in the efficacy of the democratic process for implementing our theory of moral education in America does not rest on blind faith; it rests rather on the claim that through reflection people will recognize the implications of the concept of moral agency for themselves. It follows that the application of our theory of moral education to the United States might succeed if the dialogue that generated the theory were to continue and widen to include the whole of the American public.

Economic Institutions

While American economic institutions have helped produce unprecedented amounts of wealth and provide the nation's members with a very high standard of living, they have raised questions about other aspects of their operation. Spates of unemployment, hazardous working conditions, and low wages have cast doubt upon the labor market. Cigarettes, alcoholic beverages, "fast" foods, and other products contributing to public health problems raise concerns about the retail market. The increasing control of the lives of individuals by corporations prompts one to wonder about the place of these institutions in our economic life. Finally, the unhappiness and emptiness of individuals who have spent their lives in acquiring fortunes indicate that wealth is not an adequate standard for guiding one's life.

The nation's labor and retail markets are popularly supposed to be guided principally by freedom. That is, they are presumed to be regulated primarily by the freedom to accept or reject employment freely offered by others and to buy or reject goods freely offered by others. Supply, demand, and competition will set wages, prices, and quality; economic need and the profit motive will provide all the incentive that is required for people to participate in these markets. Yet, as the theory and actuality of free markets reveal, such markets involve more than freedom as a major regulator. Knowledge is also a major principle. Laborers are supposed to know about wages and working conditions; employers are assumed to be cognizant of workers' skills and reliability. Buyers are presumed to be informed about the quality of goods; sellers are supposed to know about the worth of bills of exchange. Thus, one function of formal labor contracts is to make certain conditions of employment matters of common knowledge.

Dishonesty and fraud, which thwart knowledge, are major vices in markets. If, however, participants in free markets freely and wittingly act with respect to one another, they act as moral agents. Consequently, they are logically committed to respect, not only in themselves but in all other moral agents, freedom and knowledge and thus to respect all other traits of moral agency.

It follows that the implementation of our theory of moral education in the United States does not require an upheaval in the latter's market system. The implementation demands only that the system operate according to the moral principles that it logically entails. If the system did follow these principles completely and consistently, it would create no conflict between the moral character we want Americans to have and the competences and attitudes they must have in the economic sector of their lives. Indeed, the system would be an area where that moral character would be at home; it also would reinforce the moral education that we advocate.

The corporate organization of economic activity has flourished in market economies because it has provided greater efficiency than its predecessor, the enterprise identifiable with the individual human beings who are its owners. Corporations have amassed amounts of capital that noncorporate businesses never could. They have kept prices of raw materials and finished products down because of their enormous capacity for mass production. In addition, they have made a more efficient use of workers by stabilizing the labor market, at first by working with labor unions and subsequently by implementing their own benefit programs for workers. In bringing greater efficiency to the economic world, however, corporations have also reduced or eliminated the human agent's freedom in that world. Unless people in a mass production society are wealthy, they must ignore their respective tastes, their eccentricities, and settle for conformity. As employees of corporations, people act mainly as occupants of positions, not as particular human beings. Hence, they have to relate to one another not as complete human beings but as position holders; they have to act according to bureaucratic regulations, not according to their own evaluations and deliberations. Moreover, the loss of individual freedom has not been confined to the economic sector of American life; it has extended to education, health, recreation, and other institutional areas that have adopted corporate organization in order to gain more efficiency.

Nobody wants to say that the loss of individual freedoms to the corporate organization of American economic life has been entirely or mostly bad. Not only has that organization contributed to the enormous rise in our standard of living, but that increase has provided most Americans with opportunities which were not even imagined during the last century. Nevertheless, Americans have an uneasiness about business corporations; they suspect that they have lost control of them. Because these institutions came into being simply as means for improving the nation's material life, they originally had only instrumental value. But since the last century they have tended to become autonomous, taking on an intrinsic value. Economic efficiency is the social good of the business corporation; profit is the good of the corporation for its owners. That corporation, however, has been granted, by economists and business leaders, its own special purpose and good, which is its growth. A shrinking or static corporate enterprise is a bad one; the supreme aim and good of such a business is its expansion, whether measured by profit, capital, or market. The mission of corporate leaders is to promote the growth of their institutions.

To be sure, the growth of a business corporation is not a necessary evil. Growth frequently enhances efficiency and thus the material welfare of people; it often increases returns for owners. The ultimate problem with growth as the overriding purpose and good of a business corporation is the same as the ultimate problem with efficiency or profit as its principal purpose and good: As a goal sought above all others, growth, efficiency, or profit justifies any means for its attainment. Thus, growth has been attained through monopolistic practices, reducing competition and quality while raising prices. It has been gained through huge debts, at times upsetting financial markets and boosting the cost of money beyond the means of ordinary people. It has been reached through restructuring, leaving unemployed workers with dislocated lives and reduced livelihoods. It has been attained through the marketing of harmful or wasteful products. Moreover, it has been reached through bribery, illicit campaign contributions, and other forms of criminal activity. When corporations seek growth, profit, efficiency, or any other goal by any means, they plainly do not respect the values, rights, and duties of moral agency. If, therefore, American business corporations persist in having any purpose to be reached by any means, they will pose obstacles to the moral education we have proposed for the nation's members. They will support that education as long as they regard it as serving their interests; they will oppose it when they see it threatening their interests. Moreover, because people will wonder why they should act by the norms of moral agency when corporations do not have to, they are likely to question the supremacy of moral standards and thus the worth of moral education.

Corporate enterprise, however, does not have to be abolished to be kept from interfering with the moral education we have conceived for Americans. Indeed, it can be enlisted into maintaining and nurturing the development of that education. Even though corporations are usually not taken by social scientists and policymakers as moral agents, they may be understood as such. Corporations, of course, obviously differ from human beings; the former are, for instance, artificial and abstract while the latter are natural and concrete. Nevertheless, corporations are willful agents in that they act freely and wittingly, at least in the sense that they voluntarily do things through their officers. This point has long been recognized in law, which regards corporations as persons, that is, as entities with interests, rights, and responsibilities. In addition, business corporations are moral agents in that they act voluntarily with respect to other voluntary agents, corporate or human. If, consequently, economists, policymakers, business leaders, and others stopped thinking of corporations as nonmoral agents and started to recognize them as moral agents, they would be in a position to reconstruct and guide them according to the norms of moral agency. When operating as moral agents, American business corporations logically will respect the moral values, rights, duties, and virtues of Americans. In addition, they logically will encourage the moral education of Americans not because their doing so is good for business, but because their doing so is what they will want to do as moral agents.

That wealth does not necessarily bring a meaningful life is an old lesson, dating at least since the days of King Midas. But wealth with morality does not necessarily make such a life either. If all Americans were morally virtuous and materially well off, and the nation's markets and corporations functioned according to the norms of moral agency, Americans still would not necessarily have meaningful lives. The explanation for this possibility concerns the nature of wealth and that of morality. As usually understood, wealth is merely a means. It is for obtaining other things; it has no intrinsic worth. According to our analysis of the matter, morality simply provides a normative structure for regulating the conduct of voluntary agents towards one another. It tells what is good or right for us as moral agents, but it does not tell us what meaning to attach to life. Thus, while morality sets limits on how wealth is to be acquired and specifies that at least some wealth should be used for charity and the public moral good, morality otherwise does not say what to do with our material goods. Questions about the meaning of life, therefore, must receive their answers from some source other than economics and morality. Theology and metaphysics are traditional sources of those answers.

So, even if our theory of moral education becomes the actual basis of moral character development in the United States, it alone will not enable Americans to have meaningful lives. It will furnish them with guidance in their conduct toward one another, but it will not provide them with a vision of life or with goals to pursue. Americans, consequently, will have to look to theology, metaphysics, or someplace else for guides to their happiness. This is not to say, however, that the moral education of Americans will have no significance for their search for a meaningful life. With the character of moral agents, Americans will have sufficient order and freedom for seeking and enjoying worthy lives. Moreover, because Americans as moral agents will recognize the supremacy of moral standards, they will accept only those visions of life that are consistent with the norms of moral agency. Their moral character, therefore, will be a constituent of each of their individually chosen modes of life. It also will ensure that their respective visions of life will be compatible with one another.

Selected Bibliography

Ackerman, Bruce. *Social Justice in the Liberal State*. New Haven, CT: Yale University Press, 1980.

Alexander, Lamar, comp. *America 2000: An Education Strategy Sourcebook*. Washington, DC: U.S. Department of Education, 1991.

Auletta, Ken. *The Underclass*. New York: Random House, 1983.

Barber, Benjamin R. *An Aristocracy of Everyone: The Politics of Education and the Future of America*. New York: Ballantine Books, 1992.

Bennett, William J., ed. *The Book of Virtues: A Treasury of Great Moral Stories*. New York: Simon & Schuster, 1993.

Bellah, Robert N., Richard Madsen, William M. Sullivan, Ann Swidler, and Steven M. Tipton. *Habits of the Heart: Individualism and Commitment in American Life*. Berkeley, CA: University of California Press, 1985.

Bettelheim, Bruno. *Love Is Not Enough*. New York: The Free Press, 1950.

Bloom, Allan. *The Closing of the American Mind*. New York: Simon & Schuster, 1987.

Bricker; David C. *Classroom Life as Civic Education: Individual Achievement and Student Cooperation in Schools*. New York: Teachers College Press, 1989.

Callan, Eamonn. *Autonomy and Schooling*. Kingston and Montreal, Canada: McGill-Queen's University Press, 1988.

Caplow, Theodore, Howard M. Bahr, John Modell, and Bruce A. Chadwick. *Recent Social Trends in the United States, 1960–1990*. Montreal, Canada: McGill-Queen's University Press, 1991.

Chazan, Barry. *Contemporary Approaches to Moral Education: Analyzing Alternative Theories*. New York: Teachers College Press, 1985.

Coleman, James S., et al. *Equality of Educational Opportunity: Summary*. Washington, DC: U.S. Government Printing Office, 1966.

Dewey, John. *Democracy and Education: An Introduction to the Philosophy of Education*. New York: Macmillan Company, 1916, 1958.

———. *Human Nature and Conduct*. New York: Random House, 1950.

———. *The Public and Its Problems*. Denver, CO: Alan Swallow, 1954.

———. *The Quest for Certainty*. New York: Minton, Balch & Co., 1929.

Dworkin, Ronald. *Taking Rights Seriously*. Cambridge, MA: Harvard University Press, 1977.

Eisner, Elliot W. *The Educational Imagination: On the Design and Evaluation of School Programs*. New York: Macmillan Company, 1981.

Etzioni, Amitai. *The Spirit of Community: Rights, Responsibilities, and the Communitarian Agenda*. New York: Crown Publishers, 1993.

Feinberg, Joel. *Rights, Justice, and the Bounds of Liberty*. Princeton, NJ: Princeton University Press, 1982.

Frankena, William K. *Ethics*. Englewood Cliffs, NJ: Prentice-Hall, 1963.

Freire, Paolo. *Pedagogy of the Oppressed*. New York: Herder and Herder, 1972.

Friedman, Milton, and Rose Friedman. *Capitalism and Freedom*, 2nd ed. Chicago, IL: The University of Chicago Press, 1982.

Gewirth, Alan. *Reason and Morality*. Chicago, IL: The University of Chicago Press, 1978.

Gilligan, Carol. *In a Different Voice: Psychological Theory and Women's Development*. Cambridge, MA: Harvard University Press, 1982.

Ginsberg, Ruth Bader. "Realizing the Equality Principle," in William T. Blackstone and Robert D. Heslep, eds., *Social Justice and Preferential Treatment: Women and Racial Minorities in Education and Business*. Athens, GA: The University of Georgia Press, 1977.

Glendon, Mary Ann. *Rights Talk: The Impoverishment of Political Discourse*. New York: The Free Press, 1991.

Glickman, Carl D. *Renewing America's Schools: A Guide for School-Based Action*. San Francisco, CA: Jossey-Bass, 1993.

Goldscheider, Frances, and Linda Waite. *New Families, No Families? The Transformation of the American Family*. Berkeley, CA: The University of California Press, 1992.

Green, Thomas F. *The Activities of Teaching*. New York: McGraw-Hill, 1971.

Gross, Ronald, and Beatrice Gross, eds. *Radical School Reform*. New York: Simon & Schuster, 1969.

Gutman, Amy. *Democratic Education*. Princeton, NJ: PrincetonUniversity Press, 1987.

Heslep, Robert D. *Education in Democracy: Education's Moral Role in the Democratic State*. Ames, IA: Iowa State University Press, 1989.

Hirst, Paul, and R.S. Peters. *The Logic of Education*. London: Routledge & Kegan Paul, 1973.

Hobbes, Thomas. *Leviathan*. New York: E.P. Dutton, 1950.

Hodgkinson, Harold L. *A Demographic Look at Tomorrow*. Washinton, DC: Institute for Educational Leadership, 1992.

Jackson, Philip W., Robert E. Boostrom, and David T. Hansen. *The Moral Life of Schools*. San Francisco, CA: Jossey-Bass, 1993.

Janowitz, Morris. *The Reconstruction of Patriotism: Education for Civic Consciousness.* Chicago, IL: The University of Chicago Press, 1983.

Jencks, Christopher, and Paul E. Peterson, eds. *The Urban Underclass.* Washington, DC: The Brookings Institute, 1991.

Kant, Immanuel. *Fundamental Principles of the Metaphysic of Morals*, translated by Thomas K. Abbot. New York: The Liberal Arts Press, 1954.

Kilpatrick, William K. *Why Johnny Can't Tell Right from Wrong: Moral Illiteracy and the Case for Character Education.* New York: Simon & Schuster, 1993.

Kohlberg, Lawrence. *The Philosophy of Moral Development: Moral Stages and the Idea of Justice*, Vol. 1 of *Essays on Moral Development.* New York: Harper and Row, 1981.

Kotlowitz, Alex. *There Are No Children Here.* New York: Anchor Books, 1991.

Lickona, Thomas. *Educating for Character.* New York: Bantam Books, 1992.

MacIntyre, Alasdair. *After Virtue*, 2nd ed. Notre Dame, IN: Notre Dame University Press, 1984.

Maslow, Abraham. *Dominance, Self-Esteem, Self-Actualization: Germinal Papers of A.H. Maslow.* Monterey, CA: Brooks/Cole, 1973.

Moore, G.E. *Principia Ethica.* Cambridge, England: Cambridge University Press, 1954.

Moynihan, Daniel Patrick. "Defining Deviancy Down," *The American Scholar* (Winter 1993), pp. 17–30.

Murray, Charles. *Losing Ground: American Social Policy, 1950–1980.* New York: Basic Books, 1984.

National Commission for Excellence in Education. *A Nation at Risk: The Imperative for Educational Reform.* Washington, DC: U.S. Government Printing Office, 1983.

Nussbaum, Martha C. *Love's Knowledge: Essays on Philosophy and Literature.* New York: Oxford University Press, 1990.

Piaget, Jean. *The Origins of Intelligence in Children*, translated by Margaret Cook. New York: W.W. Norton, 1952.

Raths, Louis, Merrill Harmin, and Sidney Simon. *Values and Teaching: Working with Values in the Classroom*, 2nd ed. Columbus, OH: Charles E. Merrill, 1978.

Rawls, John. *A Theory of Justice.* Cambridge, MA: Harvard University Press, 1971.

Rescher, Nicholas. *Introduction to Value Theory.* Englewood Cliffs, NJ: Prentice-Hall, 1979.

Rogers, Carl. *Freedom to Learn: A View of What Education Might Become.* Columbus, OH: Charles E. Merrill, 1969.

Ryle, Gilbert. *The Concept of Mind.* New York: Barnes & Noble, 1949.

Sandel, Michael J. *Liberalism and the Limits of Justice.* Cambridge, England: Cambridge University Press, 1982.

Shklar, Judith. *Ordinary Vices.* Cambridge, MA: Harvard University Press, 1984.

Sichel, Betty A. *Moral Education: Character, Community, and Ideals.* Philadelphia, PA: Temple University Press, 1988.

Slavin, Robert. *Cooperative Learning*. New York: Longman, 1983.

Taylor, Charles. *Sources of the Self*. Cambridge, MA: Harvard University Press, 1989.

Tocqueville, Alexis de. *Democracy in America*, edited by Phillips Bradley. New York: Vintage Books, 1954 (two volumes).

Whitehead, Alfred North. *The Aims of Education and Other Essays*. New York: Mentor Books, 1955.

Wilshire, Bruce. *The Moral Collapse of the University: Professionalism, Purity, and Alienation*. Albany, NY: State University of New York Press, 1990.

Wilson, William Julius. *The Truly Disadvantaged: The Inner City, the Underclass, and Public Policy*. Chicago, IL: The University of Chicago Press, 1987.

Index